DATE DUE

ISBN 978-0-260-07067-8
PIBN 11022032

1 MONTH OF
FREE
READING

at
www.ForgottenBooks.com

By purchasing this book you are eligible for one month membership to ForgottenBooks.com, giving you unlimited access to our entire collection of over 700,000 titles via our web site and mobile apps.

To claim your free month visit:
www.forgottenbooks.com/free1022032

English
Français
Deutsche
Italiano
Español
Português

www.forgottenbooks.com

Mythology Photography **Fiction**
Fishing Christianity **Art** Cooking
Essays Buddhism Freemasonry
Medicine **Biology** Music **Ancient
Egypt** Evolution Carpentry Physics
Dance Geology **Mathematics** Fitness
Shakespeare **Folklore** Yoga Marketing
Confidence Immortality Biographies
Poetry **Psychology** Witchcraft
Electronics Chemistry History **Law**
Accounting **Philosophy** Anthropology
Alchemy Drama Quantum Mechanics
Atheism Sexual Health **Ancient History**
Entrepreneurship Languages Sport
Paleontology Needlework Islam
Metaphysics Investment Archaeology
Parenting Statistics Criminology
Motivational

BARTLETT'S LIFE AMONG

WILD BEASTS IN THE 'ZOO'

ORTRAIT BY JOSEPH WOLF, TAKEN DECEMBER 10, 1849.

BARTLETT'S LIFE AMONG

WILD BEASTS
IN THE 'ZOO'

BEING A CONTINUATION OF

WILD ANIMALS IN CAPTIVITY

THE HABITS, FOOD, MANAGEMENT AND TREATMENT
OF THE BEASTS AND BIRDS AT THE 'ZOO'

WITH

Reminiscences and Anecdotes

BY

A. D. BARTLETT

LATE SUPERINTENDENT OF THE ZOOLOGICAL SOCIETY'S GARDENS
REGENT'S PARK

COMPILED AND EDITED BY

EDWARD BARTLETT, F.Z.S.

LATE CURATOR OF THE MAIDSTONE MUSEUM, AND OF THE SARAWAK MUSEUM
ETC.

ILLUSTRATED

LONDON: CHAPMAN AND HALL, Ld.

1900

Richard Clay & Sons, Limited,
London & Bungay.

THE· EDITOR,

By permission, dedicates

THIS BOOK TO

SIR W· H. FLOWER, K.C.B.

PRESIDENT OF THE ZOOLOGICAL SOCIETY OF LONDON

WHO, IN KINDLY GIVING THIS PERMISSION, WRITES

THAT HE WAS "FOR EXACTLY FIFTY YEARS IN PRETTY

CONSTANT ASSOCIATION WITH HIM," THE EDITOR'S FATHER,

"AND SO HAD AMPLE OPPORTUNITIES OF

OBSERVING HIS UNTIRING DEVOTION

TO THE ADVANCEMENT

OF ZOOLOGY."

PREFACE

THE thought has suggested itself to me that, by connecting the "fragments" left over from *Wild Animals in Captivity* with some further scraps, jottings and letters upon which, since the publication of that book, I have alighted by a happy chance, I might be able, by the aid of some of the most interesting of the scientific papers read by my late father at the meetings of the Zoological Society, to compile a companion volume to *Wild Animals in Captivity*, which would be interesting alike to the general reader and to the zoologist.

I have, therefore, to the best of my ability endeavoured to place before my readers, who I trust will be indulgent, a second series of my father's zoological notes, anecdotes, etc., for assistance in the publication of which I am much indebted to the gentlemen to whom I referred in my preceding work.

I may here state, on good authority, that it was not my father's intention that his work should be of the serious order, nor did he wish it to be wholly scientific, but that it should be acceptable to both the naturalist and the non-scientific reader; he gave no thought to the captious critic.

At this stage of my preface it would, I feel, be ungenerous of me not to gratefully acknowledge, which I now beg to do, the very kind references to my father in many of the biographical sketches which appeared in various periodicals.

There is one statement only in an article which I read in the *Leisure Hour* of August 1897, p. 662, which I feel sure the writer will forgive me for correcting, viz.—

" We have all heard of the extraordinary prices given for eggs of the Great Auk, a bird now supposed to be as extinct as the Dodo. In fact there are catalogues of all the Auks' eggs known to collectors, and the fabulous sums paid when any of these come into the market do not surprise us. But in his young days Bartlett told us that he had often in his possession real living specimens of the Great Auk itself. One of these he sold to a dealer, who re-sold it at an immense advance to the Lord Derby of that day for his museum at Knowsley. If still there, and if it were brought to an auction room, what would the bird fetch, when its eggs are sold for such ridiculous sums ? "

The sentence which I desire most respectfully to set right is—" Bartlett told us that he had often in his possession real living specimens of the Great Auk itself." If the words "often" and "living" were omitted, the facts as related would be correct. Professor Newton tells us that the last two Great Auks were killed in Eldey in Iceland, between the 2nd and 5th of June 1844. I have given under the title of Great Auk, all the details referring to that bird which I have been able to gather from my father's papers. With regard to his having possessed living specimens, I need hardly say that, from my own knowledge, there must have been some misunderstanding on the subject. I feel it necessary to set this matter right, otherwise it might possibly lead hereafter to many zoological errors.

I may observe in passing, that the portrait, or frontispiece to *Wild Animals in Captivity*, was reproduced from a unique plate taken about the time stated by my brother-in-law, the late Mr. Anthony Ranson. This was long before my father changed his mode of cultivating his beard. In fact it was often remarked that his features were leonine, a similar instance of which happened to the old keeper of the lions, Cocksedge, whose features became in course of time like those of a lion.

I find that an accidental omission occurred in *Wild Animals in Captivity*. It should have been stated that the "excellent portrait" of my father was by kind permission reproduced from one taken by my late nephew, Mr. Henry Goodwin.

28 Prince's Road, Notting Hill, W.

CONTENTS

PART I.—MAMMALS

PART II.—BIRDS

PART III.—REPTILES

FISHES

APPENDICES

LIST OF ILLUSTRATIONS

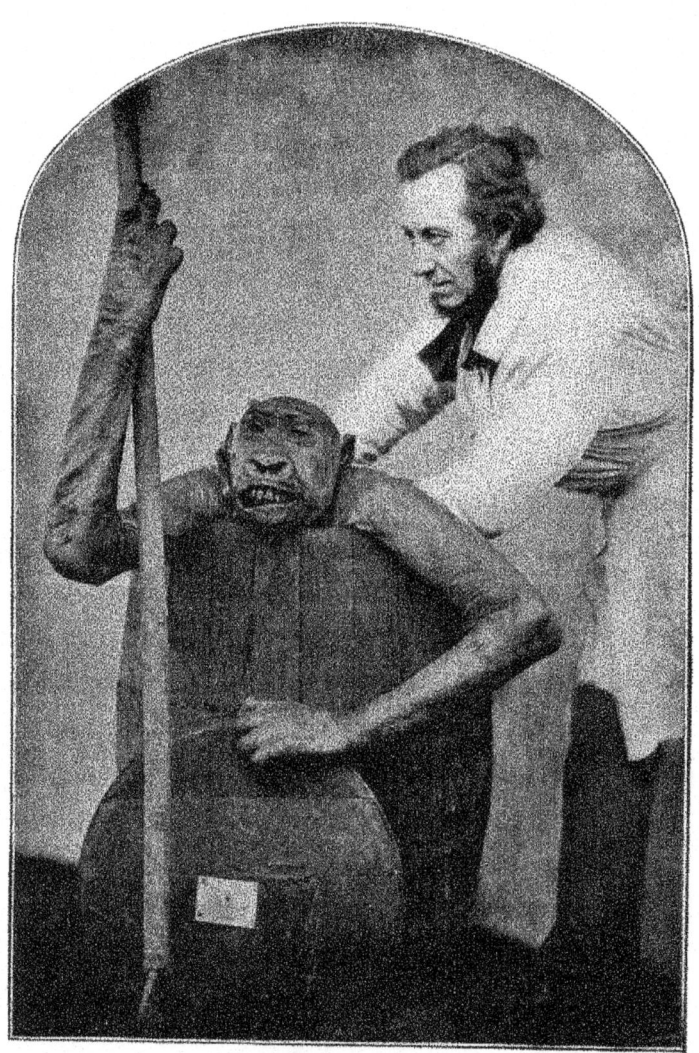

MY FIRST GORILLA.
PORTRAIT OF A. D. BARTLETT, WITH GORILLA IN TUB.
Taken by Peter Ashton in 1858.

PART I.—MAMMALS.

WILD BEASTS IN THE 'ZOO'

CHAPTER I.

GREAT APES.

GORILLAS.

THE first Gorilla with which I had to do came into my hands whilst I was engaged at the Crystal Palace in November 1858. It was sent to the British Museum in a barrel of spirits, and Professor Owen placed it in my possession to preserve and mount for the National Museum; after I had preserved it I, by permission of the trustees of that museum, exhibited it at the Crystal Palace, and delivered various lectures on it and the larger apes.

The first mention of the Gorilla was made by Hanno, the Carthaginian traveller, 2300 years since, but it remained unknown to modern *savants* until a few years ago, when Dr. Savage, travelling in West Africa, found the upper part of a skull which the natives had been worshipping on a pole. Perceiving, at once, that it was much larger than that of a Chimpanzee, he obtained it, with considerable trouble, and forwarded it to Professor Owen for examination, who at once recognized it as that of the lost Gorilla, and from this imperfect source described the remaining structure of the animal so precisely that the

3

arrival of other remains verified in the most extraordinary degree his scientific prediction.[1]

After describing those animals whose formation, until this last discovery, approximated nearest to that of man, I gave a description of a Chimpanzee, whose intelligence I endeavoured to train; the most favourable result, however, of its skill was its capability of spinning a humming top, although I believed, but for the physical weakness of its thumb, that it would have threaded and used a packing needle.

The long and, apparently, interminable contention that was kept up respecting M. Du Chaillu's exploits, called forth much correspondence that was quite useless in determining the truth. Many of the remarks and objections that were brought forward on both sides are totally futile and also inaccurate, and tend to obscure the facts.

I will endeavour to explain some of them away, and at the same time make an attempt to throw some light upon the subject, which I admit is involved in great obscurity.

I will commence with my first introduction to M. Du Chaillu himself, having been called upon by him to assist him with my advice, through Professor Owen, who wrote—

"*British Museum, March* 26, 1861.

"MY DEAR SIR,—M. Du Chaillu is desirous to have his largest Gorilla skin properly stuffed. I know no one better qualified to put him in the way of getting this properly done than yourself. Any information, or help you can render, will oblige,

"Yours truly,

"RD. OWEN."

---

[1] The Gorilla above-mentioned was fully described by Professor Owen in the *Transactions of the Zoological Society*, 1866, p. 243 plates 45, 46. It was received at the British Museum on September 10, 1858.

At Du Chaillu's request I went to Mr. Murray's to see the skin unpacked; having done this I conveyed the same to my office for the purpose of making a thorough and careful examination of it, and to report upon it. I invited my pupil and assistant, Mr. F. W. Wilson, to meet M. Du Chaillu and me and consult with us upon the matter. At this interview I called M. Du Chaillu's attention to the face of the animal, which I told him was not in a perfect condition, having lost a great part of the epidermis. In reply he, M. Du Chaillu, assured me that it was quite perfect, remarking, at the same time, that the epidermis on the face was quite black, and that the face of the skin being black was a proof of its perfectness.

I, however, then and there convinced him that the blackness of the face was due to its having been painted black; finding I had detected what had been done, he at once admitted that he did paint it at the time he exhibited it in New York.

The question that arose in my mind upon making this discovery was, did M. Du Chaillu kill the Gorilla and skin and preserve it? If so, he must recollect that the epidermis came off; supposing he did forget this, he must have been afterwards reminded of the fact when he had to paint the face to represent its natural condition. These facts (to which I had a witness) led me to doubt the truthfulness of M. Du Chaillu's statement, and it occurred to me that he was not aware of the state of the skin, and probably had not prepared it himself.

The skin was in a wretched condition, and was much decayed, and as my examination was not directed to ascertain by what means this animal had been killed, I took less notice of the wounds than I otherwise should have done.

Upon this latter subject I beg to offer a few remarks.

5

The first object of a taxidermist is to render all the damages or wounded parts of a skin as perfect as possible, and this can be done by a skilful operator in such a manner as to render the detection of the damaged parts next to impossible. Had the beast been shot in the *back*, the bullet hole could have been easily closed while in a fresh condition, but not so easily after the skin was hard and dry.[1]

While on a visit to Charles Waterton I carefully examined a specimen which he had labelled "Martin Luther," with donkey's ears. This specimen I identified as a young gorilla, which came to England alive while Waterton was a young man, and which had been overlooked by naturalists of the day.

CHIMPANZEES.

THE BALD APE (*TROGLODYTES CALVUS*).

The Chimpanzee "Sally."

I suppose that no one individual ape was ever a subject of more interest or created more amusement than "Sally." Black as she was, she had a far more intelligent face than some of our own species. It is to be hoped that all the members of this extraordinary species may prove as intellectual as "Sally," or even more so.

"I have paid considerable attention to the Anthropoid Apes, and from the opportunities I have had of seeing a very large number of living and dead specimens, not only in England, but at the different Zoological Gardens, Menageries and Museums, I have arrived at the con-

---

[1] See my remarks on "reducing bullet hole," *Wild Animals in Captivity*, p. 209.

BALD-HEADED CHIMPANZEE—'SALLY.'

elusion that my acquaintance with them is sufficient to enable me to offer a few remarks upon an example now [1] living in the Society's Gardens. This animal was purchased in Liverpool, October 24, 1883, together with an adult male of the well-known Chimpanzee. When received, she was quite immature, not having shed any of her sucking-teeth. At that time, however, she exhibited many well-marked characters, differing much from the well-known common Chimpanzee ; and as she advances towards the adult condition these differences are becoming more fully developed, and thus render a description of them less difficult.

' In the first place, I may remark that the colour of the face, hands and feet in the Chimpanzee are *white*, or *pale flesh-colour ;* the same parts of the animal under consideration are *black* or *brownish-black.* Another well-marked difference is to be observed in the hair upon the head and face. In the Chimpanzee the hair on the top of the head, and passing down from the centre (where it divides) to the sides of the face or cheeks, is tolerably long and full, forming what may be considered rather bushy whiskers ; whereas the figure before you clearly shows the front, top and sides of the head and face to be nearly naked, having only a few short hairs on the head, quite destitute of any signs of the parting so very conspicuous in the Chimpanzee. Another striking difference may be noticed in the size and form of the head and ears. Out of the number of Chimpanzees I have seen and examined, both old and young, none have possessed the large flat ears so conspicuous in this individual. The form of the head, the expression of the face,

[1] June 16, 1885. Reprinted from the *Proceedings of the Zoological Society.*

the expanded nostrils, the thicker lips, especially the
lower lip, together with the more elevated skull, cannot
fail to distinguish this animal from the common Chimpanzee. There are other external characters that I pass
over, as they require to be described anatomically. Again,
the habits of this animal differ entirely from those of the
well-known or common Chimpanzee. She has always
shown a disposition to live upon animal food. Soon after
her arrival, I found she would kill and eat small birds;
seizing them by the neck, she would bite off the head
and eat the bird—skin, feathers, and all; for some months
she killed and ate a small pigeon every night. After a
time we supplied her with cooked mutton and beef-tea;
upon this food she has done well. I have never found
any ordinary Chimpanzee that would eat any kind of
flesh.

"Another singular habit was the producing pellets, or
'quids,' resembling the castings thrown up by raptorial
birds. I have here a few of them, taken from her mouth.
They are composed of feathers and other indigestible substances, that had been taken with her food. Moreover, she
is an expert rat-catcher, and has caught and killed many rats
that had entered her cage during the night. Her intelligence is far above that of the ordinary Chimpanzee.
With but little trouble she can be taught to do many
things that require the exercise of considerable thought
and understanding ; she recognizes those who have made
her acquaintance, and pays marked attention to men of
colour, by uttering a loud cry of *bon, bun, bun.* She is
never tired of romping and playing, and is generally in a
good temper.

"I have no doubt but that M. Du Chaillu obtained
specimens of this animal,—for I perfectly recollect seeing
in his possession some damaged skins, the heads of which

were quite bald, that is, destitute of hair ; but his statements were so vague that it was impossible to say to what species he attached the different names he used. I am therefore, I think, justified in regarding the animal in question as distinct from the well-known or common Chimpanzee; and as the term *Troglodytes calvus* implies a bald-headed animal, it appears to me that the animal under consideration is fully entitled to its application.

"Since writing the above, I have examined the specimens in the British Museum obtained from M. Du Chaillu, and, notwithstanding the shrivelled condition of the face and ears, I am perfectly satisfied of the identity of this specimen with the animal under consideration.

" Another consideration is, however, forced upon me, with reference to this subject, and, to give an illustration, I may ask you for a moment to call to mind a fable of the Monkey who had seen the world. Now, supposing the Monkey to have been a collector of animals, and in Europe to have obtained some *white people with red or fair hair*, and upon his arrival in Africa to have met with the Negroes *black as jet*, with *flat noses, thick lips and black woolly heads*, I think he would have been justified in regarding them as a very well-marked and distinct species. We are, however, in a position better able to understand that *time, climate, food* and other *circumstances* may so change the condition and appearance that the original type may be said to have disappeared altogether. I venture to say this change is now taking place, however slowly it may be. It is noticeable in America, and doubtless in a few generations (without fresh arrivals of Europeans) the descendants of Europeans will gradually develop the peculiarities of the original natives of that country.

" In conclusion, I feel it is necessary to offer a few words in defence of naming animals that are nearly allied and calling them by new names, in order to constitute them as species. This practice has of late received a check, and it appears to me a very reasonable and proper mode of treating the subject to consider a large number of the animals that exhibit a few trifling differences to be only local varieties of the same species. At the same time, we must bear in mind that in order to do this we should seek for intermediate forms or individuals that may be regarded as uniting two extremely different creatures. In the present instance I have failed to find any animal showing this tendency to be intermediate between this animal and the well-known Chimpanzee."

After the above appeared, Mr. W. B. Tegetmeier wrote a very able article on what I said in the *Field*, adding :—
" The Bald Chimpanzee must be regarded as one of the most interesting animals, not merely on account of the species, but also from the peculiarities of its habits and food, and its being one of the few anthropoid apes that have passed through two winters and approached maturity in our unfavourable climate."

At the death of " Sally," a very interesting series of articles and letters of sympathy were published in the various papers and journals, showing how widespread her reputation had travelled. These would be too extensive to add now.

APES' PALACE.

In building a house for Anthropoid Apes, the first consideration must be the strength necessary to contain adult specimens of these powerful animals. It would be also necessary to provide for the safety of the keeper, by having each den so constructed that the animals could be shut away, in order that the keeper may enter the

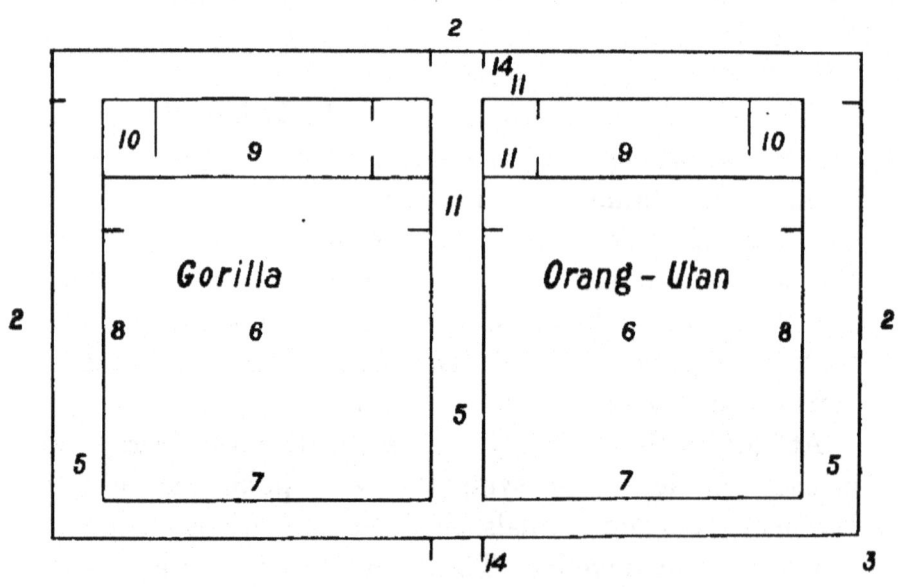

North

. 12

2

14
11

10   9   11   9   10
11

11

Gorilla   Orang - Utan

2   8   6   5   6   8   2

5   7   5   7   5   3

14   14

2

13

South

GROUND PLAN OF APES' PALACE.

den for the purpose of cleaning, etc. It would be desirable to have a glass front between the dens and the visitors, the glass being sufficiently far away from the den to prevent the animals reaching it, and also to enable the attendant to keep the glass clean. The portion of the house inhabited by the animals should be kept at a much higher temperature than the part occupied by the visitors. The divisions between the dens of each species should be opaque, to prevent the animals seeing each other, as the different species will not agree, or very rarely so, but when very young they can be placed together.

I think a sufficient number of compartments should be allowed, although the known species of ape are few, viz. :—

The Gorilla (*Troglodytes gorilla*, Sav.).

The Bald-headed Chimpanzee (*Troglodytes calvus*, Du Chaillu).

The Chimpanzee (*Troglodytes troglodytes*, Gmel.).

The Orang-utan (*Simia satyrus*, Linn.).

The Lesser Orang-utan (*Simia morio*, Owen).

Perhaps a third species of Chimpanzee ?

The Gibbons, although a much more numerous family, and highly interesting, should no doubt have a home in the same house with their larger relatives, the Apes, more especially on account of the temperature, which is an all-important factor in keeping alive those animals accustomed to a climate like West Africa, Sumatra and Borneo.

The portion of the building for these Apes should be so constructed as to shut out all draught at night and to be closed, during bad weather, in the day-time. We know for a positive fact that all these wonderful denizens of the hot jungle never suffer from draughts in a wild state, but the least draught or cold wind blown upon them in captivity results in death.

The cages which are made for the Gibbons could be occupied by some of the larger Baboons during the absence of the former, but these cages require to be made strong enough to hold both.

The question regarding light, sunshine and open air is not within our power to successfully cope with in a building. In the first place, I know all these Apes live in the open air in the dense forest, they can remain in the hottest sun, or hide themselves in the shade of a thickly-leafed tree, and still be in the open air day and night; but in captivity an unnatural heat is produced by the sun's power upon a glass roof which can only be avoided by having a false, movable roof above the glass to prevent (shut out) the burning rays of the sun from falling upon the living occupants, and, at the same time, admit sufficient light from the front of the house. One of the most important elements, fresh air, cannot, as well as heat, be supplied under such circumstances to these animals in captivity, and greater moisture with the heat will assist both, there-fore tropical plants and palms should be abundantly used.

The cages, which should be so formed as not to be like dungeons, should be double cages, back to back, so that the keeper can always see the animals night and day. The floor should be of wood three feet from the ground; any other material is too cold for these delicate beasts. The hot-water pipes should be placed back and front of the cages. I give a plan of two cages, showing the style of apartments which would in a country like this be much suited to tropical Apes. The house should be in pro_portion to the size of the animal, *i. e.* the length of a full-grown Gorilla, or Orang-utan's fore-arm.

1. Outer wall, with windows and doors.

2. Visitors' hall, where they can walk all round the glass screen.

3. Glass screen surrounding the cages.
4. Lobby and entrance doors.
5. Passage round each cage.
6. Large cage, with tree trunks, etc.
7. Wire front, with large mesh.
8. Side, either blank or small mesh to prevent the hand protruding.
9. Sleeping apartment, used by keeper when cleaning the large cage.
10. Box for bed.
11. Doors.
12. Windows; all these, back and sides, should be permanent, *i. e.* not to open, this will prevent draught.
13. Window to open in fine weather.
14. Closed doors.

CHAPTER II.

MONKEYS AND LEMURS.

CHILL OCTOBER.

THE arrival at the Gardens of a large number of monkeys is as good an indication that winter is approaching as is the appearance on our coasts of large flocks of wild fowl. A flock of monkeys would, in this country, be a curious sight, yet it happens that, at this season of the year, a flock of these "funny people" arrive at the Zoological Gardens as regularly as the flocks of wild fowl come to our shores.

The cold, yes, the cold, that drives the poor birds to this country, causes the kind owners of pet monkeys to seek a warm shelter for the "pets" which have, during the summer, passed a happy time in gardens, outhouses and the like. On the approach of winter these active, mischief-making, trick-playing rogues are ordered off, *nolens volens*, to the Zoo, there to ponder o'er their past gay life. A few may be so much liked and so well behaved as to be allowed to remain with the servants of their masters, as sometimes they take a fancy to them, and make them "at home" in the kitchen, but, as a rule, they are sent to visit their fraternity in the Gardens. Could the monkeys be examined by an inquisitive counsellor they would, I have no doubt, astonish the world of men by the histories each could relate.

There is a queer-looking old hag, blind of one eye, that for fourteen or fifteen years amused admiring audiences in the streets of London, and, it is said, made the fortune of more than one Italian. Her last owner, on his retirement into private life, with kind consideration for her years of activity and intelligence, presented her to the Society to enable her to pass the rest of her days in quiet enjoyment. It was suggested that application should be made to the committee of the Theatrical Fund to obtain for her a secluded nook at the delightfully situated home, on Woking Common, for decayed actors, but it was ruled that Jenny would be more at home with "persons of her own class of life." Others there are, which, like our street arabs, are a pest and a trouble. One of these Jack the sailor brings home as a pet and usually presents to his sweetheart, or, maybe, his mother, who accepts the mischievous imp with much misgiving as to the propriety of so doing, but from love of the donor cannot refuse, and finds out, alas! too late, the awful destruction of property the possession of one of these entails, the smashing of crockery, the upsetting of ink over clean white linen, the pilfering of jam, killing the canary, and, in one recorded instance, making a finale by upsetting the clothes-horse on to the kitchen stove and setting fire to the house.[1]

The variableness in the habits and dispositions shown by the monkeys selected for performing is well worthy of notice. Many of the different genera are mentally, so to speak, far removed from each other; some of them are capable, by training and education, of being taught and made to understand the various duties that the teacher imposes upon them; while others, as among ourselves, are found devoid of the power of learning.

The trainers of monkeys well know the species best

[1] A fact!

adapted to their various purposes. For the mimic performances in the streets the monkeys of South America (any of the species of the genus *Cebus*) are mostly selected; and for exhibition in the circus (for horse-riding, rope-dancing, and tumbling) the genus *Macacus* and *Cynocephalus* of the Old World are best suited; they being larger, having more strength and courage, and requiring another mode of training, being less intelligent than the others.

That these animals often enjoy the fun they create there can be no doubt, and any one who has witnessed the tricks of the monkeys at the Gardens on Easter Monday must be at once convinced of this fact, on seeing these imitative rascals playing at blind-man's buff, a thing they never attempt to do unless surrounded by a crowd of youngsters, who roar and shout at the fun, and the greater the merriment the more active the monkeys; a pocket-handkerchief stolen from one of the young monkeys who enjoy the privilege of bearing a Christian name being used for the purpose.

It is a laughable sight to see a monkey, especially if it be a large and powerful one, introduced for the first time into a cage or room full of monkeys. The interloper is offered by the smallest of the monkeys, encouraged by the larger ones, every insult and annoyance it is possible to think of, and if the one insulted should be so unfortunate as to lose his self-possession and dare to resent any of the insults, he is at once pounced upon by the larger occupants and thrashed most unmercifully, reminding one of one's early school-days when the new-comer was hustled about, and the younger boys pushed against him by the older in order to create a breach of the peace.

The lively and beautiful marmozets and squirrel monkeys of South America are, strange to say, far from intelligent, although the brain is in far greater proportion to the size of the body than in most other monkeys. Many never become tame, and those most tame rarely or never can be taught. They are, in a wild state, great destroyers of insects, living much on caterpillars, moths and butterflies; they also devour fruit, seeds, occasionally small or young birds, eggs, mice and other animals. Sometimes they breed in captivity, but require much warmth and change of food.

BARBARY APE.

(*MACACUS INUUS.*)

This hardy and powerful monkey, the only species of monkey found wild in Europe, has from time immemorial inhabited the Rock of Gibraltar. It is found also in North Africa. The adult male is a formidable and savage animal; his canine teeth are, when fully developed, of large size, and have sharp and pointed cutting edges.

This ape has been found to thrive better and live longer when exposed to the open air (in the coldest weather) than when kept in a warm house. It is dangerous to allow the adult males to be placed with any other species of monkey, their savage disposition being apt to manifest itself in a very painful manner. One habit exhibited by most of the larger male monkeys is the display to each other of their powerful canine teeth, this they invariably do on seeing a new arrival; this performance is gone through by sham yawning, which is not attempted by those whose teeth have been cut off, or otherwise damaged. It is, therefore, evident that the exhibition of these formidable weapons is intended as a threat, or, perhaps, as a caution to the new-comer.

The collection contains generally one or two specimens of the Barbary Ape, but it is only the young of this species which are permitted to associate with the other monkeys, it being very dangerous to trust the adult in the same cage.

The looking-glass in the large cage in the monkey-house affords much amusement, not only to the visitors but to the inquisitive monkeys, who for a long time seem puzzled at seeing themselves reflected in the glass; they are constantly trying to look behind it, no doubt expecting to find one of their own species.

The Andaman monkey met a rival for favour in the shape of a rare *confrère* from the interior of Asia. This new rival, a Cashmere monkey (*Macacus pelops*), was a lively little thing, and became a favourite both on account of its good-nature and of the nimble manner in which it springs, acrobat fashion, into mid-air.

WHITE-WHISKERED LEMUR.

(*LEMUR LEUCOMYSTAX.*)

In size this animal nearly equals the Ruffed Lemur (*Lemur macaco*), which animal it also much resembles in form and habits.

A living specimen was purchased for the Society from a dealer in Liverpool, in the month of October 1861, and was in the menagerie at the time this was written. It was stated, by the person who brought it to this country, that the natives of Madagascar, from whom it was obtained, said it was a very rare kind and that it had been kept as a pet upwards of two years in that country.

I have compared this animal with the descriptions and specimens that I have been able to find in the British Museum and several other museums on the Continent, and I feel satisfied that this animal is specifically distinct from any that I have met with. I, therefore, proposed to call it the White-whiskered Lemur (*Lemur leucomystax*)—a name that will, I think, enable any one to recognize the species, it being remarkable for its long and perfectly white whiskers, in which its ears are almost entirely concealed; the face is greyish-black, darkest on the nose and back part of the head; the feet are brown, inclining to black on the toes. The prevailing colour of the body, limbs and tail is reddish-brown on a grey ground, darkest on the middle of the back; on the lower part of the back, at the base of the tail, is a white patch; the tail is lighter in colour than the body, the underside and tip nearly white; the belly is greyish-white; the eyes are yellow-brown. On examination, I find the animal is a female; and I imagine, from her voice, which is a kind of hoarse croaking bark rapidly and frequently repeated, that the male would probably produce a louder and more powerful note.

I am led to infer this from having repeatedly heard the voice of both male and female of *L. macaco.* The voice of the male of this species is certainly very astonishingly powerful, and can be heard a great distance; while the voice of the female, although loud and discordant, is comparatively weak. Nevertheless it is a very unpleasant series of loud, grunting, grating barks, sufficient to alarm a nervous traveller should he be in the forest at dark, and unacquainted with the size and nature of the animal producing these loud and dismal sounds.

MONTEIRO'S GALAGO.

(*GALAGO MONTEIRI*, BART.)

In the month of November 1862 I had occasion to call at the house of Mr. L. A. Monteiro, and that gentleman showed me an animal which I at once told him was new and unknown to me. I took every opportunity of ascertaining if I were right in so saying, and I called again upon Mr. Monteiro, who kindly lent me the animal with permission to exhibit and describe it. I at once proceeded to the British Museum to compare this animal with the species in that collection, but nothing like this specimen was to be found there. I have also the opinion of Dr. Gray, who has for some time devoted much attention to this group of animals, and who kindly assisted me in this examination, to the effect that he believed the animal to be unknown and undescribed. It differs from the known species in being larger and lighter in colour and in having a much longer tail. Mr. Monteiro informs me that it was sent to England by his son, Mr. J. J. Monteiro, who obtained it at Cuio Bay, to the south of Loando, in Angola. It is very gentle and sleeps much during the day, feeds on *fruit, bread, milk,* and other sweet things, particularly bananas.

The entire length of the animal is 28 in., of which the tail measures 16 in. The colour is light chinchilla grey all over the head, body and tail, nearly white on the throat; the toes and feet are dark brown, nearly black; nose black; the eyes greyish-brown; the ears nearly black, 2 in. long, 1½ in. broad at the base. The animal has the power of turning its ears back and folding them up when at rest. When moving about or in search of food, they spread out and stand upward and forward, reminding one of the Aye-aye; but when folded back and down, the animal's face bears a strong resemblance to the Douroucouli. The pupils of the eyes are oval and vertical.

This animal is considerably larger than the specimen in the British Museum known as *Otolicnus crassicaudatus;* but as I am unable to determine the exact structure of its teeth, in order to say positively that it belongs to that genus, I propose to name it *Galago monteiri*, in order to identify it with the gentleman who has added from time to time many rare specimens to our collection.

AYE-AYE.

(CHIROMYS MADAGASCARIENSIS.)

A fine adult female of the Aye-aye (*Chiromys mada-gascariensis*) arrived in this country on the 12th of August 1862. On the voyage, this animal produced a young one which lived about ten days. On arriving here she was in poor condition and very feeble; she soon, however, began to feed freely, and gained considerable strength, as was shown by the timber destroyed in the cage in which she had been kept.

This animal is much blacker, and appears larger, than the male of this species now in the British Museum; the long hairs on the back of the neck, extending to the lower part of the body, have white points; these white points are thickest above, and become less numerous towards the limbs and tail, which appear quite black; the hairs of the tail, however, are white or grey at the roots (this can only be observed by separating them); the chin and throat are dirty white, which colour extends over the chest; the short hairs on the face are a mixture of dirty grey and white; the long hairs are black; the eyes light brown, surrounded by dark-coloured hairs; the nose and muzzle are of a dirty flesh-colour; the lips pink; the ears, shining black and naked, but thickly studded with small protuberances; the feet and toes are sooty black, with the under surface and claws lighter, inclining to flesh-colour. The situation of the mammæ is remarkable. They are two in number and placed at the lowest part of the abdomen (the animal differing in this respect entirely from the Lemurs and Bats, the teats of which are on the breast).

The Aye-aye sleeps during the day, and the body is then generally curved round and lying on its side; the tail is spread out and flattened over it, so that the head and body of the animal are almost entirely covered by the tail.

It is only at night that the Aye-aye exhibits any activity. I hear her crawling about and gnawing the timber when, to me, all is perfectly dark; and I have been surprised to find that upon the introduction of a light, directed to the face of the animal, she does not exhibit any signs of uneasiness, but stretches out her arm and tries to touch the lamp with her long fingers. She frequently hangs by her hind legs, and in this position cleans and combs out her large tail, using the slender hook-like third finger with great rapidity, reminding one strongly of the movements of the large Bats (*Pteropus*). This skeleton-like finger is used with great address in cleaning her face and picking the corners of the eyes, nose, mouth, ears and other parts of her body; during these operations the other fingers are frequently partially closed.

In feeding, the left hand only is used, although she has the full use of her right one. The mode of taking her food requires careful attention, in consequence of the very rapid movement of the hand during the process. The fourth finger (which is the longest and largest) is thrust forward into the food, the slender third finger is raised

26

upwards and backwards above the rest, while the first
finger or thumb is lowered so as to be seen below and
behind the chin; in this position the hand is drawn backwards rapidly, the inner side of the fourth finger passing
between the lips, the head of the animal being held sideways, thus depositing the food in the mouth at each movement; the tongue, jaws and lips are kept in full motion
all the time. Sometimes the animal will advance towards
and lap from the dish like a cat, but this is unusual. I
have never heard her utter any cry, or produce any vocal
sound, during the many hours at night in which I have
watched her habits, nor has she appeared shy or angry at
my presence.

With reference to food, this creature exhibits no inclination to take any kind of insects, but feeds freely on a
mixture of *milk, honey, eggs,* and any *thick, sweet, glutinous
fluid,* rejecting meal-worms, grasshoppers, the larvæ of
wasps, and all similar objects. Consequently I am inclined
to think that this animal is not insectivorous. Its large
and powerful teeth lead me to infer that it may possibly
wound trees, and cause them to discharge their juices into
the cavity made by its teeth; and that upon this fluid it
probably feeds. This appears to me the more likely, as I
observe that our specimen returns frequently to the same
spot on the tree which she had previously injured. I am
also strengthened in my opinion by noticing the little
attention paid by the animal to its food. It does not watch
or look after it, for I have on several occasions removed the
vessel containing its food during the time the animal was
feeding, and the creature continued to thrust its hand
forward, as before, upon the same spot; though after a
while, finding no more food, she discontinued the action,
and moved off to search for more elsewhere. This apparently stupid act is so unlike the habits of an animal

intended to capture or feed on living creatures, that I am inclined to believe that the Aye-aye feeds upon inanimate substances. I have frequently seen it eat a portion of the bark and wood after taking a quantity of the fluid food.

The excrement of this animal much resembles the dung of small rabbits, being in separate, nearly round, balls.

CHAPTER III.

LIONS AND TIGERS.

(*FELIDÆ.*)

THE lion (*Felis leo*) appears to breed more freely than any other species of *Felis*, and the number of young at a birth is greater, not unfrequently four and sometimes five being produced in a litter. It is remarkable that these animals breed more freely in travelling collections (wild-beast shows) than in zoological gardens; probably the constant excitement and irritation produced by moving from place to place, or change of air, may have considerable influence in the matter.

The Tiger (*Felis tigris*) has rarely bred in confinement, but there are several well-authenticated instances of the female Tiger breeding with the Lion. The hybrids lived, and in due time arrived at maturity. Animals of this mixed breed have been exhibited in a travelling menagerie kept by Mr. Atkins, and the appearance of the animals at once bespoke their mixed origin.

I have more than once met with instances of the male Jaguar (*F. onca*) breeding with a female Leopard (*F. leopardus*). These hybrids also were reared recently in Wombwell's well-known travelling collection. I have seen some animals of this kind bred between a male black Jaguar and a female Indian Leopard; the young partook strongly of the male colouring, being almost black.

The Leopard is not unfrequently bred in captivity, many

29

having been bred and reared in the Society's Gardens, and elsewhere.

The Puma (*F. concolor*) has bred frequently in the Society's Gardens. This species appears to produce generally two only at a birth, in some cases only one; they rear their young without difficulty.

The Ocelot (*F. pardalis*) has also bred two or three times in the Society's Gardens.

As far as I am able to ascertain, the period of gestation in the foregoing species is *sixteen weeks*. The young of some of the species bear a great resemblance to each other, thus, for instance, the young of the Lion is indistinctly spotted all over; the young of the Puma is also spotted with large and well-marked patches, which the figures, drawn by Mr. Wolf from young Pumas born in the Gardens, well exhibit.[1]

The Cheetah (*F. jubata*) never to my knowledge has bred in England. Dr. Günther, however, informs me that this species has bred in the Gardens in Frankfort. From all that I have experienced with reference to this beautiful species, I consider it one of the most difficult of the family to keep, and consequently the chances of its breeding are rare. This animal is generally gentle, timid, and very excitable. I am inclined to think the want of sufficient space and exercise, together with over-feeding, are the cause of convulsions and fits, to which this species is liable; I have witnessed the death of two or three of these animals from excitement after a full meal.

The young of the Tiger is striped like the adult, but, of course, less distinctly. The young Leopard also resembles the adult in its markings. Not only in the large Cats, but in all the smaller species of the genus *Felis*, the spots, stripes, or markings are always present in the young of

[1] See *Zoological Sketches*, 1861–67.

those species that are so marked in the adult state ; and, as far as my knowledge extends, the young of all (except the *domestic* cat) exhibit traces of spots or other markings, although they disappear in the adult animals.

A very extraordinary malformation or defect has frequently occurred among the lions produced during the last twenty years in the Regent's Park. This imperfection consists in the roof of the mouth being open—the palatal bones do not meet; the animal is therefore unable to suck, and, consequently, always dies. This abnormal condition has not been confined to the young of any one pair of lions, but many lions that have bred in the Gardens, not in any way related to each other, have from time to time produced these malformed young, the cause of which appears to me quite unaccountable.

THE LATE CHARLES JAMRACH.

Upon one of my frequent visits to the establishment of the late Charles Jamrach, I found Mrs. Jamrach in a very serious condition, she was suffering from a very alarming fright, the cause of which was as follows :—Jamrach had purchased three small lion cubs, they were in a very poor and emaciated condition, and thinking that they might recover, he had them conveyed to a small room at the top of the house, the windows of which were barricaded with strong iron netting on the inside. These animals were placed under the charge of his principal man, Clarke, whose duty it was to feed and attend to them. Under Clarke's care the animals rapidly improved in condition, and time passed on. The attention which he had to bestow upon his three or four establishments so occupied his time that Jamrach had, in all probability, not often visited the lion cubs. He heard from Clarke that the young lions were growing fast and were much improved, and he felt satisfied that they were increasing in value, and would ultimately well repay him for their keep; so the time went on. Of the length of time they remained in this place of captivity I have no perfect knowledge, but they had grown to a considerable size and had kept perfectly tame, and had become accustomed to be attended daily by Clarke. It happened, however, that Clarke was required by his master to go early one morning to the docks for the purpose of either shipping some animals or landing them, which would probably cause him to be absent for the day. Upon leaving he reminded his master that the lions up-stairs had not been fed. "Oh," said Jamrach, "all right, I'll feed them." In the course of the day Jamrach proceeded up-stairs, carrying with him the lions' food. Upon opening the door and entering the room the three lions (to his great astonishment) took fright at the sight of a stranger, and before Jamrach had time to think what would happen they rushed past him and blundered headlong down the stairs. Fearing that the door at the bottom of the stair-case leading into the parlour might be open, and that his wife would be terrified if they were to rush into the room, he called with all his might, "Mary, Mary, the lions are coming down-stairs." "Mary" closed the door in time to prevent their entrance. If I am not mistaken there was a glass panel in the door, which enabled her to see the brutes in the small passage at the foot of the stairs. She at once realized the awkward position in which her husband and herself were placed; she watched the lions with intense anxiety, and in a few minutes she saw them quietly ascending the stairs, they having found there was no exit. Thinking that her husband might be then in danger, she quietly opened the door and called out,

"Charlie, they are coming up-stairs." "Charlie" not being anxious to meet them beat a hasty retreat, as they were growling and appeared in a very angry mood; he took possession of the room they had lately occupied, closing the door after him, thus giving himself time to consider what was best to be done under the circumstances. After a time, when they found they could gain no admittance, they beat another retreat, and as he heard them a second time blundering down-stairs, he with caution took a glance at the situation. Once more the staircase was ascended by the animals, and "Mary" again signalled their upward progress. How often this performance of ascending and descending the stairs was repeated I am unable to say, but the signals between "Mary" and "Charlie" were very frequently exchanged. The lions, however, were no longer perambulating the staircase, but had taken possession of the bedroom on the second floor, thus enabling Jamrach to descend and close the door upon them. There they remained until the reappearance of Clarke, who at once proceeded to coax them to return to their former safe and suitable abode. The above was communicated to me by both Jamrach and wife, who assured me that her most severe illness, from which she never properly recovered, was only the result of the most awful fright she experienced on that occasion.

CHAPTER IV.

BEARS AND HYÆNA.

BEAR STORIES.

In the Bear-pit in the Gardens a male Black Bear of America (*Ursus americanus*) was kept for a long time with a female of the European Brown Bear (*Ursus arctos*). In the month of May 1859, these bears were seen to copulate, and on December 31 the female produced three young ones, which when born were *naked* and *blind*, and about the size of a full-grown rat.

The mother was seen to carry one of these young ones in her mouth a day or two after it was born, and, as it disappeared, it is supposed that she devoured it. Probably it was not healthy. The other two remained and continued to grow, and at the age of five weeks were as large as a common rabbit. Their eyes began to open by this time, and their bodies were covered with a short thick fur and were nearly black.

On examining these young bears it was found they were male and female, and the number and situation of the teats appeared somewhat remarkable. The female had six teats, four of them placed in front between the fore-legs, and two of them in the lower part of the abdomen. Another singular fact was, that the female during the time she was suckling these young ones fed most sparingly, and rarely took any drink. From the before-mentioned observations we may infer that the period of gestation of the Bears is about seven months.

A young female Malayan Bear which was in my possession had only four teats, they were rather far apart between the fore-arms or breast, without a trace of any on the lower abdomen.

For many years the Polar Bear was described and considered to be the only one of the family that was strictly carnivorous, and was believed to exist entirely upon animal substances, and natural history books, copying one another, perpetuated this erroneous idea. One of the Arctic explorers, however, observed that the Polar Bears during the Arctic summer grazed upon the short vegetable growth on the banks and hilly parts of the country; he at first thought, as they appeared to him at the distance, that they were a flock of sheep.

Since that time it is found that during the summer these bears will eat grass and other vegetable food.

Two Frenchmen, who were for some time about London with a large bear, came finally to grief. A nervous old lady at Brentford took fright and called the police to her assistance. The consequence was an altercation with the gentleman in blue, who did not understand exactly the French language, and who rudely tried to take the two Frenchmen and the bear into custody. The men and the beast, however, did not feel disposed to comply with the aforesaid gentleman's rough treatment, and made a *little resistance*, which *being represented* to the magistrate the unfortunate foreigners were consigned to a month's imprisonment.

A great difficulty now arose, for although the poor Frenchmen were easily locked up, what was to be done with the bear, which stoutly declined to be separated from his master, and which scratched and fought at any one who attempted to take any liberty with him. So the first night the two men, the bear and a large dog slept together. On the following day the chairman of the magistrates applied to the authorities of the Zoological Gardens for assistance to take "in charge" the beast and dog. Having obtained permission to place them in the Zoo, the next proceeding was their removal from Brentford. Now although every one of our policemen had become adepts at carrying off unlucky dogs, they had as yet to learn the cost of muzzling bears and leading them to prison. In their first attempt they failed. In order to make sure of Bruin they obtained an omnibus, and softly, as they thought, shut him in and started; but the bear preferred to ride outside, so making free with the glass windows, which he soon broke, and getting out, he stopped the omnibus by hanging on the hind-wheel; as his chain had been fastened on the inside of the 'bus he was prevented from making off altogether. Under these trying circumstances the frightened police had to return and get the two poor Frenchmen (although sentenced to a month's imprisonment) to help them to cart the bear to its own prison in the Zoo!

One of the bears which was brought to England by H.R.H. the Prince of Wales, thought proper on one occasion to make his way out of the den in which he had been kept during the voyage from India, and in which he remained after his arrival at the Zoo.

This animal had been a great pet on board the *Serapis*, and was known as "George." Like all bears "George" had, when young, been a very funny, playful little fellow, but he had now grown to a considerable size, and his strength had increased accordingly; he was, therefore, able to bend the iron bars that were before too strong for him, and escape.

This he managed to do at night-time, to the great alarm

of the night-watchman, who aroused me and others in the hope of recapturing him. For some time no trace of the runaway could be found. The first information we received of his whereabouts was from the driver of a cab, whose frightened horse was in a nervous state of excitement, having met Master Georgie in the outer circle of the Park, on his road to the well-known "York and Albany." This was enough, and we were on his track like lightning. The man who had charge of him on the voyage, and who was always on the most friendly terms with him, approached near to him, calling him by his name. Instead of being pleased at meeting his old friend, Master "George," with an angry growl, made direct for him, but was met with one or two sharp blows from a heavy stick on his tender snout, causing him to change his mode of procedure; being again called by his name, and in an angry tone threatened with more punishment, he gave up further resistance, and allowed his captors to put a cord over his head, fasten it round his neck, and lead him in triumph to a safer place of confinement.

THE PANDA.

(*AILURUS FULGENS.*)

On May 22, 1869, the subject of this notice was received at the Gardens. I found the animal in a very exhausted condition, not able to stand, and so weak that it could with difficulty crawl from one end of its long cage to the other. It was suffering from frequent discharges of frothy, slimy fæcal matter. This filth had so completely covered and matted its fur that its appearance and smell was most offensive.

The instructions I received with reference to its food were that it should have about a quart of milk per day, with a little boiled rice and grass. It was evident that this food, the change of climate, the sea voyage, or the treatment on board ship had reduced the poor beast to this pitiable condition.

My first object was to endeavour to support the little life that remained by a change of food. I first tried raw and boiled chicken, rabbit, and other animal substances, all of which it refused to eat. I found, however, it would take arrowroot, with the yelks of eggs and sugar mixed with boiled milk; and in a few days I saw some improvement in its condition. I then gave it strong beef-tea well sweetened, adding pea-flour, Indian-corn flour, and other farinaceous food, varying the mixture daily. The appetite of the animal for sweet food was remarkable, and by adding a little sugar to the meat that had been boiled to make the beef-tea, it was induced to eat it freely.

Finding a great improvement in the strength of the panda, and the weather being fine, I gave him his liberty, by letting him out of his cage into the garden in front of my house (having a boy to see that he did not escape); he soon began to eat a few leaves and the tender shoots of the roses, and finding some unripe apples that had fallen from the trees, greedily devoured them. I had a fear they might disagree with him; this, however, was not the case, for he rapidly improved in condition. At night his usual supply of beef-tea, etc. was given to him in his cage, and this was always consumed by morning.

We have in the Gardens two or three trees upon which grow bunches of yellow berries (*Pyrus vestita*). Upon giving some of these to the panda, I noticed his fondness for them. He would grasp the bunch in his paw, holding it tightly, and bite off these berries one by one; so delighted with this food was he, that all other food was left as long as these berries lasted. I have every reason to believe that berries, fruit, and other vegetable substances constitute the food of this animal in a wild state.

Upon this food the animal became more vigorous, the old ragged and matted coat was thrown off, and the beautiful new fur began to grow rapidly. One important operation was performed almost every morning, that of a shower-bath, administered by means of a garden syringe; this was done before letting him out of his cage; it induced him to bask in the sun, to clean and dry himself. The biting, scratching, and shaking to get rid of the old and clotted fur was a sure sign of good health. Animals recovering from sickness show signs of improvement by their attempts to clean themselves, and it is of the utmost importance to aid them, by judicious means, to accomplish this object. Many valuable animals are lost in consequence of their neglected condition; they fret and die more on account of the filth about them than from actual disease, although disease is a sure attendant upon animals allowed to become filthy.

This individual was not disposed to become a pet, for, notwithstanding every attempt to induce it to be caressed, it continued to exhibit a rather fierce and angry disposition —probably only an individual peculiarity, and not at all characteristic of the species.

When offended, it would rush at me and strike with both feet, not, like a cat, sideways or downwards, but forward, and the body raised like a bear, the claws projecting, but not hooked or brought down like the claws of a cat; for although the claws are partly retractile, the animal cannot use them in that manner. At the moment of making the attack, it would utter a sharp spitting hiss; this, and a weak, single, squeaking call-note, are the only sounds I ever heard it utter.

Its mode of progression on the ground corresponds with that of the kinkajou, otter and weasel—running on all fours, or jumping with a kind of gallop, its back rather arched. In climbing, the panda is not quite so expert in trees as the kinkajou, the prehensile tail of which renders the animal much assistance in swinging from branch to branch. The kinkajou has also a far higher intelligence.

In forming an opinion of the affinities of the panda from its general appearance and habits, as far as it is possible to judge of these by observing an animal in captivity, I am led to remark the strong resemblance to the kinkajou in its movements, running, walking, climbing, mode of feeding, and its food. In drinking, it inserted the lips and sucked up the fluid after the manner of bears; it does not lap like the dog or cat.

At the same time the fur of the panda, not only in quality but also in the colour and marking, especially that of the tail, exhibits a remarkable affinity to the coati, raccoon and binturong. I am, however, inclined to think that its affinities are greater with the kinkajou than with any other animal. The coati and raccoon are far more carnivorous than the panda, kinkajou, or binturong; they are also less nocturnal than these last-mentioned species.

In the use of the front paws the most perfect of the animals alluded to in this paper is perhaps the raccoon, of which the naked toes form a strong contrast with the thickly muffled foot of the panda—the fur covering the whole of the underside of the foot of this animal, except a space about the size of a small pea in the middle pad. This thick clothing of the paw would lead one to doubt whether the panda could grasp with its paw as firmly and perfectly as I have seen it do.

The eyes of the panda are small and bear-like. It does not appear to have the power of smelling well developed, like the coati or raccoon; it is also much slower in all its movements than those animals.

I must not omit to remark that the voice of the panda, kinkajou, otter and coati are wonderfully alike, especially the short faint squeak, or call-note.

I submitted a small portion of the hair or fur of the panda to my friend Mr. Richter, in order to have it examined under the microscope, and to obtain his opinion. I give an extract from his letter, which was accompanied by the following drawing.

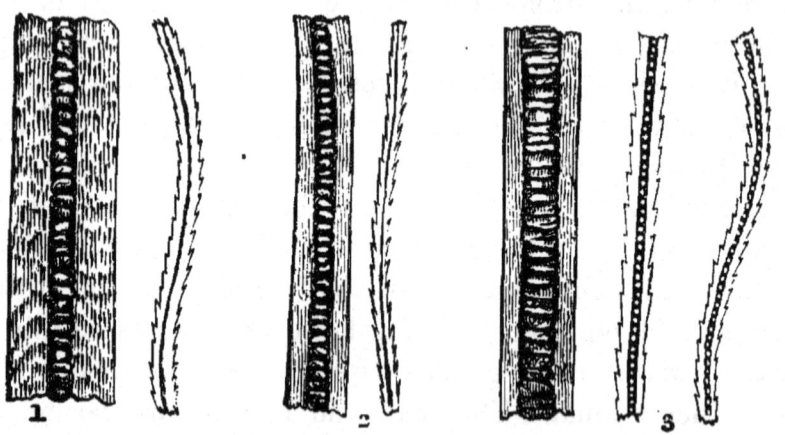

1. Hair and wool of *Ursus piscatur*, magnified.
2. Hair and wool of *Cercoleptes caudivolvulus*, magnified.
3. Hair and wool (two varieties of) of *Ailurus fulgens*, magnified.

"I have examined the hair of the panda, and compared it with that of some of the bears. I send you a sketch of some of these hairs. The panda is evidently a more woolly animal than most of the bears, and its hair shows a larger development of the medullary cells; but these differences are of very slight consequence, so little, indeed, that they might only signify a mere specific distinction. If the hair of the panda were to grow a little harsher, and include rather less wool, it might, as to construction, be that of a true bear. You say that the bear grows its hair in *tufts;* this is certainly the case with the panda. The hairs of the panda are quite simple, like those of any other mammal, and each one proceeds from its own follicle; but the follicles being collected into groups, and not evenly dispersed over the surface, the tufted appearance is caused at once.

"I do not know if this is the case with the kinkajou. I think the panda's hair is more like that of a bear than the kinkajou's."

At a meeting of the Zoological Society in 1870, papers were read by Professor Flower and myself, the former upon the anatomy, and the latter upon the habits of the panda (*Ailurus fulgens*). It is very satisfactory to find the close agreement in the opinions expressed as to the affinities of this very singular and rare animal, and argues well for the truthfulness and accuracy of our observations. Although no communication had passed between us, we independently arrived at the same, or nearly the same, conclusion as to the real position of this remarkable animal in the natural system.

THE AARD-WOLF.

(*PROTELES LALANDII.*)

A rarely obtained animal, the Aard-Wolf (*Proteles lalandii*) is little known, although not one of extreme rarity: the first living example was received October 26, 1868, at the Gardens, and since that time others have been received; the beast is undoubtedly an aberrant form of hyæna; the remarkable difference, however, consists principally in the very feeble dentition, especially in the molar teeth. These teeth in the hyænas proper are, considering the size of the animal, unequalled by any known mammal, while in the *Proteles*, or Aard-Wolf, the molar teeth are mere rudiments, and so small as to be almost useless for the purpose of mastication.

But the habits of the true hyænas require these massive and enormously powerful grinders, seeing that their office is most frequently the crushing up the bones of other animals. The hardest and largest bones of a horse are broken and eaten by them with apparently little trouble, while the diminutive Aard-Wolf is contented to eat the putrid flesh and soft parts, and in consequence of this vulture-like habit becomes so offensive that it requires a very enthusiastic and strong-stomached collector to screw up his determination to so high a pitch that he can undertake to remove the stinking jacket from the more stinking body of this foul-feeding brute for the purposes of the naturalist, and hence the rarity of specimens in museums. The smell is, perhaps, the only offensive quality of this creature, for it seems very harmless, and will not attack or kill other animals, but appears content to wait not only till they die, or are killed, but to allow them to become perfectly soft before they attempt to make their filthy feast. The specimens now in the Gardens, however, having become more civilized by being fed upon finely-chopped fresh meat, the foul and unpleasant odour has quite left them, and they appear in good health and to bear their altered condition perfectly well.

CHAPTER V.

SEALS AND WALRUS.

STELLER'S SEA-LION.

(*OTARIA STELLERII*.)

In the *Field*, 1892, Mr. W. B. Tegetmeier tells us:—
" There is a very remarkable sea-lion on view at the
Zoological Gardens, which is well worth a visit from those
interested in the group; it is that known to zoologists as
Steller's Sea-Lion (*Otaria stellerii*). Its preservation is
entirely due to the practical skill of Mr. Bartlett. The
animal, which is of a very large size, was received by Mr.
Cross, the well-known importer of and dealer in live
animals at Liverpool, who was desirous of placing it on
deposit in the Gardens, in which there are several ponds
devoted to the seals. This, however, was not done, and
the animal passed into the possession of Mr. Bostock, of
the travelling menagerie known formerly as Wombwell's;
but here a difficulty occurred. The animal, since its capture, refused to feed, and had certainly gone many weeks
without any food whatever, and was gradually losing flesh.
This may appear incredible, but it is well known that the
male fur seals (*O. ursina*) of the Pribiloff Islands remain
on land for three months, never leaving their families
during the breeding season. This Steller's seal was, however, absolutely wasting away for want of food, but refused
every fish offered to it. Its large size and strength and

formidable canine teeth rendered any attempt at forcible feeding impracticable. But Mr. Bartlett is not readily baffled, and he determined to try the *Otaria* with living fish; so, clearing out the common seals from their pond, he had the new species placed in it, and, sending to Billingsgate, purchased a dozen pounds of the largest eels he could obtain. These were placed in the pond with the *Otaria*. They instinctively recognized their danger, and swam rapidly round the shallow margin of the concrete pond, but in vain. Their presence whetted the appetite of the seal; he pursued them with the most marvellous activity, and in less than five minutes they were all captured and devoured. The desire for food, once raised, has continued. *O. stellerii* is as great a feeder as the old Patagonian species in the next cage, and a dozen whiting disappear at one time with marvellous celerity. Not only will fish be eaten, but flesh, a portion of which was given as a restorative after his long fast. This was readily accomplished by dipping lumps of flesh into the pail containing the dead whiting, by which it acquires a good fishy flavour, and is swallowed as soon as it is dropped into the mouth.

"After his feast of eels this large seal was left in the pond during the night, but, to the consternation of the keeper, was missing in the morning; it had climbed over the three-feet high iron railing, then investigated another pond, again climbed the second enclosure, and made its way into the swans' pond, where it was found amicably located with the lawful possessors, and from whence it was driven by the keepers armed with birch brooms, which implements Mr. Bartlett regards as the most effective and harmless weapons with which to face carnivora, as the thrust of the broom in the face is not appreciated by the animals."

THE WALRUS.

(*TRICHECHUS ROSMARUS.*)

A young male Walrus (*Trichechus rosmarus,* Linn.) was purchased on November 1, 1867, of Messrs. Alexander Stephen and Co. of Dundee, for the sum of £200. The animal had been captured in Davis's Straits by Captain Richard Wells of the steam whaler '*Arctic,*' on August 28, 1867.

"On my arrival at Dundee on October 29, I found the young Walrus in a very restless state, and, as I thought, hungry ; it was being fed upon large mussels, about twenty being opened at a meal, and the poor beast thus fed about three times a day.

"I immediately told the owners that I thought the animal was being starved, and suggested that some fish should be tried. To this Mr. Stephen at once agreed, and a codfish was procured from the neighbourhood, and by me cut into long thin strips. On offering the pieces of cod to the animal he greedily devoured them. Since that time I have fed the Walrus upon *fish, mussels, whelks, clams,* and the *stomachs* and *intestines* and other soft parts of *fishes,* cut small ; for I find that it cannot swallow anything larger than a walnut. I am now convinced that the food of the Walrus is strictly animal substance, and from what I have observed during the last seventeen days, I feel certain that the creature will feed freely upon almost any kind of animal matter.

"I am also inclined to believe that even carrion or decomposed flesh would not be refused. This probably has led to the frequent remark upon the disgusting state of the contents of their stomachs. May not these creatures be

46

the scavengers of the Arctic Seas, the vultures among mammals ? The remarkable dentition reminds one of the carrion-feeding *Proteles*. May not the strong bristles on its muzzle have much to do with this kind of food as well as shrimp-catching, the mode of brushing backwards and forwards with these bristles the food and other substances on the ground, and sucking everything up it swallows ?

" I notice that indigestible portions or substances taken with its food pass off in the excretion; and probably in the adult animal, when shells, seaweed, and other substances are collected, these creatures, like other carnivorous animals, have the power of ejecting these indigestible bodies from the stomach.

" The fragments of shell, small stones, the byssus of the mussels, and the opercula of whelks, together with fragments of seaweed attached to the byssus of the mussels, pass freely from this animal. The terminal portion of the intestines must be of large size, judging by the size of the excretion."

The subjoined poem commemorates this walrus and his food :—

ON THE MALE WALRUS

(*Baptized " Jemmy "*)

AT THE ZOOLOGICAL GARDENS, REGENT'S PARK.

BY ROBERT ADAMS, F.Z.S.

To M.

We must some day—next week—together go,
When air is warmer, dry, and winds don't blow,
To see the lions, monkeys, bears, and seals,
And how young Jemmy Walrus takes his meals.

He lost his mother in a piteous way.
Ah! killed she was on iceberg far away,
Some sailors haul'd her o'er the ice-bound shore,
And dragg'd her through the sea—a mile or more.
Fond Jemmy followed close upon her wake,
And saw the wicked men her body take
With ropes, which round her head and tail did slip,
And hoisted all he loved into a ship.

Oh! sorrowful and sad was this poor boy.—
An uproar then was heard—" All hands ahoy!"
The crew loud shouted, "There is one alive!"
Then round his body seamen did contrive
To pass some cords, quite carefully and soft,
And drew him from the sea, by ropes, aloft.

From Davis' Straits he voyag'd to Old Dundee,
In wooden cage, confined, obliged to be.
On fat of pork this mongrel fish did feed;
For piggy kind of stuff he show'd no greed.
Quite agonized with grief and hunger too,
Until kind Mr. Bartlett came to view
This treasure from the regions bleak and cold,
And bought the burly beast with notes and gold.
The anguish of his state no words can tell,
But kindly treatment quickly did dispel
Much fear of man from Jemmy's mind and thought,
And to his future home was safely brought;
Where all, both old and young, may go and see
This wondrous stranger from the Arctic Sea.

Molluscous food he likes, all soft as pap.
With aid of whiskers he contrives to lap
Some mussels—whelks, all shell'd, and in a bowl,—
(He cannot bolt a single herring whole.)
His stomach takes of these six quarts per day,
And ten he would devour if that he may.

48

Amphibious monster, without legs or paws,
A roundish face, with bristling bearded jaws.
He has a short and apoplectic neck,
His body brownish, without spot or speck.
With fins for legs he manages to crawl,
Attempts to climb the fence and e'en the wall.

His length may reach to sixteen feet and half,
For now he measures eight, and is a calf.
And as he grows by feeding on mollusks,
From out his jaw will come two ivory tusks,
With which to rake the sand and tangl'd weeds,
To stir up things on which the Walrus feeds.

May Jemmy live a long and happy life.
Perhaps, in time, they'll bring to him a wife !

CHAPTER VI.

RODENTS.

HARES AND RABBITS.

HARE CHEWING THE CUD.

"Sir,—You will much oblige me by giving me information upon a subject, which from your position you will be well able to do. I presume that you have among the collection of animals at the Gardens 'the Hare.' I am anxious to know in reference to this animal whether it 'chews the cud.' In the *Times* newspaper of to-day, there is an assertion made by Bishop Colenso, founded on the authority of Professor Owen, that it does *not* chew the cud. In the eleventh chapter of Leviticus, sixth verse, it is stated that the Jews were forbidden to use it as an article of food because it does chew the cud.

"Explanations are given in books I have referred to, stating that from a peculiar movement of the mouth it appears to do so,—but it does not. Cowper the poet describes one of his own, which during the day, when in his garden, 'either slept or chewed the cud till the evening.' I am giving you trouble, I fear, in thus writing to you, but *actual observation* surely is the best means of judging.

"Is it in appearance only, or is it a fact? The Bible says it is the fact, and I entirely believe it. But naturalists deny it. By giving me the above information I have requested, you will much oblige me, etc., etc.

"H. Battiscombe."

"*Zoo, April* 3, 1863.

"Dear Sir,—In reply to your letter respecting the Hare, I beg to say that I have several living in the collection, having for some years carefully studied these animals in every stage of their existence, in order if possible to obtain a cross between this animal and the rabbit, to which it is nearly allied. I have in consequence become well

50

acquainted with its habits and structure, both external and internal; my frequent examinations of the stomach and intestines have convinced me that these animals have not the power to, and consequently do not '*chew the cud.*'

"The structure of the stomach of all ruminating animals is remarkable, and well known to comparative anatomists ; and this peculiar structure does not exist in any of the order *Rodentia* to which the Hare belongs.

"The animals possess very fleshy lips, and the muscles of the mouth are largely developed ; by these means the parts are moved with great ease and kept in almost constant motion, and thus, when noticed by persons whose knowledge of the subject is limited, might easily lead them to believe that the animal was chewing, and this has doubtless led to the mistake made by the early writers.

"Believe me to be,
"Dear sir,
"Yours faithfully,
"A. D. BARTLETT.

"Rev. H. Battiscombe,
"18, *Lee Park, Blackheath.*"

ON THE SUPPOSED HYBRID BETWEEN THE RABBIT AND HARE.

For a long time the question of the "supposed hybrid between the rabbit and hare" had occupied the minds of many naturalists, therefore Buckland and I had determined to expose the imposture, which culminated in the following correspondence : [1]—

Mr. A. D. Bartlett writes me :—"I have just seen another supposed rabbit and hare hybrid, and forward you the following communication, which I lately received—'Will you inform me if the hybrid between hare and rabbit is known to you ; also if you know of the hybrid doe breeding ? I had a buck hare, taken off a gentleman's estate, given to me, quite small, and I have produced

[1] *Land and Water.*

51

by him, out of a double-lopped grey doe rabbit, six in number; also produced by him, out of a small silver-grey doe, four in number. If such a circumstance is not known by you, and you would like to see either of the specimens named, I shall feel pleasure in bringing them over some evening.'"

Mr. Bartlett writes upon the receipt of the foregoing :— "It struck me this was the most positive instance of a cross that I had ever heard of or had an opportunity of fully investigating. I made my way immediately to the stables where these animals were to be seen. The owner, Mr. Foulger, was very pleased to see me, and immediately opened a hutch, in which were the adult animals that he said were the first two hybrids that had been produced. They are both bucks, and they have all the characteristics of the so-called *Leporines* that I had years ago received from France. 'I have seen sufficient now,' I said, 'and the only thing I care to see is the father of them, the buck hare.' He went with me to the adjoining stable, and opening another hutch, drew forth a fine large buck, at which I have no doubt I looked somewhat startled. 'Is that what you call a hare?' said I. 'Yes, it is a hare. I had it when small from a gentleman's park, and there can be no doubt it was a wild hare, and having kept it two years it is perfectly tame.' I at once said, 'I am very sorry to spoil your story, but the animal before me is nothing more than a buck rabbit.' The man was astounded. He looked at me for some seconds, apparently unable to utter a word. At last he said, 'Is it possible that I could for the last two years have kept an animal as a wild hare that now turns out to be a rabbit? Where is the difference between this and other hares?' 'Well,' said I, 'the front legs are not above half the length of the common hare, and when I turn up the fur on the back the hair next the skin is nearly black. If you go to the first poulterer's and put your hand on the back of a hare you will find the fur is white.' The man appeared then somewhat better satisfied that I was giving him what he asked for—true information. 'But,' said he, 'do you think the long confinement has shortened the legs and darkened the hair on his back?' I at once told him this was quite impossible, and finding that he was, I believe, a perfectly honest truthful man, but mistaken, I invited him to call on me at the Gardens, and I would be able to show him specimens to convince him that he had been labouring under a remarkable delusion for the last two years."

"I have just seen in *Land and Water* a paragraph headed, 'Supposed Hybrid between Rabbit and Hare.' I bought in the spring of last year a buck and doe (*Leporidæ*) at the Jardin d'Acclimatation in Paris. I was assured that they would breed, but they did not do so until the doe had been mated with a lop-eared rabbit and the buck also; but now I am in possession of several thoroughbred hybrids. My breed is of the Angora, and can be seen any day at Kearsney Abbey, near Dover."—E. G.

"Your correspondent 'E. G.' has no doubt bought in France the same breed of rabbits, called *Leporines*, that have for many years been sold as hybrids. I have had many of them, and always found them to be nothing more than rabbits, with a slight resemblance to their near relation the hare. May I ask 'E. G.' the condition of the young at birth, as this is a most important question, for the rabbit at its birth is naked and blind, and continues in this helpless condition for two or three weeks; whereas the hare is produced in a most perfect condition, well clothed, its eyes open, and able to run about and feed on the second day after its birth."—A. D. BARTLETT.

HIMALAYAN RABBIT.

(LEPUS NIGRIPES.)

A RABBIT SUPPOSED TO COME FROM THE HIMALAYAN MOUNTAINS.

This animal is smaller than the domestic rabbit, being shorter and more compact; its body is pure white, the nose, ears, legs and tail are of a dark brownish-black, the eyes dark red.

The fur is much shorter and more nearly equal in length than in the common rabbit. The young are perfectly white all over until they are five or six weeks old, at which time the nose and tail begin to get dark-coloured; the feet soon afterwards get dark, and lastly the ears turn black.

In their movements they appear quicker than other rabbits, and they jump a considerable distance; some in my possession I have seen leap upon objects three feet from the ground. The first specimens of these animals that came under my notice were obtained by Mr. Baker, who informed me that they came from the Himalayas. I have since seen a large number of them, and in no instance have I observed any variation in the colour or markings. They are prolific breeders, and appear extremely hardy.

Having some recollection of hearing a furrier once speak of the skins of the Polish rabbit, I took an opportunity a few days since to examine a large lot of these skins at a fur warehouse, when I found that they were beyond all doubt from the animal now under notice. Upon inquiry I was told that these skins are imported into this country in large numbers, and extensively used as a substitute for ermine, which fur they much resemble. I find in Mulsant, *Cours Elémentaire d'Histoire Naturelle*, the following:—"The fur of the white rabbit, even that of the Polish rabbit, is easily distinguished from that of the ermine, by its less cylindrical hairs, which are considerably longer than the down." I am also informed that they are bought at the great sale of furs that takes place annually at Leipsic; to this great fair skins are brought from all parts of the world, and I think it highly probable that these skins are imported from the mountainous parts of Asia.

I have not at present examined the skull of this animal, but should I find sufficient difference upon comparing it with the skulls of the other known species, I shall then propose for it the name of *Lepus nigripes*, or black-footed rabbit.

On June 23, 1857, at the evening meeting of the Zoological Society, I called the attention of the meeting to some rabbits, known as the Himalayan Rabbits, and proposed provisionally to call the species *Lepus nigripes*.[1]

Soon after my paper was published, I received a letter from a gentleman at St. Ives, informing me that this kind of rabbit could be produced by crossing the dark *wild silver-grey* rabbit with a breed known as the *Chinchilla* or light silver-grey. This at the time appeared to me strange and unlikely, nevertheless I determined to make the trial; and having during the last two or three years produced by these means a large number, and fully established the fact, I beg leave to bring them before your notice.

. I have here a light *silver-grey male*, a dark *silver-grey female*, and *two young* of a litter of *five*,—*two* of the number being of the Himalayan variety, the other *three* silver-greys; I have many other examples of the same thing.

[1] *Proceedings Zoological Society*, 1855, p. 159.

Now, if the white or Himalayan varieties are removed and kept together, the result will be all Himalayan, thus showing a tendency to increase this variety at the expense of the silver-greys, because, although you may remove and destroy all the white specimens, still the silver-greys from which they originated will continue to produce white young ones, while, on the other hand, the white variety never produces silver-greys.

I mentioned in my former paper that large numbers of the skins of the white variety were imported to Europe annually, and these are probably bred in Asia. I now beg leave also to mention that for many years a large trade has been carried on by two or three merchants, who buy all the skins of the silver-grey rabbits, and export them to *Russia* and *China;* these skins realize a very high price, some of them 36s. per dozen in this country.

With reference to the origin of the light-coloured silver-grey or Chinchilla rabbit, I am only able to say that they came from the Continent to this country, being met with in the south of France and Belgium, but, as far as I am aware, always in a state of domestication. Observing that we receive large quantities of the skins of these white rabbits, and that the skins of the silver-grey rabbits are sold to the Russians and Chinese at a large price, I am led (from the experiments that I have tried) to think it highly probable that at some period the silver-grey rabbit existed in *Russia* or *Asia* (and hence the taste or fashion for their skins), and that this breed has been lost and replaced by the white variety whose skins we now receive in such abundance—finding, as I have before remarked, that these have a strong tendency to out-number the *greys.*

. In conclusion, it is deserving of remark that, in all instances, the young of the silver-greys are quite black for the first five or six weeks, at about this age the grey hairs beginning to make their appearance on the breast and sides; while the young of the Himalayan or black-footed kind are always perfectly white until they are five or six weeks old, at which time the black hairs begin to appear on their noses, feet, ears, and tails.[1]

CANADIAN BEAVER.
(*CASTOR CANADENSIS.*)

NOTES ON THE BEAVER IN THE ZOOLOGICAL GARDENS.

During one of the heavy storms of wind and rain that prevailed during the last month (Oct. 1862) a large willow-tree was partly blown down. The limbs and branches of this fallen tree were given to many of the animals, and to them proved to be a very acceptable windfall. To the Beaver, however, I wish to direct special attention, as this animal has exhibited in a remarkable manner some of his natural habits and intelligence. One of the largest limbs of the tree, upwards of twelve feet long, was firmly fixed in the ground, in the Beaver's enclosure, in a nearly upright position, at about twelve o'clock on Saturday last (Oct. 1862). The Beaver visited the spot soon afterwards, and walking round this large limb, which measured 30 inches circumference, commenced to bite off the bark about 12 inches above the ground, and afterwards to gnaw into the wood itself. The rapid progress was (to all who witnessed it) most astonishing. The animal laboured hard, and appeared to exert his whole strength, leaving off for a few minutes apparently to rest and look upwards, as if to consider which way the tree was to fall. Now and then

[1] See Darwin, *Animals and Plants under Domestication*, vol. i. p. 109 : 1868. Also *Porto Santo Rabbits*, vol. i. p. 114 : 1868.

he left off and went into his pond, which was about three feet from the base of the tree, as if to take a refreshing bath. Again he came out with renewed energy, and with his powerful teeth gouged away all round the trunk. This process continued till about four o'clock, when suddenly he left off and came hastily towards the iron fence, to the surprise of those who were watching his movements. The cause of this interruption was soon explained; he had heard in the distance the sound of the wheelbarrow, which, as usual, is brought daily to his paddock, and from which he was anxiously waiting to receive his supper. Not wishing to disappoint the animal, but, at the same time, regretting that he was thus unexpectedly stopped in his determination to bring down this massive piece of timber, his usual allowance of carrots and bread was given to him; and from this time until half-past five he was engaged in taking his meal and swimming about in his pond. At half-past five, however, he returned to his tree, which by this time was reduced in the centre to about two inches in diameter. To this portion he applied his teeth with great earnestness, and in ten minutes afterwards it fell suddenly with great force upon the ground.

It was an interesting sight to witness the adroit and skilful way in which the last bite or two were given on the side on which the tree fell, and the nimble movement of the animal to the opposite side, at the moment, evidently to avoid being crushed beneath it. Upon examining the end of the separated tree, it was found that only one inch in diameter was uncut; and it was of course due to the nearly erect position in which the tree was put into the ground that it stood balanced, as it were, upon this slender stem. After carefully walking along its entire length as it lay on the ground, and examining every part, he commenced to cut off about two feet of its length, and by seven o'clock the next morning he had divided it into three pieces; two of these he had removed into the pond, and one was used in the under part of his house.

The Beaver, the subject of the foregoing remarks, was presented to the Society by the Hudson's Bay Company, in the autumn of 1861, and was probably then about six months old. It is, no doubt, less vigorous than the large wild animals of this species, who would, in all probability, bring down trees of much larger dimensions in a shorter time. In fact, it was evident that our Beaver was a novice in the undertaking, as he more than once slipped and rolled over on his back in his eagerness to accomplish the task. It was impossible to witness the actions of this animal without being struck by the amount of skill and intelligence exhibited. When the space cut through towards the centre was too narrow to admit its head, its teeth were applied above and below so as to increase the width from the outside towards the centre, until the remaining parts above and below formed two cones, the apices of which joined in the middle. Again and again the animal left off gnawing, and standing upright on its hind legs, rested its front feet on the upper part of the tree, as if to feel whether it was on the move. This showed clearly that the creature knew exactly what it was about.

See "Beavers at Work," *Wild Animals in Captivity*, p. 99, showing method of felling trees.

CHAPTER VII.

THE LARGER QUADRUPEDS.

SUMATRAN RHINOCEROS.

(*RHINOCEROS SUMATRENSIS.*)

THE steamship '*Orchis*' arrived at the Victoria Docks from Singapore on December 7, 1872, having on board an adult female Sumatran Rhinoceros (*Rhinoceros sumatrensis*). About seven o'clock in the evening of that day the keeper was surprised to hear a feeble squeaking voice proceeding from the den containing the Rhinoceros. He was soon made aware of the cause of this small voice, for upon examining the den he found the beast had produced a young one, which was still fixed or attached by the umbilical cord, and, while looking at it, he distinctly saw the mother turn her head towards the young one and with her teeth bite or sever the connecting band. He found also that the mother, who had been always rather savage, appeared quite quiet and, as he called it, perfectly tamed; she allowed him to enter her den and milk her, and afterwards place the young one in a position that enabled it to suck. Having carefully closed the canvas all round and over the den, he left, thinking that rest and quietness would perhaps be desirable for the then tired and exhausted mother.

It appears, however, that the little Rhinoceros was not

inclined to be shut up in the den, and was found soon afterwards walking about in the dark and rain on the deck of the ship. The cold and wet had produced the effect of almost depriving it of the use of its limbs, but it was soon restored by being rubbed all over and placed in warm blankets. On the following morning I found the mother and young one on board the ship and about to be landed. I advised having the little one removed from the den, fearing that, during the lifting and moving to the van or trolley, the mother might be thrown or tumble on to the little one and crush it. No sooner, however, was the den safely landed on the carriage, than she exhibited restlessness, and it was thought desirable that the young one should be replaced with its mother; this was done, and the keeper, Mr. Auguste Engelecke, entered the den and remained with the animals during the journey from the tidal basin of the Victoria Docks to the Commercial Road.

On arriving at the stables of Mr. Rice, in the Commercial Road, it required some time to unload the large den from the trolley and get it into a stable; and, in order to prevent accident to the young one, we again removed it from its mother and conveyed it at once into the house, taking it in blankets into the parlour, where there was a good fire. Here we had quite enough to do to keep it from running all over the room, so strong and determined it appeared to be. As soon as the mother was safely lodged in the stable the little one was carried in a blanket by two men and placed with its mother, and it immediately went to her and commenced sucking. A very remarkable circumstance connected with the mother was her unexpected quietness; for she had, previously to the birth of the young one, been inclined to attack the keeper or any one who went near her; but after the young one was born, she allowed the keeper to enter the den and milk her as quietly as would the tamest cow; and moreover, after she was in the stable, I with others went inside with her and the young one, patting and caressing her with our hands as though she were a tame old pet that had been used to receive this marked attention from visitors. It has since occurred to me that she was probably in the sulks, because I remember the account of the Hairy-eared Rhinoceros when being removed in Calcutta. She turned sulky and laid down in the street, and it was with the greatest difficulty that she was dragged, or rather slid along, over the muddy road to the stable; so stubborn and determined not to move was she that, although hundreds of pails of water were thrown over her, she would not rise. Was the animal now under consideration quiet by being under the influence of the sulks? I think this must have been the case, since she allowed the men to enter the den, some to push at her nose, others to pull her ears to back her out, and all this was done without any attempt being made on her part to resent the liberties or injure her tormentors.[1] Now, according to the statement of Mr. Engelecke, this animal had been captured but little over seven months on her arrival in the docks, and he told me that her captors had witnessed the act of her copulation just before she was caught in the pitfall; we may presume, therefore, that the period of gestation does not differ much from that of the hippopotamus.

In appearance the young Rhinoceros reminds one of

[1] My suspicion was fully confirmed; for only a few days afterwards her savage disposition and temper caused Mr. Rice and his assistants the utmost alarm, lest she should escape from the stable or kill some of the men who attended to her; for she broke and smashed almost everything within her reach, and they had the greatest difficulty in getting her into the den in which she was shipped to America.

a young ass, viewing its long legs and general mode of
moving its large long head and meagre-looking body.
The front horn on the nose is about ¾ of an inch high,
the posterior horn is not developed; but a smooth spot
indicates its position. Nearly black and covered with
short crisp black hair, its ears very hairy inside as well as
outside, the tail quite like a brush at the tip, it was thin
and bony, looking much like a starved pig. One thing
appeared to me remarkable—the condition of the hoofs;

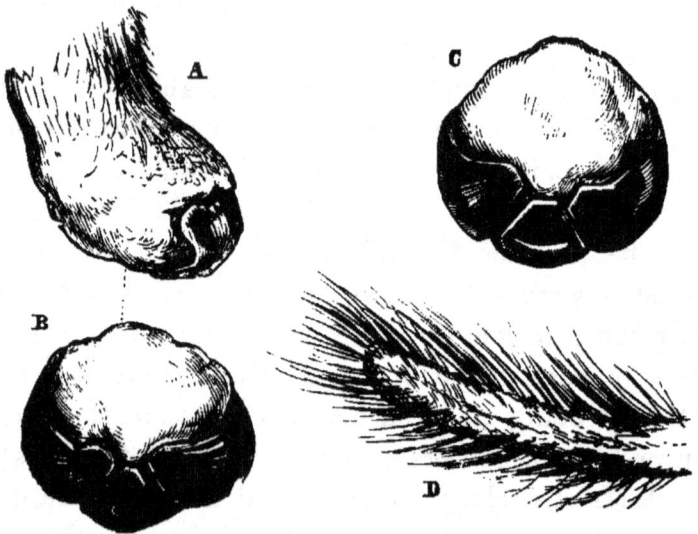

A. Side view, and, B, sole of the right fore-foot of the young Rhinoceros.
  C. Sole of right hind-foot of same. These three figures show how
  the nails or hoofs are long and inturned immediately after birth, as
  described above. D. Sketch of the tail of the adult male.

they were turned under the feet, as will be seen by the
drawings (Figs. A, B, C). The extreme points of the hoofs
were quite soft, like the same parts of a newly-born calf.
It is quite evident, from the manner of the turning-under
of these horny appendages, that, as they are worn through,
the proper form is produced by the pointed portion being
got rid of.

It was 3 ft. in length, 2 ft. high at the shoulder; and its weight, as near as I was able to judge by lifting it, was rather over 50 lbs.

I observed that as soon as the young one had sucked sufficiently it walked away from its mother and entered a dark corner in a box provided for it and lay down to sleep; by this I am led to think that in a wild state it would be left by the mother in the same way that many vegetable-eating animals leave their young while they roam about in search of food, returning to suckle their young at the proper time.

RHINOCEROS FROM BORNEO.

Mr. Alfred R. Wallace, F.Z.S., exhibited at a meeting of the Society some Rhinoceros-horns, sent from Borneo by Mr. Everett, and read the following letter addressed to him by Mr. Everett concerning them :—

" Sarawak, March 12, 1874.

" I have forwarded to you, through Dr. Jessopp, of Norwich, two Rhinoceros-horns, obtained in the Bazaar at Sibu, the principal station of the Sarawak Government in the Rejang river.

"These specimens, together with three others, the largest of which measured perpendicularly stood $8\frac{1}{2}$ in. high, were brought probably from the country about the head-waters of the Koti; but there is reason to believe that the animal is distributed (though not abundantly) throughout the upper course of the Rejang, Kapuas, Koti, Baluñgan, and, perhaps, all the larger streams of the island. Both horns and teeth are brought to Sibu by natives, arriving from the above district for purposes of trade; and these articles being valued by Chinese and Malays for their supposed medicinal properties, at once command a ready sale, so that they disappear generally beyond hope of recovery.

"The Kayans call the animal 'Temadu'; and the country at the head of the Rejang, *i.e.* for the last five days of its course, would seem to be well suited to be the habitat of this bulky herbivore, being described as destitute of any settled human population, and as affording stretches of tolerably level and grassy country which affords pasture to herds of a species of wild ox. The horns of the latter are often purchased at Sibu ; but I have never seen a skin or skull. The general close affinity between the faunas of Borneo and Sumatra suggests that a Bornean Rhinoceros would be found to be furnished with two horns ; and, in fact, natives describe it as being so.

"It is very long since I have seen the horns of any species of Rhinoceros ; but, so far as my memory serves, the large one I send is unlike that of the *Rhinoceros sumatrensis*."

I exhibited a similar horn, but a larger example, which I had obtained from a friend, along with some Dyak weapons, twenty years ago, and which was stated to have been received from Borneo. I remarked that these specimens left no doubt of the existence in Borneo of a Rhinoceros which was probably allied to *Rhinoceros sondaicus*, but of smaller dimensions.

THE HORSE.

HORSE-FLESH AS FOOD.

Frank Buckland having written the following, I will give it just as he penned it :—

"Not long since an exceedingly fine young horse was sent to the Zoological Gardens as food for the lions. The owner of the horse insisted, for certain private reasons, that the animal should be destroyed, which was done accordingly (it was shot dead by my son Edward with a single bullet in the forehead), although the horse was in perfect health. The next day my friend, Mr. Bartlett, resident superintendent of the Gardens (with whom I had often talked over the subject of hippophagotomy), invited me to lunch ; two exceedingly fine hot steaks were placed on the table. 'Now Buckland,' said he, 'one of those steaks is horse, and the other is rump-steak proper; I shall not tell you which is which, make your lunch of that which you think is best.' Accordingly I set to work upon that dish which I fancied from taste was the rump-steak, and I thought I was right, for Mr. Bartlett also partook of the same dish. His daughters all the time were laughing at us both ; I tried in vain to get a clue from them as to whether I was eating horse or beef ; but it was no good, not a hint could I get, for whether I tried one dish or the other, my attempts to make a meal only produced shouts of merry laughter at my doubts and difficulties. However, luncheon over, and the dish I had chosen being quite empty, I said, ' Now then, Bartlett, which have I eaten ? ' ' You have made your lunch *off horse*,' said he. ' Uncommon good it is too,' I replied, though I confess, as far as the idea was concerned, I had much rather I had made my choice the other way."

Some time after the above, I wrote as follows :—

" Sir,—All true Englishmen must deplore the alarming condition of his country with reference to the multitude of criminals that flourish, and keep us all in a perpetual state of fear. This subject, I know, causes the most able and wise of our kingdom an amount of anxiety and never-ending trouble, and I beg to throw out a suggestion with a view to lessen this gigantic evil, which I trust will be received and taken into consideration. I have long known and tried the use of ' horseflesh,' and find it excellent ; the highest and best authorities declare it wholesome and fit for food of man. It is used extensively on the Continent, and, unsuspectedly, at home. Upon this point I could give some astounding facts, but my object at the present moment is to point out the horror that the lower classes of this country have to be fed on what they consider as ' cat's meat.'

"Now, I am certain that many of the criminals now

filling our gaols would be industriously at work earning their bread by the sweat of their brow, had they thought or suspected that the allowance of animal food supplied in prison was horseflesh. Be assured these fellows who would garrote you, murder your wives and children, or commit the most fearful crimes, would shudder at the thought of dining upon horseflesh. No ! They, or most of them, would die of starvation rather than be reduced to this most dreadful necessity.

"Let me, therefore, under the head of ' Practical Natural History,' ask you to call the attention of the proper authorities to, and to advise them to take into their consideration, the desirability of using a very salutary and easy mode of emptying our prisons, and of saving a very large amount now paid for oxflesh, which is eaten by the people who are the curse of the country.

"From long experience I feel able to say that the most fastidious people in this country on the subject of food are the very lowest classes. True it is, they eat the most common and worst, and suffer in consequence, but they eat it without having any prejudice or suspecting it to be inferior; but offer them the most delicious rump-steak, and tell them it was cut from a dead horse, they, however hungry, would shudder, turn pale, and feel sick at the thought of eating it; I am certain this is the feeling with most of them. A crust of bread and a drink of water would be preferred, therefore take advantage of this and use it for the good of the public. Let the criminals in all our prisons be fed upon horseflesh, and we shall soon find the benefit of the alteration in food, for I am certain the fear of a prison life does not, and never will, decrease the number of prisoners, but the change of food will reduce not only the expense of keep, but the number to be kept.—DAB."

When I wrote the above I fully expected to get a crowd of writers down on me for suggesting anything of the kind; however, Mr. R. G. Moger wrote to *Land and Water,* Nov. 6, 1869 :—

"Sir,—The great help that would be given to the supply of nutritious and wholesome animal food to our now ill-fed poor, by doing away with the vulgar prejudice against horseflesh, no reasonable man can doubt; but first the animal must be properly prepared for slaughter, and only those selected which are healthy, but unfit by accident or incurable lameness for active work, and these would be many if taken away from their labours at an early period, instead of being cruelly and shamefully worked until they are brought into the wretched condition described in my letter of last week. I therefore do not agree with your correspondent 'Dab,' who recommends horseflesh for the food of criminals. This would only serve to throw an additional brand-mark on the more general use of horseflesh among the poor. 'Dab' declares it to be 'excellent and wholesome and fit for the food of man.' In this opinion I quite concur; but then it must be well prepared and carefully selected, and this can only be done by proper feeding and inspection of the carcases."

Without meaning to give any offence I sent this reply :—

"Sir,—Your correspondent Mr. Moger appears to differ from me in my proposition to feed criminals on horseflesh, thereby reducing the cost of their keep and diminishing their number. Now, as I wrote from long experience among the poor, and knowing their great antipathy to that food, I am willing to assist Mr. Moger in trying the experiment (and testing the truth of my assertion). If

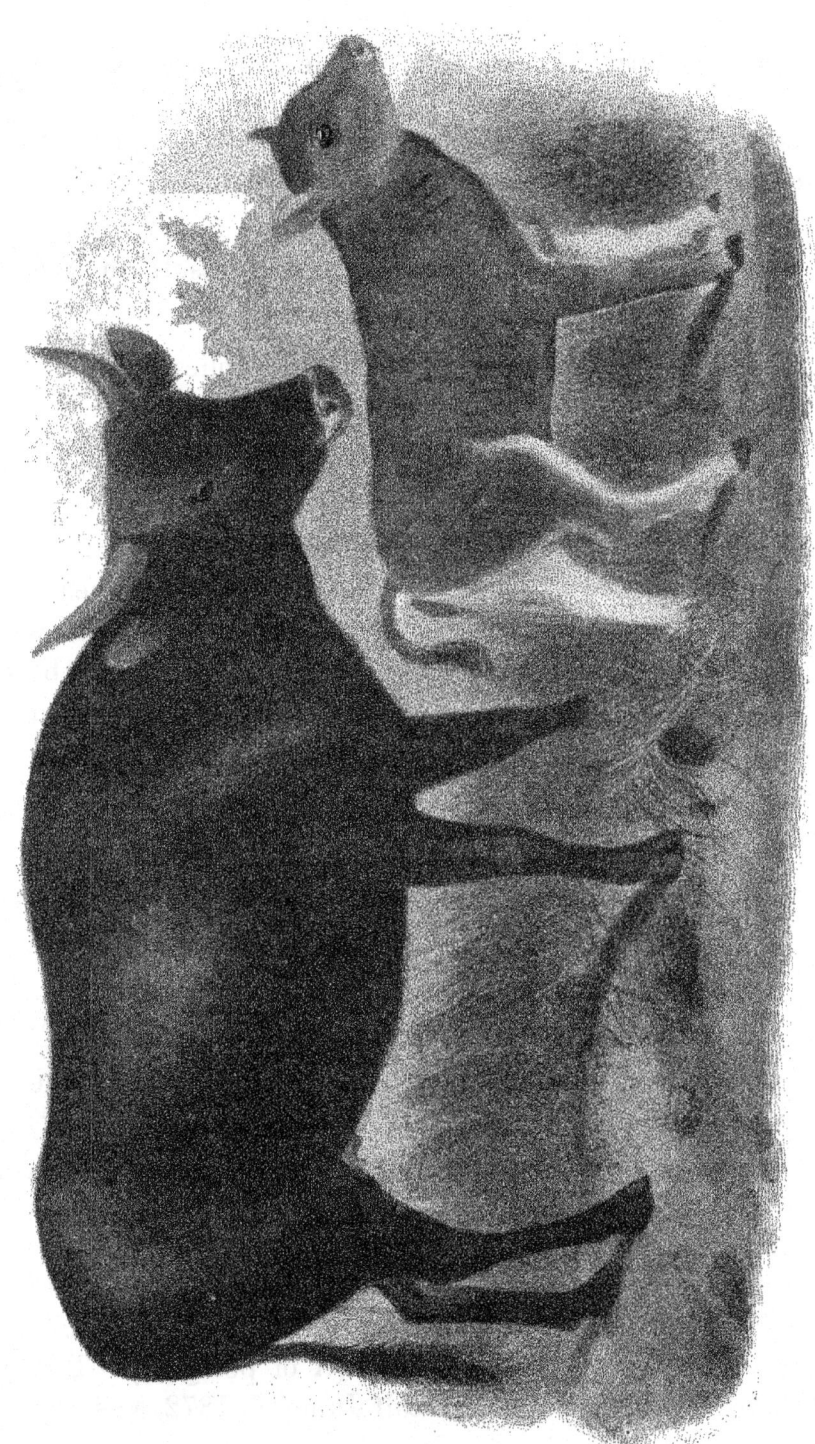

A.   HYBRID BOVINE.   B.

he will find fifty poor starving people (not criminals) to partake of a dinner off horseflesh I will forward him, free of cost, 50 lbs. of the finest horseflesh that can be obtained, with an equal quantity of potatoes. At the same time all I ask is that three persons of reliable integrity shall be present at the feast, and report the result in the columns of *Land and Water.*—DAB."

To which Mr. R. G. Moger sorrowfully replies, Nov. 27, 1869 :—

" SIR,—It appears that my advocacy of a more humane treatment of (too often prematurely) worn-out and useless horses has led to my receiving a challenge from your correspondent 'Dab,' which I am by no means inclined to accept, knowing well that his very generous offer of 50 lbs. of 'the finest horseflesh that can be procured,' even accompanied by 50 lbs. of potatoes, and cooked in an artistic style, would, under the existing very just and natural feeling against such food, remain untasted even by the starving, or at any rate half-starving poor."

BOVINE ANIMALS.

HYBRID BOVINE ANIMALS.

I wish to call attention to the production of some remarkable Bovine animals in the Society's Gardens.

I will endeavour, by the aid of the pedigree on p. 72, to explain the order or manner in which they were produced.

In the first place, the bull Zebu (*Bos indicus*) was introduced to the cow Gayal (*Bibos frontalis*), and a female hybrid was born October 29, 1868 (A of pedigree). This animal (A) produced her first calf June 16, 1872, a second one October 16, 1873, a third one January 5, 1875, a fourth March 11, 1876, a fifth November 2, 1878; these five calves were the produce of this female hybrid Gayal with the Zebu bull. She was now introduced to the male American Bison (*Bison americanus*), and on May 21, 1881, she produced a female No. 2 (B of pedigree).

It will be seen that this animal (B) is the product not only of the intermixture of three well-marked species, but, according to our present definition, of three distinct genera.

PEDIGREE OF HYBRID BOVINES.

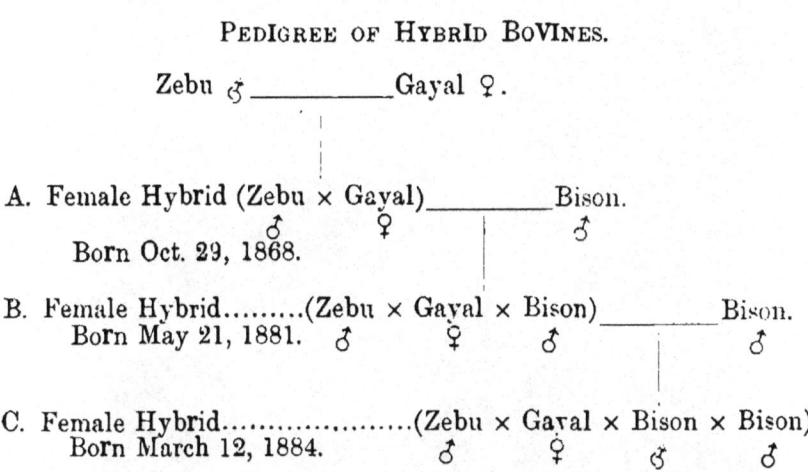

Zebu ♂ _____ Gayal ♀.

A. Female Hybrid (Zebu × Gayal) _____ Bison.
   Born Oct. 29, 1868.

B. Female Hybrid.........(Zebu × Gayal × Bison) _____ Bison.
   Born May 21, 1881.

C. Female Hybrid...................(Zebu × Gayal × Bison × Bison).
   Born March 12, 1884.

This remarkable animal, the result of the triple alliance, was last year introduced to the bull Bison, and on March 12, 1884, she produced a female (C of pedigree). This last individual, now eleven weeks old, is undistinguishable from a pure-bred Bison of the same age.

Having placed before you the facts of the wonderful fertility of this hybrid race, and the remarkable display of what I think may be called the plastic properties that are capable of producing by artificial selection a variety of races, I think I may venture to say that the hybrid

C.

HYBRID BOVINE.

Gayal and Zebu would have bred with any true bovine animal.

For many years I have carefully considered the subject of hybrid animals, having a strong suspicion that some of our domestic animals (for the origin of which our most able observers fail to fully account) have been produced by a mixture of species. And in support of this opinion I will call your attention to some of the species of the equine and asinine group of animals. And I shall endeavour to show some very remarkable points to be found in confirmation of my ideas upon the subject.

During my visit to Norway I was much interested in noticing the multitudes of ponies in that country. By far the greater portion of them were dun-coloured, varying from dark dun to a pale cream-colour; but the most striking peculiarity was the striped or zebra-marked legs, together with *one* or *two*, and sometimes *three, shoulder-stripes;* most of them had also the dark medial line running from the mane down the back, ending in the tail.

These characters appear frequently among individuals of the common domestic ass, and also among mules, the produce of the horse and ass.

The former Earl of Derby published in the ' *Knowsley Menagerie* ' plates of several hybrid animals belonging to this family, the most remarkable one being of a double mule that was born in the Gardens of this Society. This mule had in its composition the *Zebra*, common *Ass*, and *Horse*. You will observe in the figure of the mule —and I can say from my own knowledge it is a most accurate representation of that animal—that the long hair commences from the base of the tail, like that of the horse, whereas all the zebras and asses have the long hair at the extremity of their tails only.

My object in bringing forward this part of the subject is in the hope that it may induce experiments to be made that will lead to some important and useful discoveries. Having such positive proof of the fertility of some hybrids, I feel anxious that the old superstition should be entirely removed. The belief, so general, that all hybrids or mules are barren and useless for breeding purposes is simply a stupid and ignorant prejudice, and has been the means, in my opinion, of preventing many valuable discoveries.

The late Mr. Darwin, in his *Origin of Species*, calls particular attention to the zebra-like markings observable in a number of animals of the equine and asinine family, and it appears to me to be highly probable that the horse was originally produced by the mixture of species, seeing the unlimited variation in *size, colour*, form and marking, and bearing in mind that no wild animal has been discovered that fairly represents the horse.

The zebra-markings, so common among the very ancient stock of ponies in Norway, seem to indicate their remote origin to be connected with a striped animal, the traces of which are still visible.

I intended to extend these remarks, and to add a list of the hybrids that are known to be fertile, but finding that there are some valuable experiments being carried out by Mr. Day and others, in the hope of producing a non-migratory salmon, by the mixture of other species of the *Salmonidæ*, I have deferred doing so in order to make the list more complete.

THE PRONGBUCK.

(*ANTILOCAPRA AMERICANA.*)

REMARKS UPON THE AFFINITIES OF THE PRONGBUCK.

Notwithstanding that this remarkable animal has been
the subject of considerable notice, I believe few naturalists
have felt perfectly satisfied with its supposed affinities;
none, however, appear to have hesitated to place it among
the hollow-horned Ruminants. Once there, its most interesting structure and economy were altogether overlooked and unsuspected. No writer, that I can find, has
ever stated that this animal carries deciduous horns. This
character has always been considered to belong exclusively
to the Cervine group of Ruminants, and, however much
the Prongbuck differed from the Antelopes, still it has been
retained among them upon this supposed distinctive character. I will now endeavour to prove that this animal's
affinities are closer to the genus *Cervus*, to which I think
it more nearly allied, than to the Antelopes. Although it
does possess to a great extent the characteristics of the
hollow-horned Ruminants, still I think I shall be able to
show that the horns of the Prongbuck are a modification
of the horns of *Cervus*, with a strong resemblance to, and
with an intermediate character approaching, the hollow-
horned Ruminants. In support of this statement, I adduce
the fact that the Prongbuck sheds its horns; and the evidence I am now able to produce is positive and unmistakable, although this has been denied repeatedly by many
authorities. I call attention to the following words of
Messrs. Audubon and Bachman in their second volume of
the *Quadrupeds of North America*, p. 198:—

"It was supposed by the hunters of Fort Union that

the Pronghorned Antelope dropped its horns; but as no person had ever shot or killed one without these ornamental and useful appendages, we managed to prove the contrary to the men at the Fort by knocking off the bony part of the horn and showing the hard spongy membrane beneath, well attached to the skull, and perfectly immovable."

Another well-known and eminent writer and naturalist, the late Sir John Richardson, in his *Fauna Boreali-Americana*, says of the Prongbuck, at p. 268 :—

" The females are stated by some American writers to have horns like the males, although smaller; but in one gravid and therefore at least nearly full grown individual which I have examined, there was merely a short obtuse process of the frontal bone, scarcely to be felt through the fur and not covered with horn."

This was probably the first horn, which is doubtless covered with hair in its early stage of growth.

But in his work upon the Mammals of North America, contained in the Pacific Railway reports, Professor Baird says (p. 667) :—

" The female sometimes has no horns externally; frequently, however, there is a short horny tubercle of a few lines, occasionally 2 in. long; it does not show any curve, however, although usually warty at the base. When horns appear wanting in the female, they may sometimes be found concealed among the hair of the head."

Many will remember that in the month of January 1865, a living male Prongbuck was purchased by this Society and placed in the Gardens. The animal, at that time, was thin and in poor condition, probably owing to the voyage it had so recently made from North America. Its horns were about 3 in. long, and exhibited no signs of the prong. This, however, could be felt among the hair at the base of the then growing horn. The animal made but little progress or improvement in condition till about the month of April. At this time it much improved, and the horns showed signs of rapid growth, apparently becoming complete with the prongs at midsummer. This condition continued until about the middle of October, at which time the horns appeared to have again commenced growing : not only were they increased in length, but they spread wider apart at the points.

On the morning of November 7, the keeper, somewhat

Fig. 1.—Perfect horn when shed, November 7th.

alarmed, called my attention to the fact that one of the horns of the Prongbuck had fallen off (Fig. 1). I hurried to the spot immediately, fearing that some accident had happened, and reached the paddock in time to see the second horn fall to the ground. My astonishment was much increased at observing that two fine new horns were already in the place of those just dropped, that these new horns were soft and covered with long, straight, smooth and nearly white hairs, and that the bony core (that I had expected to see) was thickly covered with soft new horny matter. These new horns appeared larger than the hollow portion of the horns just cast—an appearance due to the fact of their having pushed off the shed horns by their growth. The long hair at the base of the horns (see Fig. 2) had concealed the separation that was taking place.

I will again quote Messrs. Audubon and Bachman. In their volume previously referred to, they remark (p. 204) :—

"As to the shedding of the horns of this species, I

Fig. 2.—Old horn in process of being thrown off, showing the separation between the old and the new horn.

never was able to ascertain it; but a fine buck we killed late in November had a soft space between the head and the horn, over the bone, that looked as if it had grown that length in one season."

As a proof that the shedding of these horns was not the result of any disease or accident, I may remark that whenever the hollow horn of any Ruminant is broken or torn from its bony support, a copious discharge of blood immediately follows; and the horn so removed is never replaced by any subsequent growth. This remark applies equally to any injury done to the outer or velvety covering during the progress of growth of the solid horns of the genus *Cervus*, of which innumerable instances can be found. I will mention the following, which may be deemed sufficient to illustrate the truth of this statement.

A young male Nylghau (*Portax picta*) accidentally struck off the horny covering when these parts had become nearly full-grown, leaving the bony cores bare and bleeding; the bleeding continued a short time, and the bony stumps when dry became nearly black; the animal continued in good health, and bred with the females, and lived several years without the slightest sign of horny covering making its appearance.

I will not dwell upon this point, feeling it unnecessary, but proceed to direct your attention to the various forms and the differences in size to be found among the horns of the Prongbuck.

Now this variation in form is more in accordance with my notions of *Cervus* than of the Antelope type, in which no great diversity of form is found in the same species, while in the Deer tribe the most remarkable variation is to be found in almost every species.

The Cervine characters consist, however, not only in a mere resemblance on account of diversity of form in the horns, but in the fact of their being deciduous, together with the hairy covering. But, in speaking of the affinities of this animal, I am struck by the peculiar resemblance it has to the giraffe, not only in the structure of its horns, but in its legs and feet, the total absence of false hoofs, glands, etc. Nor can I avoid noticing the resemblance it bears to some of the wild sheep both in colour and general appearance, and in the thickness and structure of its coat.

Here, again, its likeness to the Deer tribe is most strongly marked—the white patch on the rump,[1] the brittle hair, the fine legs, the elastic gait, the full, dark eye, and the almost erect horns. But here, again, the chamois is seen, in fact it does appear to me that we have in this animal the elements of all the group—forcing one to call to mind the extinct monster *Sivatherium*, whose wonderful remains indicate to us a beast with four horns of great size, and, from their form, probably partaking of the characters of several different existing forms; and the remarkable difference in form of the pair of horns in the fore-part of the skull as contrasted with those behind, affords the ground for much speculation upon this subject.

But to return to the animal under consideration. May it not be one of the remnants of an extinct race, whose diversity of characters point out to us by a very easy method how one form may slowly glide to the right or to the left, as it were, and by little alteration become a *Stag*, an *Antelope*, or a *Sheep?*

The consideration of the peculiar structure and remarkable variation in the size and form of the horns of the Prongbuck has led me to believe that this animal may approach more nearly to the genus *Cervus* than to any other; and this idea prompts me to suggest that the hairy covering in which the newly-formed bony core is enveloped during the growth of the stag's horns is the homologue of, and should be regarded as representing, the horny part which is more strongly developed on the bony cores of the hollow-horned ruminants, or, in other words, that the so-called solid-horned ruminants (*Cervus*) shed their horny, hairy, dried, vascular covering at the completion of the growth of the bony core.

[1] A gland of considerable size exists in the back of this animal, immediately over the white patch.

This explanation of the process of the development of all horns appears to me more probable and natural, inasmuch as the covering of the deciduous horns is always, or nearly always, hairy, while these hairs have their terminal roots upon the inner surface, and this character is carried out in a most remarkable manner in the horns of the Prongbuck.

The hairs connected with this structure are not only very numerous, but pass completely through the horny structure, extending from the base of the horn upwards above the prong. In proof of this, I was myself astonished when taking a cast of the internal part of the hollow horn; the cast, upon being withdrawn, presented the appearance of the specimen now before you.

It is probable there may be objections offered to this theory of the growth of the so-called solid horns, seeing that, in the early condition of the budding forth of the new horn, the parts are largely supplied with numerous blood-vessels, and from their power to deposit rapidly the bony matter, the increase of which carries out at a marvellously rapid rate this vascular and cuticular or tegumentary covering. By the rapid growth of bone, the outer covering becomes thin and the circulation is cut off at the base by the increase and development of the burr. As its functions cease it soon becomes withered and is shed, leaving the branching bony structure to fall off after the rutting season.

If this be the correct explanation of the growth of some of the structures now under consideration, I think a considerable difference will be found in the growth and formation of the horns of the Prongbuck; it will be seen that the bony core is much smaller, when compared with the cavity or hollow space in the horny casing, than in any other hollow-horned ruminant that I am acquainted with. This fact, I think, will show that the space admits of the growth and formation of the new horn, the bone being thickly covered with vascular integument, and the hairs appear to grow upon the surface of this, beneath the old horn; the extreme point appears first to put on the horny matter (see Fig. 4); this increase of growth, acting like a wedge, forces the old horns upwards and outwards until they fall off.

An examination of the cast horn from the living specimen at the Gardens shows clearly the structure and the singular manner in which the hairs pass through the horny substance ; that they do so is clearly to be seen by the casts now on the table. Being a little puzzled, on looking into the cavity of the cast horns, at the small size of the hollow, I determined to take a cast of the interior ; for this purpose I melted some gutta-percha and filled up the hollow space, and as soon as it had become hard, I withdrew the specimen before you, covered, as you see, with the hairs in the same manner as the new horns on the head of the living animal: the roots of these hairs having become fixed in the gutta-percha, were drawn through the minute openings in the horn. This can be done easily upon any of the specimens of the shed horns of this animal.

With reference to the frequency of the shedding of the horns of this animal, I can only offer a surmise. Judging from the rapidity of the growth of the young horn, I reasonably conclude that it occurs annually. In support of this, it may be remembered that our animal's horns in January were barely 3 inches in length, while by June of the same year they were fully formed, and measured 8 inches; they were cast the first week in November— that is, on the seventh; the new horns on that day (see Fig. 3) were about 4 inches long; they are now, this day, 6 inches long, having grown 2 inches in twenty-one days (see Fig. 4).

Besides this, we have the testimony of Messrs. Audubon and Bachman, as previously quoted, that in the month of November they found in the buck killed by them the soft

Fig. 3.—New horn, as it appeared when the old horn had been shed.

space between the horn and the skull, which they supposed to be due to that year's growth. A still further proof bear-

Fig. 4.—New horn after twenty-one days' growth.

ing upon this conclusion is furnished by a fine specimen belonging to Mr. Moore, from the Derby Museum at Liverpool; this example is evidently from a larger and older animal, as is shown by the superior size of its horns. The core upon which the freshly-developed horn rests has been removed from the hollow horny cavity, and it will be seen that it has already attained a length of 6½ inches, in this respect being larger than that of the Society's animal when first shed.

One remarkable feature yet unnoticed is the absence in the new horns of the curved or hooked point. This part of the subject necessarily requires further observations during its growth, but I have already noticed that the extreme horny point is movable at the apex of the bony core. This suggests to my mind the possibility of the point assuming a contrary direction during its growth, probably by an accident; and this would well account for the remarkable disposition of the specimen now before you from the Liverpool Museum. described and figured in the Society's *Proceedings* for 1855 (p. 10), by Dr. Gray, under the name of *Antilocapra anteflexa*. I am therefore inclined to believe that this individual does not represent a different species, but a deformity of growth.

Having, I hope at least, proved beyond all doubt the deciduous nature of the horns of the Prongbuck, and alluded to what I consider its affinities, and these considerations being founded principally upon the character of the horns, I am obliged to admit the great difficulty I see in the classification or arrangement of the *Ruminantia* upon this character only, seeing that in both deer (*Cervus*) and antelopes the females, in some instances, carry horns, and in the smaller members of the family the males as well as females are without these appendages. Nevertheless I believe there is no other character of equal importance, and that by an increased knowledge of these structures a nearer approach to the perfect arrangement of this important group will be made.

In concluding, I think I have shown—

1st. That the Prongbuck is not a true bovine animal.

2ndly. That this animal sheds its horns.

3rdly. That the structure of these organs appears to be imperfectly understood.

£120 FOR AN ANTELOPE.

I give this story just as it appeared, at the time, in one of the papers. It is perfectly true:—"The Superintendent of the Zoological Gardens once gave as much as £120 for a remarkably fine specimen of an antelope, without having the opportunity of first obtaining the sanction of the Council to make his bargain. The circumstances were these. He was on board a vessel that had just brought some rare animals into the docks, and two or three dealers were there too. The captain told the Superintendent that he would rather the Society should buy a magnificent antelope that was on the ship at the price offered by the dealers. There was no time for him to go to Hanover Square for instructions, so he took upon himself to purchase the antelope. Afterwards he was somewhat sternly reproved by one of the Fellows of that learned Society, who hinted that the bargain might be repudiated by the Council, and asked the Superintendent how he thought he would stand then. The reply was, 'In that case I shall simply be a gainer of £30, as I have already received an offer of £150 for the beast, if he is mine to sell.'"

CHINESE SHEEP.

These sheep differ from all others that I have seen in not possessing external ears. In size they are equal to ordinary sheep; the wool is perfectly white, rather *coarse and mixed with long hairs;* the head and face are smooth, and covered with white hair; they have no horns; the tail is short, rather broad, and turned up at the tip; the profile is very convex.

My attention was first called to these sheep from the fact of their great reproductive power. I find they breed twice in a year, and produce four and, sometimes, five at a birth, the three ewes in the Society's Gardens producing in one spring *thirteen lambs.* These lambs are very easily reared by hand, and are perfectly hardy. Upon referring to Miss Corner's *History of China,* published in 1847, it appears that since the introduction of the cotton plant into China (which took place during the Ming dynasty, about 500 years ago), the breeding and rearing of sheep have been neglected, as the following extract will show :—

"The extended cultivation of cotton was one of the causes that led to the almost entire disappearance of sheep from the southern provinces, for it was found that it would take much more land to supply a certain number of persons with mutton and wool, than with rice and cotton. Then the pastures were gradually turned into rice and cotton plantations, while sheep were banished to the mountains and less fertile parts of the country. For the same reason cattle, horses, and other domestic animals are scarce; the few that are kept for the purposes of husbandry are poor and ill-fed; for there is not a common on which they can graze, so that they are tied up in stalls when not employed in the field. Dairy farms are unknown in China, where people use neither milk, butter, nor cheese."

In a recent letter from China, the writer mentions, among other matters, that in giving a good dinner to some distinguished friends, one of the choicest dishes was a leg of mutton, the cost of which was equal to 30*s*.

Having submitted specimens of the wool of this animal to my friend Dr. Price, who kindly forwarded the same to Mr. Darlington, the Secretary to the Chamber of Commerce at Bradford, for the purpose of having it examined by the most competent judges, the following report from these gentlemen was received. They say, "That the sample of sheep's wool from China enclosed in Dr. Price's letter, is a class of wool which would be extensively used by the manufacturers of this district for goods of low quality; that it appears to be wool suitable for combing purposes, and would now command about one shilling per pound."

That the wool does not appear to offer any great inducement for its introduction will be seen by the above report. I, however, think it is highly probable that by cultivation and judicious crossings, a great improvement may be fairly looked for. It is, however, to us a matter of the utmost importance that we should possess animals whose power of reproducing is greatest, in order to supply the increased demand for meat.

The origin of our domestic animals has been a subject of much discussion. The remote period of their domestication involves us in much doubt and this mystery and obscurity will probably never be satisfactorily cleared up. It is, however, interesting to find, in a country whose civilization is of such ancient date as China, the most perfect of domestic animals. I mean by this, the animals that are furthest removed from their natural condition.

Now, knowing what wonderful changes can be, and are, produced in the vegetable kingdom by skilful modes of propagating, cultivating and artificially treating plants,

causing them completely to change their nature, producing all kinds of variety of monstrous growth, double
flowers, fruit and seed in enormous abundance;—all this
being done by the interference of man;—may I ask, is
it not probable that a people like the Chinese, whom
we know to have practised these arts for ages, may
have by artificial means induced a similar power in
these domestic animals? As we find, for example,
the pigs, the fowls, the geese and the sheep of China
more prolific than the same animals in any other part
of the world. Instances of Chinese sows producing
twenty-two at a litter have come within my own observation; their fowls are certainly unequalled for the
number of their eggs, and their geese, as reproducers,
stand unrivalled.

It is almost needless to say that the result of cultivation,
whether as applied to plants or animals, has produced an
unnatural and abnormal condition; instances too numerous
to mention may be found, but it will be sufficient to notice
the pigeons and ducks. The former in a wild state produce
only two broods in a season, while, in a state of domestication, they continue to breed all the year. The domestic
ducks not only produce a much larger number of eggs, but
one drake is sufficient for a number of ducks, five or six,
while, in a state of nature, they universally are found in
pairs.

Experience has proved that by a careful admixture or
crossing in the breed of the Chinese pigs, geese and fowls,
the mixed races are much improved in quality and size,
while they retain the reproductive power undiminished,
and the animals are more hardy. As regards poultry, I
cannot admire the celebrated Cochin China breed in their
pure state, but I have abundant proof of their great value
for breeding and crossing; the least possible trace of the

breed appears sufficient to impart all that is desirable, and, by after-breeding, the improvement that may be made is as astonishing as it is undeniable. As crossing the breed in the animals before mentioned has been attended with so much success, there is no reason why crossing the sheep should not also produce a favourable result.

It must not be supposed that, because the Chinese have banished their sheep (having found cotton and rice more suited to their climate and better adapted to their wants), they are unworthy of our notice, taking into consideration that in this country we cannot grow cotton or rice.

Having witnessed the many attempts that have been made to reduce some of the existing wild animals to a state of domestication, and observing the utter failure in all instances of producing what may fairly be called a domestic variety of any true species, I am inclined to believe it is necessary, as a means of reducing wild animals to a domestic condition, that they must be crossed with nearly allied species; by this means the creatures are rendered unnatural, and consequently dependent on man. Different varieties would doubtless be produced, according to the manner in which they were crossed, and permanent varieties would be thus established. Such is the opinion at which I have arrived, after a long and mature consideration of this extremely interesting subject.

CHAPTER VIII.

DEER.

CERVIDÆ.

OCCASIONALLY the males of the Deer tribe (*Cervidæ*) when they have grown their horns become, in confinement, extremely fierce and dangerous, attacking at every opportunity those that approach them; nor are they to be trusted, at all times, with the female of their own species. At the approach of the breeding season it is necessary to cut off their horns in order to prevent them from killing or frightfully wounding the females, *i.e.* if it is desired to perpetuate a species. The operation of cutting off a stag's horns requires to be performed with considerable caution and care. The strength and determination exhibited on these occasions by a stag need to be seen to be fully understood, the assistance of five or six strong men being required by the operator to enable him to perform the operation safely. A rope of considerable strength is first thrown over the deer's antlers, and by this means he is drawn close up to a tree, post, or fence to which he is temporarily secured. The next thing to be done is to pass a soft but strong cord in a loop round the under side of the burr of the horn; the cord is then twisted until it is quite tight, and is in its turn made fast to the tree or other convenient obstacle; it is safer to do this on both burrs. Having, so far, firmly secured the animal, the rope on the upper part of the horns is removed. The operator next proceeds with a sharp saw to cut off the horns about half-an-inch above the burr. This being accomplished the cord is untwisted, and the animal, who a few minutes previously was all courage and strength, will generally walk away, apparently conscious of having been conquered, and glad to escape out of sight.

CHAPTER IX.

KANGAROO AND SLOTH.

KANGAROOS.

ON THE MOVEMENT OF THE SYMPHYSIS OF THE LOWER JAW IN THE KANGAROOS.[1]

A SHORT time ago, a lady, a frequent visitor at the Gardens, on conversing with the keeper of the Kangaroos, asked him if he was aware of the manner in which these animals used the teeth of the lower jaws to snip their food, as a person would do in snipping grass with a pair of scissors. She mentioned that she had resided many years in Australia, and seemed quite positive as to the truth of the fact that Kangaroos used their lower incisors in the manner already spoken of. The keeper, interested in what had been told him, called the attention of Mr. Bartlett to it.

Mr. Bartlett immediately examined the teeth and jaws of several skulls of Kangaroos in his possession, and, satisfied of the probable truth of the remark, took the first opportunity of observing the same in the living animals in the Society's collection.

Since then we have corroborated and added to these observations together. The following were the different species of the living animals examined for this purpose,—

[1] By James Murie, Prosector to the Society, and A. D. Bartlett, Superintendent of the Society's Gardens, 1866.

viz. the Red Kangaroo (*Macropus rufus*), the Black-faced Kangaroo (*M. melanops*), the Great Kangaroo (*M. giganteus*), the Yellow-footed Rock Kangaroo (*Petrogale xanthopus*), Bennett's Wallaby (*Halmaturus bennettii*), and the Derbian Wallaby (*H. derbianus*).

In these several species we noticed the following movements :—As the animal opened its mouth and seized the grass offered it, there was a slight though distinct separation of the lower incisors, differing in each individual according to its size,—in the large Kangaroo almost as much as a quarter of an inch.

The small mouthful of grass being seized, the green blades were cropped or nipped off, a portion being evidently cut through by the anterior free sharp edge of the two lower incisors as they pressed against the opposing concavity of the palate and the cutting-edge of the upper and anterior incisors; while another portion of the food passed between the two lower incisors, and seemed also to be snipped through, either by the closure or approach of the trenchant internal lateral edges of these, or it might be by the jerking movement of the head, which caused the morsel to be half torn and half cut through by these incisors. At other times, when the grass was in small loose bundles of a few of the stronger fibres with their roots attached, instead of chewing the latter, the animal rather rejected them; but in order to do so grasped the roots or dry portion of the stem, which it wished to disengage, with its fore-paws, using the claws in the manner a human being would the fingers and hands to clutch and drag an object. While doing this, what stalks were between the lower incisors were severed by their internal acute borders. After the grass had thus been cut through, it was passed between the molars, partly by the aid of the tongue and partly by the movement of the jaws, and then, with the ordinary side to side and semi-rotatory movement, the process of mastication was completed by the molars.

In watching the animals, it was at first difficult to notice the action of the jaws and lower incisors which we have spoken of; and this was to be accounted for by the great rapidity of the movement, which was also sometimes hidden by the retraction of the lips. The opening movement of the lower incisors seemed chiefly to occur when the animal raised its head to seize the food; for while in the act of chewing with the molars, the incisors were either closed or hidden by the lips.

With reference to the movement of the head in animals which graze or browse, as for instance in the sheep, the direction of motion while in the act of cropping the grass is nearly always upward and forward, though every now and again the reverse is the case. In the Kangaroos, however, we did not observe this latter motion, the jerking movement being invariably in a forward direction. This would seem to agree with and favour the act of the grass slipping between the open incisors; and as these are closed the short quick movement of the head would likewise tend to cut asunder the stalk or blade of the leaf. Besides the direct forward jerk, the head at the same time moved slightly laterally, though this was not so very perceptible.

From these observations, then, we are inclined to believe that the lower incisor teeth in the Kangaroos act in the manner either of a pair of cutting-forceps or short-bladed scissors (see Fig. 2, p. 100), with also occasionally a knife-like action; that is to say, the lower incisors themselves, if to a certain extent fixed, would on their closure prevent the blade of grass from slipping (from, in many cases, their points being perfectly close and their bases more open), and the jerk combined with the dragging movement would cut it through.

Upon consulting the various authorities as to what has been said respecting the movement of the teeth and lower jaws of the family of Kangaroos, we find Mr. Waterhouse stating, in his admirable work,[1] of the *Macropodidæ*, that "the lower incisors are horizontal, long, compressed, and lanceolate, and have cutting external and internal margins ; their outer surface is convex, and the inner surface is strongly convex in the transverse direction, in the middle, but concave near the margins; when the mouth is closed, the outer cutting-edge of the lower incisors is brought in contact with the cutting-edges of the posterior incisors of the upper jaw on either side, and their points shut within the apex of the foremost pair of the upper jaw. In *Macropus major* (and perhaps in some nearly allied species) the rami of the lower jaw are loosely attached at the chin, and at the apex they are free, and the animal has the power of slightly separating the lower incisors, so that their outer cutting-edges are brought more closely in contact with the upper incisors than they otherwise would be."

Although Mr. Waterhouse therefore has pointed out both the cutting-edges of the outer and inner sides of the lower incisors, and justly attributed to the closing of the lower upon the upper jaw with the separation of the lower incisors the effect of producing closer contact between the cutting-edges of both jaws upon one another, yet he has failed to notice the use and mode of application of the *inner* cutting-edges of the lower incisors.

Professor Owen, in his valuable memoir "On the Osteology of the Marsupialia,"[2] does not mention anything from which it would be inferred that the lower

---

[1] *Natural History of the Mammalia*, vol. i. p. 51.

[2] *Transactions of the Zoological Society*, 1841, vol. ii. p. 364.

H

incisors are used in the manner we have described; he says, however, among other things, that, excepting the Koala, "in all the other marsupial *crania* which I have examined, the *rami* of the lower jaw are not anchylosed at the symphysis."

Having satisfied ourselves of the occurrence of the mobility of the teeth and symphysis of the lower jaws in the living animals, it became an object of interest to ascertain in the dead ones how this was produced; and for this purpose we commenced by studying the bones in a few macerated skulls.

In one of these, an adult specimen of *Macropus major* (*M. giganteus*), the two halves of the inferior maxilla of which have been completely separated, when the symphyses are applied closely together the two lower incisors are approximated at their anterior half or points upon the inner edges; while the posterior halves of the incisors have an interval of nearly one-eighth of an inch, of a somewhat spear shape. The two margins of the incisors in apposition are worn and flattened, evidently by the continued attrition of the one upon the other. The symphysis of the bones at the part where they are most closely applied is at the posterior half; and there they unite, though loosely, by an articulation in the manner of a diaphysis.

In a *Macropus ocydromus* the symphysis and teeth of the mandible exhibit very nearly the same appearances.

The same parts in *Osphranter antilopinus* differ in the anterior and inner cutting-edges of the incisors not coming together so sharply, by reason of the points being more rounded and set outwards than in the two former species. When the teeth are separated there is an open space of fully one-eighth of an inch; there is also a diminutive ovate space at their base, which may in part be a natural deficiency; but likewise the dental tissue seems partially abraded as if worn by the action spoken of, possibly by the tearing of grasses or other harder stems.

The shape and position of the incisors of *Halmaturus agilis* approach those of *Macropus major*; the interval at the base of the teeth, however, is relatively wider and correspondingly shorter than in that larger species.

Halmaturus irma presents no remarkable difference from *Macropus major*, excepting in the mandible being

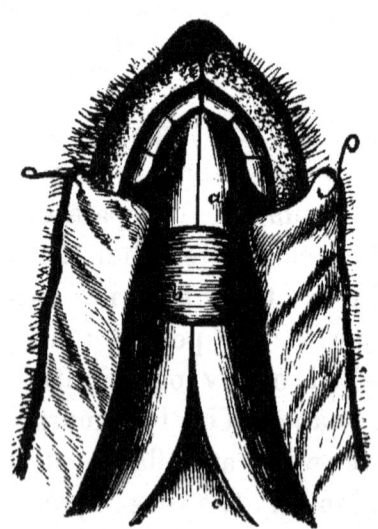

Fig. 1.—Partial dissection of the lower jaw of *Halmaturus bennettii*, showing (*a*) the incisors in close apposition, (*b*) fibres of the orbicularis oris muscle, (*c*) anterior portion of the genio-hyoid muscle of left side, the median line of separation from its fellow of the right side being hardly distinguishable.

less in dimensions, and consequently having a smaller separation of the teeth.

Besides an examination of the dried bones, we have been fortunate in having the opportunity of studying the appearances in two animals which died in the Gardens. In one of these, Bennett's Kangaroo (*Halmaturus bennettii*), a young female, the teeth of the lower jaw when close together, as Mr. Waterhouse remarks, fit within the apex of the foremost pair of incisors of the upper jaw, the two sharp inner edges of the lower incisors coming so close together that the line of separation (Fig. 1, *a*) is hardly distinguishable; but when the angles of the inferior maxilla are slightly approximated, as, for instance, by a gentle pressure of the thumb and fore-finger, then the two teeth open like the blades of a pair of scissors at their points, as much as one-eighth of an inch, and, according to what Mr. Waterhouse says, their outer

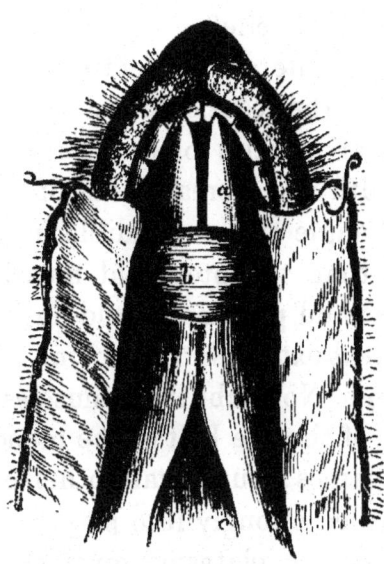

Fig. 2.—The same dissection of the mandible of *Halmaturus bennettii* as in Fig. 1, but showing (at *a*) the manner of separation of the lower incisors, and how they also override the anterior upper incisors.

cutting-edges are brought more closely in contact with the inner edge of the anterior upper incisors; but at the same time it must be remarked they can also overlap them (Fig. 2, *a*). But whether this overlapping takes place ordinarily, when the creature crops its food, we are not prepared to say, as it is not readily distinguishable, from the rapidity of the act.

In the second specimen of Kangaroo (*Petrogale brachyotis*), an adult female, the tips of the lower incisors could be separated almost one-fourth of an inch, and the structure was in nearly all respects similar to that of Bennett's Kangaroo—with this difference, that in *Petrogale brachyotis* there was an interspace at the base of the lower incisors, even when the points of the teeth were brought in contact; while in *Halmaturus bennettii* the whole of the inner edges were applied closely to each other (Fig. 1, *a*). It is possible that this slight hollow may have been caused by a wearing away of the substance; that it existed in the adult animal gives feasibility to this belief.

The next point of interest connected with this remarkable movement is the consideration of what muscular apparatus or set of muscles produces it.

The great breadth and increased size of the inner hollow of the ramus and angle of the mandible in the Marsupials at once suggest that the pterygoid muscles, from their increased purchase and position, would entirely effect this, as they do, to a great extent, in the bovine race in the process of rumination. No doubt these muscles are concerned in the motive act of the one half of the mandible upon the other in the Kangaroos; but certain other muscular fibres seem also to be called strongly into play.

The thin layer of the platysma myoides on either side appears to have a slight influence in the production of the opening of the incisors, by gently aiding the approximation of the angles of the lower jaw.

The digastric muscles, moderately strong in the specimens dissected, have their usual origin and median tendon slightly in advance of the angles. Their anterior fleshy bellies are inserted half-an-inch or so behind the posterior junction of the symphysis, so that on contraction of their fibres they serve to pull together the posterior rami, and also produce the aforesaid separation of the lower incisors.

The two mylo-hyoidei are not extraordinarily large, although broad; but their position and nearly transverse direction give them even a more direct and important action in the opening movement than the last.

The genio-hyoidei are, on the contrary, strong and well developed. Their point of traction from the hyoid bone, and apparent tenseness while the incisors are asunder, lead to the inference that they likewise modify and aid the opening movement, although mere position and the parallelism of the fibres to the medium line of divergence (at least as they appear on dissection) make one hesitate to attribute too much power to them; but they certainly act along with, and greatly strengthen the force of, the mylo-hyoidei.

By the conjoined simultaneous action of the whole of the muscles mentioned, the movement of the symphysis and separation of the incisors seemed to be effected; while the return to the state of closure follows relaxation of these, with possibly contraction of one of the pterygoid muscles. The chief agent, however, in the approximation of the anterior portions of the symphysis and the internal edges of the incisors is no doubt the transverse fibres of the orbicularis oris (here situated at the anterior portion of the bony symphysis and the root of the lower incisors), which, although delicate medially, is nevertheless well developed laterally (see Figs. 1 and 2, b).

In proof that the portions of the symphysis in close juxtaposition are the pivot or point of leverage in the movement spoken of, and that the muscles stated are those concerned in the action, a partially dissected specimen need only be experimented on, when very gentle inward pushing at the angle will be seen to produce the separation of the incisors, and a like force applied in advance of the pivot (*e. g.* where the orbicular muscle is placed) immediately and easily causes closure.

Hence, as to the point at issue, we have tried to show from our observations the analogy of the movements and use of the mandible and incisors of the Kangaroo to those of a pair of cutting-forceps or scissors, the posterior part of the symphysis being the pivot, the angles the handles, and the incisors the blades, the inner edge of which is the cutting-edge.

The manner of use, at least in confinement, we have attempted to describe; but whether the teeth are put to the same use when the animal is in a state of nature is a fact unknown to us. Mr. Gould, whose opportunities of observation of their native habits was at one time great, informs us that the food of the *Petrogale brachyotis* is often dry and tough vegetables obtained among rocky places. It is possible therefore that the cutting-edges in that case might well serve to sever dry or fibrous material.

P.S.—Since this paper was read, our attention has been called by Dr. J. E. Gray to a paragraph in *The Book of Nature*, by John Mason Good (vol. i. p. 254), where the author says—"The *Mus maritimus*, or African Rat, the largest species of this genus which has hitherto been discovered, and seldom less than a full-sized rabbit, has the singular property of separating at pleasure to a considerable distance the two front teeth of the lower jaw, which are not less than an inch and a quarter long. That elegant and extraordinary creature the Kangaroo, which we may soon hope to see naturalized in our own country, is possessed of a similar faculty."

But this statement does not seem to forestall the facts which we have observed regarding the use or manner of action of the lower incisors in these Marsupials; nor does it even express either so definitely or clearly some of the peculiarities of the movement as observations which we have quoted at length.

HOFFMANN'S SLOTH.

(*CHOLOPUS HOFFMANNII.*)

No fault can be found with the person who first gave the name of Sloth to this animal. Its life seems to be passed without the slightest attempt on its own part to improve its condition. Living as it does in the dense and gloomy forests unheard of and seldom seen, the creature passes its existence in slowly crawling under the branches of trees, feeding upon the leaves, blossoms, or fruit; no sooner are the leaves, etc., of one tree consumed, than the Sloth descends and re-ascends the nearest food tree that suits his taste; thus the animal passes his monotonous life as a vegetarian, pure and simple. Without any playful habits or lively antics, it lives a solitary, secluded existence.

For the size of the animal, its strength is very extraordinary. It is with great difficulty that a man can detach the brute from the branch of a tree to which it clings with its powerful limbs and strong claws. If one is shot dead in a tree which an Indian is unable to climb, it is left there for one day, or perhaps two days, when the limbs become relaxed, and it then falls to the ground. If, however, it is not soon picked up by the hunter, it is very quickly devoured by the ants.

ABRAHAM DEE BARTLETT,

NATURALIST,

Born October 27, 1812.

MANY YEARS SUPERINTENDENT OF THE ZOOLOGICAL SOCIETY'S
GARDENS, REGENT'S PARK.

Died May 7, 1897.

———

THIS PORTRAIT WAS TAKEN ABOUT 1886–7.
REPRODUCED BY KIND PERMISSION OF GAMBIER BOLTON, ESQ., 1898.

PART II.—BIRDS.

CHAPTER I.

TROPICAL BIRDS.

THE GREAT BIRD OF PARADISE.
(*PARADISEA APODA.*)

In the second volume of *The Cruise of the Marchesa,* by Dr. F. H. H. Guillemard (p. 340), a strange statement is made upon the authority of the inhabitants of the Aru Islands respecting the moulting and plumage of the Great Bird of Paradise (*Paradisea apoda*). It is there said that this bird, unlike its nearly allied species *P. minor,* does not wear its adult male plumage all the year, and that its beautiful plumes remain developed for not longer than two or three months.

If I had nothing but my acquaintance with the habits and life-conditions of birds to judge from, I should at once question the accuracy of these statements.

I could not really believe that two species of birds so closely allied as these two Paradise birds, having the same arrangement of their plumes, the same structural peculiarities and inhabiting the same region, could, by any possibility, differ so widely in this respect. It is, however, a great pleasure to me to be able to offer a very clear and well-established fact in proof of my previous conviction.

On October 1, 1885, I was fortunate enough to have placed under my charge a male of the larger species *P. apoda.* The bird, at that time, was in the adult male plumage; the side-plumes were not so long as in the old

109

male birds, but the feathers of the tail, together with the two long wire-like central feathers, were well developed. About the end of November the bird commenced to moult, throwing off the feathers rapidly. The head and throat soon became completely bare, the uppermost side feathers fell off first, the new feathers taking their place before the longest feathers of the plumes fell off. By the end of January the bird had moulted every feather, and the whole plumage was entirely new and beautiful. In this condition the bird was transferred on May 2, 1886, to the Zoological Gardens at Antwerp.

I feel, therefore, after giving the foregoing facts, fully justified in calling in question the statement of natives and others who may be ignorant, or from some motive wilfully attempt to mislead strangers.

In conclusion I may add, so far as I am able to ascertain, the bird was the only living species *P. apoda* ever brought to Europe.

BARTLETT'S BIRD OF PARADISE.
(*PARADISEA BARTLETTII* GOODWIN.)

The following account was given, by Mr. William Goodwin, of an apparently new species of Paradise Bird—

"I beg permission to introduce to your notice a Bird of Paradise, which I believe to be altogether unknown, or, at least, hitherto undescribed.

"I have interested myself for many years in this branch of Ornithology, and possess in my own collection twenty-nine specimens, representing all the different species known up to the present time, with the exception of *Semioptera wallacii*. I have had opportunities of inspecting the fine collections of these birds sent to England by that energetic and able naturalist, Mr. Wallace, and have searched in vain for any specimen similar to that which I have now the honour of introducing to the meeting. I, therefore, conclude it to be in all probability an entirely new and undescribed species.

"The bird, which I believe to be the female, came into my possession about twenty years ago, together with another, which I have no doubt is the male bird. This latter specimen is now in the British Museum.

"I received them both from Mr. Bartlett, and we then agreed in considering them as a young male and female of the *Paradisea papuana;* but the numerous specimens which I have examined in the collections of Mr. Wallace, consisting of males, females, and young of the latter bird, have now convinced me that they belong to an entirely distinct species.

"The male (now in the British Museum) is smaller than the *Paradisea papuana,* the length from head to end of tail being about 9 in., bill 1¼ in., wings from shoulder to tips barely 7½ in., tail 5½ in. Feathers on the head and shoulders yellow; back, tail, and wings, dark chestnut-brown; the coverts of the wings edged with yellow; the two central tail-feathers have naked shafts 15 in. in length terminating with elongated webs 3 in. long; the throat has a small patch of golden-green, which surrounds the base of the bill; the lower parts, with the exception of a small patch under the throat, white; side-feathers somewhat elongated and soft.

"Female: length from head to end of tail about 9 in., bill 1¼ in. Forehead, throat, side, and top of the head dark chocolate-brown, shading to a dingy yellow and cinnamon colour; tail-coverts tinged with yellowish-brown; tail cinnamon-brown, 4⅝ in. long, the two middle feathers narrow, pointed and curved, 5½ in. in length; the whole

England with other skins of Birds of Paradise, viz. the Clouded (*P. magnifica*), Golden-breasted (*P. aurea*), and the *Ptilorhis magnifica*.

" The locality was unknown to him, and is probably one which Mr. Wallace has not yet visited. Should he continue his researches, he may yet be fortunate enough to meet with this species.

" In conclusion, I beg to propose that the bird now brought under your notice be named *Paradisea bartlettii*, in recognition of the valuable services rendered by Mr. Bartlett to the lovers of ornithological science by his very careful researches and numerous observations."

LYRE-BIRD.

(*MENURA SUPERBA.*)

On the 9th of April, 1867, the Society acquired a fine example of the Lyre-bird (*Menura superba*). It was a young bird, having been reared from the nest, and was consequently in immature plumage; we therefore were unable to determine its sex. This bird, considering its size, is perhaps the most active and quickest-moving bird known; its large and powerful legs and feet enable it to run with amazing swiftness; it also jumps or hops not only with great rapidity, but to almost incredible distances. These facts have been repeatedly stated by persons who have seen the bird in its native haunts, and its shy and wary habits have been frequently described.

Notwithstanding the well-known wildness of the species when at liberty, the individual now under consideration is

112

most remarkable for its tameness; it will come readily to the call of the keeper and perch upon his hand or arm, and in the most gentle manner search his hand or anything he may hold in it for food. In doing this it exhibits a great amount of inquisitiveness and intelligence; if the closed hand is held near the ground the bird will grasp it with its foot, and in a very quiet way try to open it in order to obtain what may be held in the hand. The bird runs or hops upon the ground or upon the perches with equal ease; that is, it runs along the perches that are horizontal. It scratches on the ground, using the right and left foot alternately, grasping the clods of earth and pulling them over, examining the roots and under-parts most minutely for the smallest seeds or insects.

The strength of the legs and feet will be better understood from the fact that the bird will drag about large clods of peat, earth, and roots upwards of 7 lbs. weight. This I have ascertained by weighing the lumps of earth after the bird had so moved them. Unlike the gallinaceous birds, the Lyre-bird washes freely, and has never been seen to dust itself. It has a loud and fine voice, and, although I cannot say I have heard its song, the keepers, upon whose veracity I can place every confidence, assure me that the bird has frequently sung, and its notes are described as resembling those of a thrush or a blackbird in the commencement, but gradually become much louder. Its food consists of finely-chopped meat mixed with a quantity of bruised hempseed, earthworms, mealworms, ants' eggs and grasshoppers, together with a small quantity of canary and millet seed. Like most insect-eating birds, the Lyre-bird throws up the pellets, usually called castings, of the indigestible portion of its food, such as the wing-cases and legs of beetles and other insects.

Having made myself tolerably well acquainted with the

and in so doing I beg to refer to the habits as noticed in No. 45, vol. ii. of *Land and Water*, in which the writer describes the meeting of a number of male birds of this species, which he supposes were fighting and, as he says, making a most abominable noise.

A similar meeting of male birds is mentioned by Mr. Wallace as taking place with the great Bird of Paradise. Mr. Wallace says the male birds assemble together upon the tops of the tallest trees and utter their loud and not very pleasing notes.

This, together with what I have observed in captivity, both of the *Menura* and the smaller kind of Bird of Paradise, induced me to consider and search for other characters on which to found an opinion; I therefore take the *habits, voice, feathers,* and their arrangement[1] together with the skeleton. Having examined the skeleton of the *Menura* together with that of the Bird of Paradise and a true *Corvus*, I must say in general that the *Menura* and Bird of Paradise present a stronger likeness to each other than either of them exhibits towards the genus *Corvus*. In the breadth and form of the skull, the *Menura* and Bird of Paradise resemble each other remarkably.

In conclusion, I have to remark that the strong and well-marked resemblance between these birds consists in the *voice, food and mode of breeding,* the large size of the legs and feet, the form of the skull and skeleton, the structure of the feathers, and their arrangement on the body; and to this I may add, the bird belongs to the same geographical range as the true Paradise bird: I regard it as an aberrant form, or rather as the terrestrial form, the true Paradise bird being the arboreal form of the same group.

[1] See Nitzsch's *Pterylographie*, pl. 3, figs. 11—13.

KINGFISHERS.

The laughing kingfisher, or, as he is better known by the Colonist, the laughing jackass, is a fine large bird, but, unlike the kingfishers of our climate, does not inhabit the water-side to feed upon fish. It is most frequently found in the forests far away from water, living upon small birds, quadrupeds, snakes, lizards and insects of various kinds which are pounced upon and devoured by this noisy and bold bird. Three or four species of this genus are found in Australia, all of which have the powerful and harsh voice so well known in the country they inhabit.

One of the prettiest of our British birds is the kingfisher, and it is much to be regretted that the number of them is so greatly on the decline, when we take into consideration that it is the only species of the family that has made Great Britain its home. The everlasting desire to kill these handsome little birds for the sake only of their skins or feathers has reduced their number so much that it will be soon regarded as a *rara avis.* Were it not for their habit of making their nest in a hole in the banks of streams, and these being generally situated in a difficult and oftentimes dangerous place to be approached, the nests would be more frequently plundered, and the total destruction of the bird thereby eventually accomplished. The large number of fish-destroying birds of various kinds has no doubt led many of our fish-preserving friends to extremes, "that of killing and otherwise trying to reduce their numbers," and in this, no doubt, their efforts have been partly successful; however, in regard to the kingfisher, in many places this destruction is quite unnecessary and probably injurious, as these little birds eat large

115

excusable, and in some instances very praiseworthy, on the part of our fish-preservers, were their breeding-grounds visited by such monsters as the pelican, which with distended jaws and capacious pouch could gulp down at one mouthful enough young fry to stock a goodly-sized pond.

No follower of Izaak Walton, while patiently watching and trying to capture a monster pike or perch, could begrudge his lively brother fisher a few of the common little fry, and such an one must in his lonely and dull solitude be charmed by the appearance now and then of this charming little blue-jacket, the bobbing jerk and shrill chip of which must always make it welcome. Although only a single species of this group of beautiful birds is found in this country, yet their distribution over the world is universal. Many of the genera, such as *Dacelo, Ispida, Halcyon*, etc., are so well marked and so easily described that any one possessing a tolerable knowledge of ornithology would be able, at once, to distinguish them.

One of the remarkable features among birds that feed upon fish is the diversity of means employed by them to capture their slippery prey. The bill of the kingfisher is in form the same as that of the heron, but the mode of using it in each bird is singularly different. The heron stands by the water's edge, probably with its feet and legs immersed, and watches for the approach of its food, and, on its appearance, the bird, by a sudden dart of its long neck, strikes, secures, and instantly, without any preparation, swallows it. How opposite is the mode of acting on the part of the kingfisher, which, sometimes perched high above the water on a stump, a branch of an old tree, or a rail, darts with the rapidity

116

of lightning into the water, rarely missing its aim, and having captured its prey flies off to the nearest resting-place to kill it by repeated blows before making a meal. So constant and habitual is that mode of acting that even when reared and fed upon small pieces of raw meat the kingfisher always strikes it several times on a stone, or on the ground, before eating, in order to satisfy itself that it is dead, or, at least, stunned.

Who among us could have formed two animals so unlike each other in general structure as the heron and king-fisher, and destined both to catch and live upon the same kind or description of food and to inhabit the same locality, without in any way interfering with or imitating each other's mode of fishing, yet to succeed equally in the end for which they were created?

In early times, much more importance was felt to belong to the kingfisher than is now attached to this well-known bird; and in the careful and valuable work on *British Birds*, published by Mr. Yarrell, allusion is made to the ancient writers, whose notes upon the *Halcyon* are extremely interesting and curious. It is most interesting to consider how various are the adaptations of nature to the accomplishment of a desired end, and particularly so in the fish-eating birds. The heron's slow and silent watching for hours by the pool or stream, contrasts forcibly with the swift and determined energy displayed by the cormorant in the pursuit of fish under water, which to witness is a most exciting and wonderful sight. In the clear stream, the cormorant swims with almost the swiftness of an arrow; with his long neck and head thrust forward, giving the creature the appearance of a large champagne-bottle, and with legs behind, the green-eyed monster chases the terri-fied fish with marvellous speed, turning about and over-taking it in its native element. Sometimes, though rarely,

117

hooked bill of its pursuer, and is frequently dragged out and put to death. The Chinese have long since availed themselves of the abilities of cormorants in the capture of fish.

There appears to be a wide range of adaptive contrivances in the means furnished to birds for catching their food. The bills in different species vary considerably in form and construction and are used in various ways, viz. for spearing, as in the heron; for teeth-snapping, as in the merganser; for hooking, as in the cormorant; and for shovelling up, as in the pelican. Again the feet of some birds are peculiarly constructed, as in the osprey and several species of fishing eagles and owls, for grasping and holding fast their food. We have therefore, perhaps, the most complete series of organs modified and suited to perform what would appear the very difficult office of catching and retaining a very slippery and active article of food. A very remarkable fact is well known respecting the kingfisher. An adult male bird had been kept for two years in a large aviary well supplied with live fish, when a nest of young ones, five or six in number, was introduced into the aviary, and to the surprise of all, this old bird commenced to catch fish and feed them, and continued to perform the duty of the parent birds until the young birds were quite able to fish for themselves. This happy state of things was not, however, allowed to continue many months, as when the young birds appeared adult and fully able to take care of themselves, their kind friend set to work, and with his sharp bill destroyed the whole of them—evidently the solitary habits of the bird were the cause of this; as apparently the old bird in endeavouring to distribute the young ones to other localities,

118

not wishing to have a colony, had in the attempt carried his desire to get rid of the family to a fatal termination.

The hole in the bank inhabited by the kingfisher, and in which it breeds, has a nest composed chiefly of fish-bones; the bones are simply the cast pellets from the stomach of the bird. After the process of digestion the bones of the fish that have been consumed are thrown up in a ball or pellet, just in the same manner that hawks or owls throw up the pellets or castings, consisting of the hair or feathers and undigested parts of the animals they have eaten.

Nothing can exceed the beauty of the colours of the kingfishers; many have not only a plumage of exquisite tints of blue, green, pink, and almost every shade and variety and arrangement of lovely colours, but the bills of numerous species are brilliant in the extreme. Some of the genera, as in *Tanysiptera*, have their tails elongated several inches, and in this case their elongated tail-feathers are generally white or only delicately edged with pale blue, giving them a most graceful and charming appearance.

Mr. E. W. Searle tells me that he saw a kingfisher at three different times in 1883 in the Kensington Gardens part of the Serpentine. The first time the bird alighted on the notice-board " Fishing," etc., not allowed.

CHAPTER II.

VULTURES AND BIRDS OF PREY.

VULTURES.

VULTURES are, universally, in great contempt, and are regarded by the most highly civilized people as loathsome and disgusting scavengers. This feeling increases as the spots are neared where the larger species abound, and it is particularly observable in India in the neighbourhood of the burial-places. Nothing can exceed the horror that is experienced by a visit to some of these sickening and pestiferous receptacles of human remains, which are partly consumed by fire, and left exposed, to be torn and mangled by these repulsive feeders upon the most revolting of all carrion. These offensive birds appear to increase in numbers in proportion to the requirements of the situation, and their wonderful habit of appearing almost suddenly in countless numbers upon a spot where a day or two, nay, even an hour or two before, none could be seen or found, is well known. Aided by a powerful and wonderful vision, and sailing, without effort, in a circle of great diameter, in a clear, unclouded atmosphere, miles above the earth, this bird's sight, intent and keen, enables it to observe the changed and hurried movements of any others of his species which might be, as they nearly always are, in quest of food, and which in turn may be within sight of many others that again are in view of others still further off, all making towards a spot where food is to be found.

Whenever a movement is made towards the earth by one, the whole flock becomes instantly aware of it and of the direction taken; thus they concentrate in incalculable strength, in the same manner that thousands of people sometimes arrive on the field on the descent of a balloon in a part of the country that the day before seemed almost uninhabited.

There are many queer sayings connected with these hungry and unscrupulous feeders, and they are regarded by the natives of the countries in which they most abound with feelings of reverence totally at variance with the ideas of more civilized people : feeding upon the dead and thus removing the most obnoxious substances, they may be respected as scavengers provided for the benefit of other inhabitants of the soil. The Indians of Dutch Guiana have a full belief in the wisdom of the black vultures so numerous in those parts of the world; these birds, they say, give them information of the places where the turtles have buried their eggs, by walking about and scratching with their bills on the sand. Upon seeing these indications, the Indians dig out the eggs, and the vultures are rewarded by the broken ones that are sure to be left. Experience may have taught the Indians and the vultures the same lesson. The vulture's keen sight probably detects the spot on the sand that has been disturbed during the night, and in the hope of finding the eggs or endeavouring to scratch them out attracts the attention of the Indian who takes advantage of the opportunity and helps himself, leaving a few broken eggs for the original finder, and attributes this to a much better feeling or understanding between the birds and himself than ever existed; at any rate the Indian has much respect for these birds, and will not allow them to be destroyed without entering a strong protest in their

121

these birds are not produced like other birds from eggs; they are led to believe this by finding at all times and seasons vast multitudes of birds who never nest or appear to breed, and their increase is to them a mystery. The fact is the nesting-places are unknown to these people. The larger species of vultures are formidable-looking birds, but not naturally inclined to attack living animals; yet if incautiously handled, they inflict severe and dangerous wounds. A young and inexperienced collector known to the writer, came, while travelling alone, suddenly upon a large number of these birds, and finding they would not move or quit their (to him) revolting feast, he feared, although most anxious to obtain two or three of them as specimens, to kill or seize upon one of them, in case the multitude might fall upon him and reduce his frame to the miserable condition of the skeletons that were lying, in all their ghastliness, exposed to view. How is it that they live and are strong and healthy when they feed in and breathe this poisonous and pestilential air, and are nourished by the most abominable and, apparently, unwholesome food? Do they ascend into the cold pure air to rid themselves of the foul gases generated in their bodies, and thus regenerate the blood to give the strength required in order to fulfil their degraded office? Why not? The unfortunate dwellers in towns go to the seaside for change of air to enable them to continue their struggle for life.

The mode of resting or soaring in circles by these large and powerful birds has formed the subject of frequent discussions, and much has been said to account for the ease and the long-continued gliding without the slightest apparent motion of or flapping or beating with the wings, these being simply spread open to the fullest extent.

The most reasonable explanation of this wonderful power is given in the examination of the air-cells that exist throughout the entire structure, not only in the bones, but among the muscles, and between the tissues of the skin and feathers; when the bird rises to a great height the atmosphere becomes cold, and as the temperature of the bird's body is much higher than that of the surrounding air the bird fills, or rather inflates, the whole of the air-cells throughout its body by the hot air that has passed into the lungs of the bird before it reaches the chambers formed for its reception; thus the condors, or other large vultures, become like air-balloons, and float about, requiring only a slight motion of the tail to steer, rudder-like, in any direction. When the bird wishes to rest on the earth its form at once alters, the wings are no longer on full stretch, but, by contracting the muscles of the wings and body, the hot air is expelled, and the bird descends with rather a rapid, but graceful and easy movement of the wings, and alights without appearing to drop heavily to the ground. The detection of the spot where food is to be found is no longer regarded by the best authorities in these matters to depend upon the sense of smell, sight alone is the agent, and the power of which can only account for the incredible numbers of these birds that sometimes appear immediately after the death of a large animal. Endless experiments have been tried, and this fact has been, beyond all doubt, established. Vultures lay but one or two eggs, and yet their number is legion. It is a curious and noteworthy fact, that the species of birds that are most abundant are those that lay the fewest eggs at each sitting; for instance, the passenger pigeon lays but one egg, and yet that species is supposed to be the bird, of all others, the numbers of which exceed every other kind.

GOSHAWKS.

NOTICE OF SOME GOSHAWKS IN THE POSSESSION OF THE
LATE MR. HOY.

In the early part of the month of September 1839
Mr. Hoy visited London on his way to his residence
at Stoke Nayland, Suffolk. He had been on the Continent
in order to obtain some goshawks for the purpose of
hawking, to which sport he was much attached, and, I
believe, few persons better understood the nature, habits,
and the modes of training and using birds of prey than
he. He mentioned to me long since that he kept several
hobbies (*Falco subbuteo*) about his residence, giving them
their full liberty the whole of the summer and allowing
them to range about the country as they pleased, but
always accustoming them to come to him every day at
three o'clock to be fed, at which time he would walk
into a field adjoining the house, and, by whistling or
waving a glove in the air, although the birds were not
before visible, they might be seen coming towards him
with great rapidity and to alight, one after another, upon
his arm to take their meal, after which they would fly off
and perhaps not be seen until the following day. Sometimes,
when at a distance of three or four miles from the house, he
has seen one or more of them, and, by making the usual
sign, they would come to him and alight upon his hand;
but it was necessary to confine them before the season of
migration, or they would leave and not return, after they
had become wild—as was proved by trying the experiment.
During the short stay Mr. Hoy made in September last,
I called upon him for the purpose of seeing the goshawks.
There were four of them, three males and one female,—

the female, a bird of the year, was the largest and most powerful bird of the species I had ever seen; Mr. Hoy told me she could secure, with ease, a full-grown hare.

With regard to using these birds, Mr. Hoy informed me that their habits, mode of flight, etc., were much better suited than those of the peregrine falcon to an enclosed district like Stoke Nayland. When used or taken into the field, the wing of a bird, or the thin end of an ox-tail, is generally held in the hand to engage their attention, and at which they are constantly biting and tearing without being able to satisfy their appetites, as that would render them unfit for work. They do not require to be hooded, but have bells attached to their legs (for the purpose of giving notice of their situation when they alight, which would otherwise be difficult to ascertain), and a leather strap by which they are held; it is also necessary to employ spaniels to hunt up the birds, upon the appearance of which the hawk flies from the hand with incredible swiftness direct at the game, taking it generally in the first attempt, but should the bird fail to secure the quarry it will perch on some elevated situation and there remain until the game is again started, which it is rarely known to miss a second time. When the hawk has made a capture it is rewarded with a small piece of meat, or a pigeon's head, to induce it to give up the prey; if the hawk be allowed to range at pleasure, it will, on hearing its owner whistle, return to him with a swiftness truly astonishing, but finding that it cannot stop suddenly to settle without striking him with great force, it will glide past, form a circle round him, and alight with the greatest ease, and in the most gentle manner, upon his hand.—November 20, 1839.

CHAPTER III.

HERONS AND STORKS.

THE WHALE-HEADED STORK.
(*BALÆNICEPS REX.*)

THE question of the affinities of the *Balœniceps* having been discussed by so many able ornithologists, it may be interesting to know that this bird does not possess the remarkable patches of down found on each side of the breast in all the herons and bitterns.

Having had the opportunity of ascertaining this fact by an examination of the living bird, in the Society's Gardens, I am enabled to say that these patches, which are of a singular dense and close structure and are found beneath the feathers on each side of the front and fore-part of the pectoral muscles of herons and bitterns, do not exist in the *Balœniceps.* The absence of this peculiarity may, I think, assist in indicating the true affinities of this bird, as pointed out by Dr. Reinhardt, in his communication to the Society on this subject.[1] *Balœniceps Rex* arrived in the Gardens for the first time in April 1860.[2]

At a meeting of the Zoological Society I produced new evidence of the affinities of this bird, and in endeavouring to aid in settling a subject so long disputed and frequently discussed, I referred, first, to the elaborate and carefully-written paper by Mr. Parker, in which this

[1] See *Proceedings of the Zoological Society,* 1860, p. 377.
[2] *Ibid.* 1860, p. 243.

bird, after the most careful examination and comparison of its bones, is considered to be an *Ardeine*.

I observed that from an entirely different course of examination, and by the consideration of its other structures, I had arrived at the same conclusion; and I hoped, with the assistance of my friend Mr. Stewart, to prove to the satisfaction of our ornithological friends, that there is no longer any doubt in the matter.

The death of the survivor of the two birds brought home by Mr. Consul Petherick afforded me the opportunity of making a more accurate examination of its structure, and this led me to the discovery of two remarkable powder-down patches which I stated[1] on a former occasion I had failed to find in the living bird.

Upon removing the skin from the body of this bird, I was so struck by its close resemblance to the herons, that I immediately killed a heron and removed its skin also, in order to form a fair opinion by a close comparison of all the parts of these two birds. The exact form of the body and limbs was most remarkable; the structure of the hind toes (upon which so much stress has been laid) was alike, these turning backwards, forwards, or sideways in both species. The head and neck, however, of *Balæniceps*, when compared with the same part of the common heron, present some very considerable differences. These differences consist, first, of the much larger head, and consequently stronger neck, in *Balæniceps* as compared with the heron. Doubtless these modifications have reference to the food and the mode of obtaining that food. Many illustrations can be found of similar modifications. I may refer to one in the group under consideration, which results from the comparison of *Cancroma* with *Eurypyya*, and which presents, perhaps, the most extreme modifica-

[1] See *Proceedings of the Zoological Society*, 1860, p. 461.

tion in the form of the bill in two birds of the same family.

As far as I was able to examine the viscera of the *Balæniceps*, I could discover nothing that would lead me to doubt its *Ardeine* affinities ; the stomach, liver, intestines, etc., of the two birds appeared to exactly correspond in structure and arrangement.

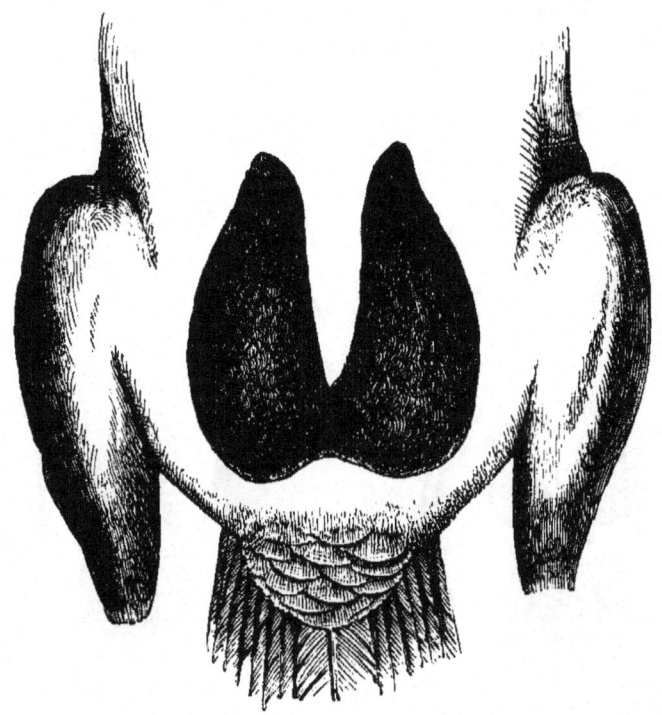

Fig. 1.

Directing my attention to the skin of *Balæniceps*, I was surprised at finding on the lower part of the back, reaching from the end of the scapulars to the base of the tail, two large, well-defined powder-down patches. The drawing (Fig. 1) represents these two patches *in situ* on the body of the bird stripped of its feathers. These remarkable patches are dark-coloured on the inside of the skin, and

128

on the outside the down is of extreme thickness, and the
quantity of white or grey powder very great. This
powder, when examined under the microscope, appears
excessively oily, and will not mix with water. It is greasy
to the touch, and is evidently produced by the growth
of the down. It appears, in fact, to be the quill-shafts of
the down, broken up; or perhaps the down-roots secrete
this powder, which is distributed over the entire plumage,

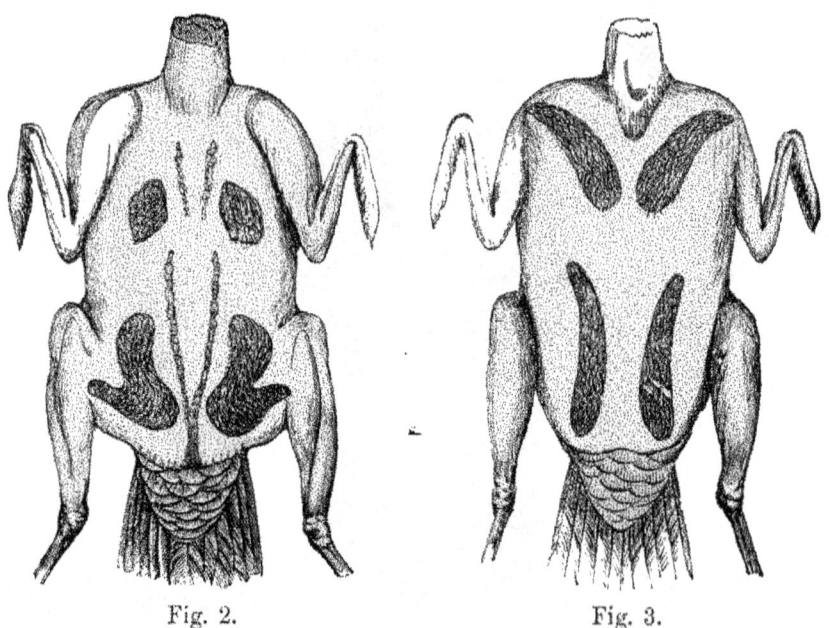

Fig. 2.   Fig. 3.

rendering the feathers impervious to water, in the same
way that the oil-glands effect this in other birds. In this
bird, however, the oil-glands are extremely small, not
larger than the oil-glands of a sparrow.

With reference to these patches, I pointed out in the
birds that I consider allied to *Balæniceps* the existence
of these patches of down; and I remarked, that the
attempt to arrange animals by such means is not new;
as, for instance, in the case of the *Ruminants*, some of

otherwise of anal and other glands and pouches.

I therefore pointed out the species more or less allied to *Balæniceps*, that exhibit these singular structures. In the New World form (*Cancroma*) this structure appears to be most fully developed, this bird having four pairs of these powder-down patches, as shown in Fig. 2, which represents the upper, and Fig. 3, which gives the lower surface of the body of this bird; while in the Old World form (*Balæniceps*) one pair only exist, as we have seen in Fig. 1.

It is worthy of notice, that the true Herons, which inhabit both the Old and New World, and which have generally been regarded as the type of the group, have three pairs of these patches; the little and certainly aberrant form of Heron, *Eurypyga*, has only one pair of these down patches; while intermediate between this bird and the herons come the bitterns, in which two pairs of these patches exist.[1]

By these remarks one is naturally led to observe the often-noticed correspondence of forms in the Old and New World; as, for instance, the ostrich of Africa represented by the rhea of America, the camel of the Old World by the llama of America, the lion by the puma, and many other similar representations.

In the work on *Pterylographie*, published by Ch. L.

[1] Having had many opportunities of studying the habits of the living examples of *Eurypyga* and *Botaurus*, I have observed a striking resemblance in these birds, particularly in the drooping and spreading out of the wings, in which position the beautiful markings upon every feather are finely displayed. I have so frequently seen this attitude assumed by both these birds, that I am satisfied it was not merely an accidental thing.

Nitzsch, the author, who evidently has paid great attention to the subject, says, that "these powder-down patches are found (but in a much smaller degree) in the genus *Tinamus*,[1] one or two parrots, and also in some of the birds of prey." I have not, however, met with them in any group except the *Ardeœ* and their allies. I can assert most positively that no traces of these patches exist in the pelicans, storks, or cranes. I have also taken considerable trouble with *Scopus*. This bird is considered by Prof. Reinhardt to be closely allied to *Balœniceps*. I cannot find anything to justify such a belief; the skins and skulls of the two birds are so entirely different, that it is useless to enter into any further details respecting them.

There is one thing, however, that I wish to remark, and I do so with considerable uneasiness lest I should be accused of casting a doubt upon the veracity of the gentleman to whom we are indebted for the first living specimens of this rare bird; and this consideration would have prevented my making the remark, had not my great desire been to call attention to the subject in the hope of obtaining a truthful explanation of what appears to me inexplicable—I refer to the statement, made by Mr. Petherick, that *Balœniceps* runs about in search of food immediately after it is hatched. If this is true, it is one of the most extraordinary facts I have yet met with.

[1] Since writing the foregoing I have examined *Tinamus*. The structure referred to by Nitzsch appears to differ so widely from the down patches of the *Ardeine* family, that I shall describe it in another paper upon this subject.

CHAPTER IV.

WATER-FOWL.

THE SELECTION OF WATER-FOWL.

At the spring of the year most persons who have couveniences for the suitable accommodation of the above kinds of birds begin to obtain a supply of them, or, should they already possess some kinds that have not answered their expectations, they seek for information as to the best sorts to keep, and how to keep them.

One of the first considerations must be the space of ground and the extent of water intended to be stocked. It will be at once seen that to keep a number of birds of different kinds, unless much space is afforded them to enable them to occupy places widely apart, great expense must be incurred in making artificial contrivances in order to separate them during the breeding season, as at that time most of them become quarrelsome, and the larger and more powerful birds kill or drive off the rest. These pugnacious habits are stronger in some species than in others, and, in remarking upon the different kinds, an endeavour will be made to point out those which are troublesome or otherwise, and, as far as possible, what are the most easily obtainable kinds and their requirements.

SWANS.

These birds, of which many species exist, are mostly strong and hardy, but require a large space; they are very quarrelsome, and unless the locality affords shelter and hiding-places for smaller water-fowl, if any be placed with them, it is useless to think of keeping and breeding the latter on the same spot. If the water is very extensive the different kinds of swans may be kept, provided that they are respectively induced to occupy localities sufficiently removed from, and so that they cannot see, each other. Nothing can exceed the charm that these beautiful creatures lend to a lake or stream; whether they be black or white, wild or tame swans, they are, from their size and grace, the most perfect finish to the scene; perhaps the most beautiful of all swans is the black-necked, the snowy-white body of which contrasts wonderfully with its black neck and head, ornamented on the forehead by the bright crimson berry and pale blue bill, so conspicuous in the breeding season. All the species can be bred in this country, but they are careful, however, in selecting secure breeding-places; a well-wooded island, with good landing-places, and a plentiful supply of dead rushes, coarse grass, twigs, moss and other nest-making materials at hand, is all that they require. The incubation occupies forty-two days, and the young are reared without trouble.

WILD GEESE.

There is so much sameness of colour in most wild geese that few persons care to possess them, and as, during the breeding season, many of them are pugnacious, it is only in large and well-divided places that the several kinds can be kept; there are, however, a few of the species that rarely do any harm to the birds around them, and as most geese are grass feeders they are not so much on the water as swans and ducks. Some are of considerable beauty, both in form, colour and marking. Especial mention may be and quiet disposition ; they do not breed freely in captivity, and it is even doubtful whether the Brent Goose has ever produced in this country. Many other instances occur in which several species of water-fowl show no inclination to breed in captivity, even under what may be considered the most favourable circumstances.

DUCKS.

Lastly, I come to the ducks, of matchless beauty and of endless variety of species, differing much in habits, food and requirements. Two well-marked divisions are exhibited in this class, viz. the swimming and the diving ducks. It must not, however, be supposed that, because so separated, the swimming ducks cannot dive, or that the diving ducks cannot swim ; the divisions depend, principally, upon a difference in the form and structure of the birds, particularly in the legs and feet. These parts in the true diving ducks are large, and placed so far behind that the body of the bird appears over-weighted in front as it walks, or attempts to walk, on the ground. The swimming duck, on the contrary, has smaller feet, is more evenly balanced, and walks on the ground with greater ease and freedom. Many other differences exist, and they may be easily distinguished by those already indicated. Among the diving ducks many species are great destroyers of fish and other fresh-water and marine animals, and those species are consequently very difficult, and, in some places, objectionable birds to keep; I intend to mention these in due course. On the other hand, many of them are perfectly harmless, and from their quick and lively movements, diving and reappearing at a considerable distance again and again, render themselves very attractive; there are also among them many species of great beauty, but they rarely breed in this country. I now come to the more delicate and smaller kinds of water-fowl, known as the swimming ducks. It must be admitted that for beauty of colour, combined with gracefulness of form, this group contains so many species, that it is difficult to select those most to be praised. To this large selection of the water birds, the delightful Summer or Carolina Duck, the grand Mandarin, the Japanese and other Teal, Wigeon, Pintail, Shoveller, and others belong; which will suffice to show the task of attempting to say more than a passing word upon each kind. Intermediate, or nearly so, between ducks and geese I find several very distinct genera or species. Of these, the Sheldrakes and Egyptian geese may be taken as examples, the plumage of the sexes of which, unlike the true ducks, are alike; at the same time they more resemble swans than geese, hence the endless attempts to classify them by the invention of new generic names. Most of them, though easily obtained and kept, are highly combative, and some are so desperate that it is dangerous to approach them in the breeding season, many of the larger species being armed with a sharp and powerful spur on the carpal joint of the wing with which they inflict dangerous and painful wounds.

List of species of water-fowl most easily obtained and kept :—

SWANS.

Common Swan (*Cygnus olor*).
Hooper or Wild Swan (*Cygnus ferus*).
Trumpeter Swan (*Cygnus buccinator*).

Bar-headed Goose (*Anser indicus*).
Bernicle Goose (*Bernicla leucopsis*).
Brent Goose (*Bernicla brenta*).
Upland Goose (*Chloephaga magellanica*).
Ashy-headed Goose (*Chloephaga poliocephala*).
Ruddy-headed Goose (*Chloephaga rubidiceps*).

SWIMMING DUCKS.

Summer or Carolina Duck (*Aix sponsa*).
Mandarin Duck (*Aix galericulata*).
Wigeon (*Mareca penelope*).
Pintail (*Dafila acuta*).
Bahama Duck (*Pœcilonetta bahamensis*).
Gadwall (*Anas stepera*).
Teal (*Querquedula crecca*).
Japanese Teal (*Querquedula formosa*).
Garganey Teal (*Querquedula circia*).
Shoveller (*Spatula clypeata*).

Of the above list of swimming ducks, it may be said they are all easily obtained, and will live and agree together upon a limited space ; they are perfectly hardy, and breed freely in captivity, if provided with good and secure hiding-places.

DIVING DUCKS.

Tufted Duck (*Fuligula cristata*).
*Scaup (*Fuligula marila*).

Red-headed Pochard (*Fuligula ferina*).
Castaneous Duck (*Nyroca leocophthalma*).
*Golden-eye (*Clangula glaucion*).
*Eider Duck (*Somateria mollissima*).
*Smew (*Mergus albellus*).
*Goosander (*Mergus merganser*).

The birds marked thus (*) are more difficult to keep than the other three species, in consequence of their feeding upon fish and other aquatic animals, while the Tufted Duck, Red-headed Pochard and Castaneous Duck feed principally on grain. They are all perfectly hardy, but rarely breed in captivity.

SHELDRAKES.

Common (*Tadorna sulpanser*).
Ruddy (*Tadorna rutila*).
Australian (*Tadorna tadornoïdes*).
Variegated (*Tadorna variegata*).

All the above are easily obtained, they are very hardy and handsome birds, but disagree with all kinds during the breeding time, consequently must be kept at a distance from smaller kinds of water-fowl. Lastly, I mention the names of the birds most objectionable, for the benefit of those who have not tried them; to such I say " Don't," for any one who has tried the Spur-winged Geese, Cereopsis Geese, and Egyptian Geese, will no doubt avoid repeating the experiment.

"The beginning of last week an exceedingly well-known character departed this life, namely 'Old Jack,' the gigantic and venerable swan, with which the public have been so long acquainted on the canal in the enclosure of St. James's Park, at the advanced age of seventy years. 'Old Jack' was hatched some time about the year 1770, on the piece of water attached to Old Buckingham House, and for many years basked in the sunshine of royal favour, Queen Charlotte being particularly partial to him, and frequently condescending to feed him herself. When the pleasure-gardens in St. James's Park were laid out 'Jack' was removed there, and his immense size, social disposition, and undaunted courage have often excited the admiration of the public. 'Jack's' strength and courage were, indeed, astonishing. Frequently has he seized an unlucky dog, who chanced to approach to the edge of his watery domain, by the neck and drowned him, and on one occasion, when a boy about twelve years of age had been teasing him, 'Jack' caught him by the leg of his trousers and dragged him into the lake up to his knees. 'Jack,' however, never acted on the offensive, and if not annoyed, was exceedingly tractable. But the march of modern improvement affected poor 'Jack' as much as it has done thousands of more pretending bipeds.

"The Ornithological Society was formed, and a host of feathered foreigners found their way on to the lake, with

[1] In *Zoological Recreations*, by W. J. Broderip, F.R.S., is an account of the death of a swan, taken from the *Morning Post*, July 9, 1840.

whom 'Jack' had many fierce and furious encounters, and invariably came off successful.

"But a legion of Polish geese at length arrived, who commenced hostilities against 'Jack.' Despising everything like even warfare, they attacked him in a body, and pecked him so severely that he drooped for a few days and then died."

There is an old adage that "Murder will out." The real circumstances of the death of "Old Jack" have never been revealed to the public until now. My old friend and colleague, the late Edward Blyth, and I were the original promoters, or rather pioneers, of the Ornithological Society. The use of the island in the ornamental water of St. James's Park was granted to us by the authorities of the Woods and Forests to carry on our acclimatization operations.

Finding that a man would be required to be in constant attendance, for fear the specimens should be interfered with by the boys, or perhaps stolen, it was found necessary to erect a house in which the caretaker could reside.

On a certain day Blyth and I, having some business on hand at the far end of the lake, took a boat and proceeded there, while all went on swimmingly until we attempted to land.

The embankment was formed of stones sloping down to the water, and Blyth, on stepping out of the boat (the stones being green and slimy), slipped back into the water nearly up to his knees. "Old Jack" was close by on the island watching his mate on her nest, and before Blyth could extricate himself "Old Jack" came down upon him, got him into deeper water, and would, in all probability, have drowned him by getting above and flapping him down with his powerful wings.

Now I must disclose what, in my opinion, was the probable cause of death of the said to be "seventy years wards we heard the sad news of his decease. We did not go to his funeral, as his body was, I believe, reserved for one of the scientific museums.

GEESE AND DUCKS.

PINK-FOOTED GOOSE.[1]

(*ANSER BRACHYRHYNCHUS*, BAILL.)

"It may be necessary, before describing the new species, to notice the three birds most nearly allied, in order more clearly to point out the distinctions existing between them; I do this in consequence of the imperfect descriptions given by authors, from which it is almost impossible to distinguish the species. I shall commence with that which is the most common.

"*Anser segetum*, Meyer. Bean Goose. Entire length 33 in.; extent 64 in.; from the carpal joint to the end of wing 19 in. The head and neck are brown, tinged with grey; back and scapulars darker brown, slightly tinged with grey, each feather being margined with greyish-white; primaries dark brown, tinged with grey; shoulders of wings and secondary quill-feathers greyish-brown; rump blackish-brown; upper tail-coverts white; tail dark brown, deeply edged with greyish-white; breast and belly

---

[1] On a new British species of the genus *Anser* (*Anser phœnicopus*). —*Proceedings of the Zoological Society*, 1839, p. 2.

dirty white ; abdomen and under tail-coverts pure white ; bill 2¼ in. long, rather slender, flattened and narrow towards the tip ; the base, sides, and nail, black ; immediately above the nail commences a yellowish-orange mark, extending a little beyond the anterior margin of the nostrils in front, and passing under and beyond the termination of them at the sides, but seldom reaching the corner of the mouth, except in very old individuals, in which this mark extends under and behind the nostrils, crosses the base of the bill next the forehead, leaving only the central part of the bill (between the nostrils) and the nail black ; which latter part is sometimes, though rarely, white ; legs and feet reddish-orange ; wings, when closed, reaching 2 in. beyond the tail. The young of this species are darker, and the markings less distinct ; the bill is shorter, the mark upon it narrower, and of a deep red colour ; the legs and feet pale orange.

"*Anser cinereus*, Meyer. Grey-Lag Goose. Entire length 35 in. ; extent 64 in. ; from the carpal joint to end of wing 17½ in. The plumage more cinereous than in the last-described species ; the shoulders and rump light grey ; breast and belly white, sometimes spotted with black ; the bill 2½ in. long ; more robust, deeper, broader, and the laminæ much more developed than in the Bean Goose, and of a dull yellow, inclining to flesh-colour towards the nail, which is white ; in summer the bill assumes a redder tint ; legs and feet, pale flesh-colour ; wings, when closed, even with the end of the tail. The young of this species are darker than the adults, but the grey upon the shoulders and rump, the form of the bill, and colour of the legs and feet, will always distinguish them from the young of any of the other species.

" *Anser albifrons*, Bechstein. White-fronted Goose. Entire length 26 in. ; extent 52 in. ; from the carpal joint to

141

end of wing 16½ in. The adult of this species may be distinguished from others of the genus by the conspicuous white mark upon the forehead and sides of the bill, and the irregular patches of black and white upon the breast and belly; the bill, 1¾ in. long, of a reddish flesh-colour; the nail white; legs and feet bright orange; wings, when closed, reaching 1½ in. beyond the tail. The young of this species are much darker than the adult; the forehead and sides of the bill nearly black; the breast and belly dirty white, spotted with brown; bill brown, inclining to flesh-colour; nail dark brown; legs and feet pale orange.

" *Anser phœnicopus*, Bartlett. Pink-footed Goose. Entire length 28 in.; extent 60 in.; from carpal joint to end of wing 17½ in. Top of the head and back of the neck dark brown; sides of the face, fore-part of the neck, and upper part of the breast light brown; back and scapulars dark brown, tinged with grey; each feather deeply margined with greyish-white; shoulders of wings and rump greyish-ash; primaries brown, tinged with grey; tail brownish-ash, deeply edged with white; lower part of belly, upper and under tail-coverts pure white; legs and feet of a reddish flesh-colour or pink; the hind toe closely united by the membrane that runs along the edge of the inner toe; the feet remarkably thick and fleshy; bill 1⅝ in. long, narrow, and much contracted towards the tip; the base, sides and nail black; the space between the nail and the nostrils reddish flesh-colour or pink; wings, when closed, reaching 1½ in. beyond the tail.

"Having thus noticed the three nearly-allied species, and described the new one, I will endeavour to point out more particularly the distinctions between this new species and the Bean Goose, to which it bears the nearest resemblance. First, the great difference in the size; the average size of the Bean Goose is 33 in. in length, and 64 in. in extent, while the average size of the new species is 28 in. in length and 60 in. in extent. Secondly, the bill is much smaller, shorter, more contracted towards the tip, and of a different colour. Thirdly, the difference in colour and in form of the legs and feet, and in the fleshy character of the foot, and the hind toe being more closely united by its membrane, has, consequently, less freedom of motion. Fourthly, the plumage on the rump and shoulders being more inclined to grey. And lastly, in the form of the sternum, which differs from that of the Bean Goose in shape, and bears a more close resemblance to that of the White-fronted Goose. In conclusion, I may remark that I have examined in all twelve specimens of this new species, four of which were alive ; one of them is now living in the Gardens of the Zoological Society, where it has been, I am told, eight years, without exhibiting any perceptible alteration in its plumage, or in the colour of its legs and feet.

"The Grey-Lag Goose is by far the most rare of the four species here referred to."

Mr. W. Yarrell also published the following remarks [1]:—

"On January 8, 1839, at the first meeting of the Zoological Society in that year, Mr. Bartlett exhibited several species of Geese in order to illustrate a paper which he communicated to the meeting on a new British species of the genus *Anser*, for which he proposed the name of *phœnicopus*, on account of the pink colour of the feet, with remarks on the nearly allied species.

"On September 10 in the same year, a communication was received by the Zoological Society from M. Baillon, of Abbeville, stating that he had described in 1833, in the *Memoirs of the Society of Emulation of Abbeville*, a new species of goose, to which he had given the name of *Anser*

---

[1] *British Birds*, vol. iii. p. 64, 1843.

brachyrhynchus, because it appeared to him that one of its most striking characteristics consisted in the shortness of the beak. This bird proved to be of the same species as the one described by Mr. Bartlett; but I believe I am correct in stating that at the time Mr. Bartlett proposed his name for this new goose in 1839, no one here was aware that M. Baillon had described and named the same species in the *Memoirs of the Society of Emulation of Abbeville,* in 1833. M. Baillon's name, of course, has the precedence, and will be adopted by others, as it has been by M. Temminck ; Mr. Bartlett's name is, however, the better of the two, since there are several species of geese with short beaks, but only one other that I am aware of that has pink legs and feet."

Some years later I wrote the following :—

"On January 8, 1839, I had the pleasure of introducing to the notice of the Society's meeting this species for the first time as a new British bird ; and although since that period many examples have been from time to time obtained, I am not aware that they have appeared in such large numbers as they now appear. Since January 3, 1861, upwards of a hundred specimens have been seen and examined by me, most of them having been killed in the eastern counties. The old males weigh about 6 lbs., the females 5 lbs., and young birds $4\frac{3}{4}$ lbs. The length of the males is about 2 ft. 6 in., the females 2 ft. 3 in., measuring from tip of bill to end of tail. The length of the bill varies from $2\frac{1}{4}$ in. to $1\frac{3}{8}$ in. in length. I mention this, as too much importance has been attached to this characteristic (in the geese), which has led Mr. A. Strickland to regard and describe the old male Bean Goose as a new and distinct species.[1] Of this latter bird I here exhibit

[1] See *Ann. and Mag. N. H.,* ser. 3, vol. iii. p. 121, where the old male Bean Goose (*Anser segetum*) is described as a new species under

an *old male* whose bill is upwards of 2¾ in. long. I also exhibit a female Bean Goose, bill 2¼ in. long; this latter is an adult female, having been kept in the Gardens of this Society nearly two years."

COMMON GOOSE.

I exhibited in 1860 a head of a variety of the common goose, in which the feathers at the back of the head were reversed so as to form a sort of ruff. It was stated that this variety had been perpetuated for several generations at the farm of J. C. Chaytor, Esq., at Croft, near Darlington, and if properly treated by judicious selection of breeding birds, might doubtless be made the origin of a new domestic breed of geese.[1]

NICOBAR PIGEON.

I at the same time exhibited the gizzard of a Nicobar Pigeon, from a specimen recently deceased in the Society's Gardens, and called attention to the peculiar stony development of the epithelial lining.

MANDARIN DUCKS.

When we seek for the origin of domestic animals the obstructions that present themselves are most perplexing, and a little consideration of the animals that determined not to be domesticated will sometimes open to us over-whelming difficulties. The Chinese, or Mandarin, Duck is a good case in point. This very beautiful bird has been

the name of the Long-billed Goose (*Anser paludosus*).—*Proceedings of Zoological Society*, Jan. 8, 1861.

[1] See Darwin, *Animals and Plants under Domestication*, vol. i. p. 238 : 1868.

and as ready to depart from us as their ancestors, it is only by the cutting of one wing that we can induce them to remain upon our ponds where they were hatched; and although fed with all the care and kindness it is possible to bestow, yet their wild nature is unaltered, and we never shall make a domestic bird of this most beautiful of water-fowl. These remarks are also intended to apply to innumerable other species of water-fowl that have been kept and bred, year after year, without the slightest alteration in their habits, appearance, or condition. The domestication of animals by acclimatization is a subject that has of late years attracted much attention, and which has produced a vast mass of interesting matter; but little progress has been made, simply on account of the deficiency of knowledge possessed respecting the early state of most of our domestic animals.[1]

DUCKS.

In 1861 I exhibited living examples from the Society's menagerie of two singular hybrid ducks, one pair being the produce of the Summer Duck (*Aix sponsa*) and Pochard (*Fuligula ferina*), and the other of the Summer Duck and Castaneous Duck (*F. nyroca*).[2]

[1] *Land and Water*, Feb. 12, 1870, p. 117.
[2] *Proceedings of the Zoological Society*, 1861, p. 44.

PAGET'S POCHARD.

(*FULIGULA FERINOIDES*, BART.)

Description of a new species of Fuligula.[1]

Paget's Pochard.—Adult male : upper part of head, neck and cheeks reddish-chestnut, tinged with purple; a small triangular spot of white at the commencement of the feathers under the bill; chin, throat, lower part of neck and breast black, darkest on the breast; back, scapulars, flank and side-feathers finely freckled with transverse lines of black on a greyish-white ground; greater wing-coverts and primaries greyish-black, the latter darkest at the tips; secondaries white, forming the speculum; tips of the feathers black, edged with white; rump, tail, upper and under tail-coverts brownish-black; belly mottled, the tips of the feathers being white, the remaining portion brownish; bill and legs bluish-slate; the tip of the former and the webs and *claws* of the latter black; the eyes straw-colour. The young birds differ in having the head, neck and breast of a lighter and brighter chestnut-red (becoming darker as the bird advances to maturity); the under tail-coverts greyish-white. Entire length, $17\frac{1}{2}$ in.; wing, from carpal joint, $7\frac{3}{4}$ in.; bill, from forehead, $1\frac{3}{4}$ in.; middle toe and claw, $2\frac{1}{2}$ in.

I have proposed the above specific name for this bird, as it appears more closely allied to our common Pochard than to any other species. I have called it, at Mr. Fisher's suggestion, Paget's Pochard, after the late E. J. Paget, Esq., of Great Yarmouth, a gentleman well known as a

[1] FULIGULA FERINOIDES. *Fulig. ferinoides fuligulæ ferinæ similis, sed magnitudine minori, colore saturatiori, alis speculo albo conspicuè notatis, oculis stramineis, tracheâ paulò longiore et angustiore, et sterno multo minore, diversâ; emarginationes tamen sterni ejus iis ferinæ sterni magnitudine æquales.*

zealous and accomplished naturalist, and one of the authors of the *Sketch of the Natural History of Great Yarmouth and its Neighbourhood,* near which place the first authenticated British specimen was obtained.

Remarks.—This bird may be readily distinguished from the common Pochard (which it most resembles) by its smaller size, darker colouring, the conspicuous *white speculum* on the wing, and the colour of the eyes. The female is unknown to me, but I presume it will much resemble the female of the Pochard, and will doubtless possess the white speculum on the wings.

The *trachea* of *F. ferinoides* differs from that of *F. ferina* in being rather longer and narrower, the tube being much narrower at the upper part, gradually enlarging towards the middle, where it is largest, and contracting gradually towards the end, which is its smallest part; the labyrinth is smaller in front, but much wider and differently formed on the left side ; the enlargement at the bottom of the tympanum is also greater than that of the corresponding part in *F. ferina :* although the sternum is much smaller, the emarginations are quite equal in size to these parts in *ferina.*

With reference to the supposition that these birds are hybrids, I beg to remark that I have paid some attention to the subject of hybrids and have compiled a list of the different species of water-fowl (as far as I have been able to collect) which have produced hybrids. On referring to this list, it will be seen that nineteen different kinds are mentioned ; five of these are referable to the *Common Goose,* and five of them to the *Common Duck ;* the remaining nine kinds are referable to species commonly kept, and which breed freely in a state of captivity. I am unable to find one instance of any species of the genus *Fuligula* (which includes no less than fifteen species) having under any circumstances crossed. These birds are most difficult to breed in a state of captivity. I have known several pairs of the common Pochard (*Fuligula ferina*) kept for years in places well suited for breeding (where many wild species and one of this genus annually breed), yet these birds showed no inclination to breed, although they were perfectly healthy and assumed the breeding dress at the proper season. As these birds have the power of suppressing and checking their desires when not in a perfect state of nature, I cannot imagine, or think it probable, that they would associate and breed, in a state of nature, with species distinct from themselves, possessing as they do the power of travelling over the globe if necessary to find a mate of their own species. Again, the fact of three specimens having been obtained at distant periods, agreeing in internal, as well as external, characters, is, I think, sufficient to prevent any one entertaining such an opinion.

List of Hybrids.

Common Goose	Hooper Swan.
	Chinese Goose.
	Canada Goose.
	Bernicle Goose.
	White-fronted Goose.
Egyptian Goose	Chinese Goose.
	Spur-winged Goose.
	Common Duck.
Canada Goose	Chinese Goose.
	Bernicle Goose.
Bean Goose	Pink-footed Goose.
White-fronted Goose	Bernicle Goose.
Common Duck	Muscovy Duck.
	Sheldrake.
	Pintail Duck.
	Wigeon.
	Egyptian Goose.
Shoveller	Garganey Teal.
Pintail	Wigeon.

Proceedings of Zoological Society, 1847, p. 48.

CHAPTER V.

THE DODO.

ON SOME BONES OF DIDUS.

THE history of the Dodo having been the subject of so much inquiry, and the exertions made by Mr. Strickland, Dr. Melville and others having succeeded in bringing together so many important facts, it might appear that there was little more to be said upon the subject; this, however, I believe is far from being the case. A few facts established upon a subject which was before obscured in doubt and error will, I trust, always act as a charm, and induce us at every opportunity to investigate that subject still further, in the hope of learning the truth. On the present occasion I am desirous of calling attention to a few bones upon the table.[1] In so doing I beg to say that, in the year 1830, a collection of bones arrived in Paris, which attracted the attention of the scientific world. These bones came from the island of Rodriguez, but on account of their being incrusted with stalagmite, little has been done with them; they were, however, the cause of search being made for more in the same locality, and two collections were made in the year 1831 by the late Mr. Telfair. One of these collections was forwarded to the Andersonian Museum in Glasgow, the other to the collection of this Society, and at the evening meeting, March 12, 1833, the bones sent by Mr. Telfair were laid upon the table.

[1] *Proceedings of Zoological Society*, Dec. 9, 1851.

I will here read an extract from the Society's *Proceedings:*—" Dr. Grant pointed out that they were the bones of the hinder extremity of a large bird, and the head of a humerus. With reference to the metatarsal bone, which was long and strong, Dr. Grant pointed out that it possessed the articulating surfaces for four toes, three directed forwards and one backwards, as in the foot of the Dodo preserved in the British Museum, to which it was also proportioned in magnitude and form."

I beg now to read a paragraph from Mr. Strickland's book. At page 52 we find :—" The bones sent by Mr. Telfair in 1833 to the Zoological Society have met with some unfortunate fate. Three or four years ago, Mr. Fraser, the late Curator of that Society, made, at my request, a diligent search for these specimens, but all his endeavours to find them were fruitless : he found the identical box sent by Mr. Telfair, but, alas ! the bones of the Solitaire, apterous as it was, had flown away, and the only bones that remained belonged to tortoises."

In the month of July last [1] an opportunity was afforded me by the Secretary of renewing this search, and I had the good fortune to find what I believe to be all the specimens sent to the Society by Mr. Telfair.

Upon my informing Mr. Mitchell of my success, that gentleman, knowing the trouble and interest I had taken to recover them, granted me permission to examine, compare, and describe them, and to bring the subject before the Society.

In the first place, we are led to believe (and I think without the slightest doubt) that these bones came originally from the island of Rodriguez. There cannot be any doubt, also, that Rodriguez and the neighbouring islands were at one period inhabited by several species of large birds.

[1] *Proceedings of Zoological Society,* July 1851.

Whether any of the same species of these birds inhabited different islands, or whether each island was inhabited by distinct species, is a question to which I beg most particularly to call your attention: the most recent publication by Mr. Strickland and Dr. Melville would lead us to believe that the true Dodo (*Didus ineptus*) was solely confined to the island of Mauritius, and another species, known as the Solitaire, was said to be its representative on the island of Rodriguez. If this be true, I should have the pleasure of introducing to your notice the bones of at least two new species of birds from that island: I do not, however, myself feel justified in so doing, but believe some of the bones sent here by Mr. Telfair belong to the true Dodo (*Didus ineptus*). There are also in the collection (I think without doubt) bones of two other species, one of these of much larger size than the Dodo, the other considerably smaller. The bones in question having all the usual and well-known characteristics of those of adult birds, we cannot therefore suppose the differences which they present to be such as might arise from age; and on the other hand, you will perceive that the proportions are too dissimilar to allow of our regarding them as having belonged to different sexes of the same species. There often exists great difference of size in the bones of the opposite sex, but I have never noticed any very evident difference of proportion. These are to me satisfactory reasons for considering them specifically distinct. But to return to the question,—Was the Dodo found on the island of Rodriguez? Sir Thomas Herbert says *it was*, and his evidence appears to me of much importance, considering the number of years he spent travelling about, visiting these islands, and collecting rare and curious things; having also repeatedly described the Dodo, and very probably brought one to England. I am therefore inclined to regard the assertions made by

Sir Thomas Herbert with more respect than they have elsewhere received. It may appear, at first sight, impossible that the same species of birds which were destitute of the power of *swimming* or *flying* could inhabit islands so far from each other; but were these islands always in the state in which we find them? May they not at some distant period have been united and formed part of the same land? In endeavouring in this manner to account for the existence of the Dodo upon the island of Rodriguez as well as at Mauritius, it has been remarked that this argument would not hold good, as the islands in question were of volcanic origin; if this be the case, to account for its existence at either place appears to me equally difficult. I am fully aware it has been the practice of late to consider the animals obtained from localities remote from each other specifically distinct; they may be so, but unless we have some certain means of distinguishing them, I do not think we ought to regard them as such.

I now venture to introduce to your notice what I believe to be the *tibia* of the Dodo (*Didus ineptus*). Its agreement with the foot in the British Museum struck me as being exceedingly remarkable and conclusive; its size and proportion, as compared with the metatarsal in question, are exactly what I should have expected upon the supposition of their belonging to the same species; they fit each other so perfectly that one might think they belonged to the same individual. With this evidence before me, I cannot for one moment hesitate in considering the *Dodo of the Mauritius to be identical with the Dodo of Rodriguez.* There are also in this collection two other bones, which, from their size and form, I believe to belong to this species; the most remarkable is the head of the *humerus*, which would indicate by its magnitude and broad attachments that it belonged to a bird of large bulk, while the sudden reduction in the size of its shaft clearly indicates a bird with small wings. The great thickness and consequent weight is sufficient to cause us to suppose that this bird had not the power of flight.

The next bone to which I will call your attention is a right metatarsal, which appears to me to have belonged to a bird known to Leguat as the Solitaire, and described by him during his residence on the island of Rodriguez. I beg to read Leguat's description, in order to point out to you its near agreement in point of size and form with the turkey, with which bird Leguat compared the bird he called the Solitaire :—

"Of all the birds in the island, the most remarkable is that which goes by the name of the *Solitary*, because it is very seldom seen in company, though there are abundance of them. The feathers of the male are of a brown-grey colour; the feet and beak are like a turkey's, but a little more crooked. They have scarce any tail, but their hind part covered with feathers is roundish, like the crupper of a horse; they are taller than turkeys. Their neck is straight, and a little longer in proportion than a turkey's when it lifts up its head. Its eye is black and lively, and its head without comb or cop. They never fly, their wings are too little to support the weight of their bodies; they serve only to beat themselves, and flutter when they call one another. They will whirl about for twenty or thirty times together on the same side, during the space of four or five minutes. The motion of their wings makes then a noise very like that of a rattle, and one may hear it two hundred paces off. The bone of their wing grows greater towards the extremity, and forms a little round mass under the feathers, as big as a musket-ball. That and its beak are the chief defence of this bird. 'Tis very hard to catch it in the woods, but easier in open places, because we run faster than they, and sometimes we approach them without much trouble. From March to September they are extremely fat, and taste admirably well, especially while they are young; some of the males weigh forty-five pounds.

"The females are wonderfully beautiful, some fair, some brown; I call them fair, because they are of the colour of fair hair. They have a sort of peak, like a widow's, upon their breasts (*lege* beaks), which is of a dun colour. No one feather is straggling from the other all over their bodies, they being very careful to adjust themselves, and make them all even with their beaks. The feathers on their thighs are round like shells at the end, and being there very thick have an agreeable effect. They have two risings on their *craws*, and the feathers are whiter there than the rest, which livelily represents the fine neck of a beautiful woman. They walk with so much stateliness and good grace, and one cannot help admiring and loving them; by which means their fine mien often saves their lives." [1]

You will perceive this bird was said to be larger and taller than a turkey. A comparison of this metatarsal bone with the metatarsal bone of the turkey, I think, will satisfactorily show the accuracy of Leguat's description, and at the same time justify our conclusion that this metatarsal bone belonged to the Solitaire of Rodriguez, to which the name of *Didus solitarius* has been applied. I trust I shall be pardoned for avoiding the use of the new generic term adopted by the authors of *The Dodo and its Kindred*, for in a group so little known, and at present so limited in species, it seems to me so much to increase the trouble and difficulty of those who endeavour to study such subjects, that I cannot help expressing my belief that many of the new names so often introduced serve only to impede and

---

[1] *Leguat's Voyage to the East Indies*, 1708, p. 71.

embarrass us, and I therefore regard them as much worse than useless.

I have now remaining the bone of a bird which when alive was much *larger, heavier,* and more *powerful* than the *Dodo.* For further examples of this bird's bones, I must refer to the plates in the work before alluded to by Mr. Strickland and Dr. Melville: Plate xv. Fig. 2, the metatarsal bone of the large species in the Andersonian Museum, Glasgow; Fig. 3, a metatarsal bone in the Parisian collection. A glance at these specimens will, I imagine, convince any one that this bird was of gigantic size, and probably double the weight of the *Dodo.* I am sure it cannot be supposed (after what has been said) that Leguat was describing this great bird when he wrote his beautiful description of the Solitaire. Another important fact will, I think, set this question at rest. Leguat states, that some of the males of the Solitaire weigh *forty-five pounds.* Now we know the weight of the largest turkeys to be considerably less, rarely reaching *thirty pounds,* while the weight of the Dodo is stated to have been at least *fifty pounds.* It cannot, therefore, be supposed, had Leguat seen birds nearly double the size of the Dodo, he could have made the statements he has, or deduced comparison between the Solitaire and turkey.

I have before expressed my great dislike to an unnecessary increase of names. I feel, however, the necessity of finding an appropriate name for this large bird, and therefore propose one somewhat familiar to all who have paid any attention to the subject, and apply the name of *Didus nazarenus* to this the largest species of the genus. In doing this I may remark that Mr. Strickland, in his work before alluded to, has considered the *Didus nazarenus* to be a phantom species, which he says has haunted our systems of ornithology from the days of Gmelin downwards.

The conclusions which I have arrived at from the examination of the bones to which I have just called your attention are these:—That there existed formerly three distinct species of apterous birds in the island of Rodriguez, namely, one which is apparently identical with the *Dodo* (*Didus ineptus*) of the Mauritius, a second, which was well described under the name of *Solitaire*, and a third, which was much larger than either of the above.

CHAPTER VI.

GAME-BIRDS.

REARING PHEASANTS.

THE work at the pheasant-coops is now (spring) in full swing; the keeper and his assistants have a busy, and for the former, an anxious time. The nesting and hatching seasons have been almost unprecedentedly favourable, and as a natural sequence great expectations are being indulged in by the sportsman. Not to disappoint these sanguine anticipations, by and by when the autumn frosts have robbed the trees of their foliage, is of course the keeper's chief object in life for the next two or three months. The work of rearing young pheasants during a wet season is very tedious and unsatisfactory, as nothing is more fatal to the birds than continuous damp. Excessive rain, or even sufficient to act prejudicially on young pheasants, has not, we feel almost certain, been experienced in any part of the country this season (spring 1870), neither has an epidemic of any kind committed its ravages on the young stock; so that with sufficient proper food and ordinary care, a keeper ought to be able to bring up a large proportion of his birds this year, unless the near future prove exceptionally unfavourable. Sufficient food and ordinary care may be considered vague and unknown quantities, and this is to a certain extent true, as many keepers have their own pet specific *régime*. I have, however, recently read some notes on the subject by a writer in the *Journal of Forestry*, which I think worthy of notice, as they bear undoubted evidence of practical knowledge. His theory regarding the desirability of allowing the young birds to remain unmolested for the first twenty-four hours after hatching coincides with my own views, because the nutriment which the young pheasant has drawn from the egg is sufficient to keep it in health and strength for that period.

The first food may be ants' eggs, and next to these in importance it is claimed may be reckoned a custard of scalded milk and fresh eggs beaten up, in the proportion of half-a-pint of the former to from nine to twelve of the latter. A good consistency may be obtained by using half-a-gallon of milk with six dozen eggs and properly setting the mixture over a slow fire. To this may be added small portions of hard-boiled eggs, either chopped very fine or grated. Before the end of a week a small quantity of Spanish meal may be used, and after that time an admixture of Caycar. Mixed meal, including a portion of best Scotch oatmeal, may gradually be introduced. At the end of three weeks some finely-kibbled maize may be given, and by the time the birds are five weeks old the strongest of them will commence picking the smallest round maize. Canary-seed is strongly recommended by some for bone-making. A small portion of biscuit, grits, and rice, millet, and hemp-seed may also be used; but the custard of new milk and eggs supplies every essential to the growth of the young bird, viz. sugar, caseine, phosphorus, phosphate of lime, sulphur and albumen. When meat is given, boiled rabbit done to rags is to be recommended as being the least relaxing.

Curds are frequently used, but when these are produced by alum they are apt to prove too astringent. For green food, finely-chopped lettuce will be found more valuable than almost any other kind. When meal is added to boiled milk, the mixture should be of the consistency of dough. A small portion of pepper will be useful in cold, wet weather.

Young birds having wet or moist food will require but little water except in the very driest weather. When water is given a little sulphate of iron may be put into it occasionally, and unless it be very pure it is better boiled first. But early in the morning the young birds may be seen pecking at the dew-drops upon the grass, and a little water from the watering-pot sprinkled near the coop will generally suffice for their wants. In wet weather the chicks should be kept in, and well fed two or three times of a morning before being allowed to roam about.

A very successful hand-rearer is quoted who keeps to custard for three days, giving additions of oatmeal and finely-chopped lettuce for four days more, and afterwards some kibbled wheat, finely-ground maize, and split grits for another fortnight; next, well-minced meat of a light kind, such as well-boiled sheep's head and pluck, and after the end of five weeks almost any well-kibbled grain, maize, wheat and barley.

When the young birds are removed to the springs or the wood-rides, with the hens confined in coops, all must be liberally fed. As they advance, the loose corn may be scattered along the feeding tracks, and small stacks of mixed grain may be built up in convenient places for future use. Barley, buckwheat, and beans in the straw may be placed upon stages raised 18 in. or 2 ft. from the ground, a few sheaves being pulled out and scattered about from time to time, the space beneath affording a good dusting-place. By commencing to feed around these stacks very early in the morning, and again from three to four p.m., the pilfering habits of other birds may be defeated. Even now a variety of food is desirable—an occasional feed of peas, buckwheat, damaged raisins, and even pulped carrots and artichokes help to keep the birds at home. Buckwheat sown towards the end of May or first week in June upon the soil from which trees have been grubbed, or worked into any bare places in the woodlands, will often supply food to the pheasants at the beginning of the shooting season. Shallow catchpools of water should be formed in abundance where there are no streams. As the acorns begin to fall, and after the stubbles are cleared, the birds will wander in spite of all precautions, and the greatest vigilance on the part of the keepers will be necessary in order to have them well together when the shooting commences.

The cost of rearing pheasants is a subject about which a dozen different preservers would probably give as many different estimates. The writer I referred to estimates that in very few cases, where great pains are taken to provide all the requisites for successful breeding—good shelter, liberal feeding, constant attention, and watching—will the birds fall to the gun at a less cost than 8s. per head; and where the shooting is rented the cost of this must be added. He quotes an instance which came under his notice in 1880, where every pheasant killed cost 12s. 6d. This was after a most successful season. Where game is reared on a large scale the payment by results seems a fair arrangement for both the owner and the head gamekeeper. In one case of this kind the keeper is allowed 10s. 6d. per bird, after bearing all expenses. Fabulous prices per head have been named, and in one well-authenticated case each bird killed had cost considerably above 30s.

Some approximate idea of their cost may be formed from the following figures:—One hundred birds in pens may be kept on about 2½ gallons of maize per day; and total cost incurred in bringing birds to the gun.

On February 13, 1868, I read a paper before the Zoological Society on the "Breeding of various species of birds in the Society's Gardens during the year 1867." Among these birds were the Barred-tailed Pheasant (*Phasianus necvcsii*), Green-necked Pheasant (*Phasianus versicolor*), and Crossoptilon, or Eared Pheasant (*Crossoptilon mantchuricum*).

It is most remarkable that the Barred-tailed Pheasants which arrived on June 22 commenced laying immediately, and four birds were hatched on August 10.

Another instance of late breeding occurred with a fine pair of Green-necked Pheasants, which arrived from Japan on July 27, 1867, and three young birds were produced on September 20. These birds were at the time considered useless and not likely to live, but two of them (hens) are strong and healthy birds, having perfectly got over the moult during the coldest part of the following winter.

Of the Crossoptilon, or Eared Pheasant of Pallas, we have reared nine fine birds, the second hatch; having lost by the gapes the first brood of seven. With reference to this species I may remark that these birds breed when only one year old.

At the first moult the young birds assume the adult plumage, the male and female being exactly alike. They are remarkably hardy and exceedingly tame.

162

THE HORNED TRAGOPANS.

(*CERIORNIS SATYRA.*)

Of this fine group of birds there are four well-known species. It may, however, be said that the most beautiful species is the one above-named, and the subject of these remarks. This species is found in *Nepal, Sikhim,* and *Bootan,* in other words, the Eastern Himalayas, while the next species in point of beauty (*Ceriornis hastingsii*) inhabits the Western Himalayas. Both species are indiscriminately called Argus Pheasants by Indian sportsmen, which name, however, really belongs to a totally different bird, which is found in *Malacca,* and certainly has never been met with near the Himalayas.

The great difficulty in obtaining and bringing living examples of these birds to Europe has been well known to all collectors whose previous efforts have failed, and only two recorded instances are known of these birds having reached England alive. Upon the first occasion one male only of *Ceriornis temminckii* arrived, and upwards of twenty years passed before a second bird of this group made its appearance. In 1857 a *female* of *Ceriornis hastingsii* was brought home by Mr. Thompson, who was sent to India by the Zoological Society to receive and bring home a collection of these and other game-birds that had been collected for the Society, and also for her Majesty the Queen. Since the above date no others have reached this country until March 31, 1863; on that day *nine* fine and healthy birds arrived—these were *six males* and *three females* (as before stated of the species known as *Ceriornis satyra*).

We are indebted to the zeal, ability, and persevering energy of Mr. John J. Stone, assisted by the Rev. W.

Smyth, and the Baboo Regrendra Mullick, for obtaining and forwarding these birds to England. The trouble and expense attending the importation has hitherto prevented many from making the attempt—the above-named gentlemen did not allow these considerations to stand in the way; hence we have for the first time the opportunity of seeing these magnificent birds in all their glory. Notwithstanding the long voyage, the birds had been so well attended and every care bestowed upon them, that almost as soon as they were liberated from the coops in which they arrived they began to show signs of breeding, and we have the gratification of being able to say that two small broods have been hatched, and several eggs were in the process of incubation, showing at least that these birds are easily adapted to their changed condition, and also that they are very likely soon to be acclimatized. It is quite impossible to convey in writing or drawing a very perfect idea of the extraordinary beauty of the living *male bird* during the short and almost momentary display he makes while courting the female, on account of the vibratory motion of the head and neck, which, of course, renders a drawing imperfect, and it is next to impossible to describe these parts and the appearance of the bird in rapid motion. It is therefore necessary, in order to understand it fully, that it must be seen.

We have reason to believe that these birds are monogamous, resembling the partridge in this respect; the eggs, however, bear a close resemblance to those of the wood-grouse (*Capercaillie*), and the young birds when newly hatched are not unlike the chicks of that bird. The wings of these chicks are sufficiently developed as soon as they are hatched to enable them to mount to the branches of trees or shrubs, much like the habits of the tree-grouse.

DISPLAY OF HORNED TRAGOPANS.

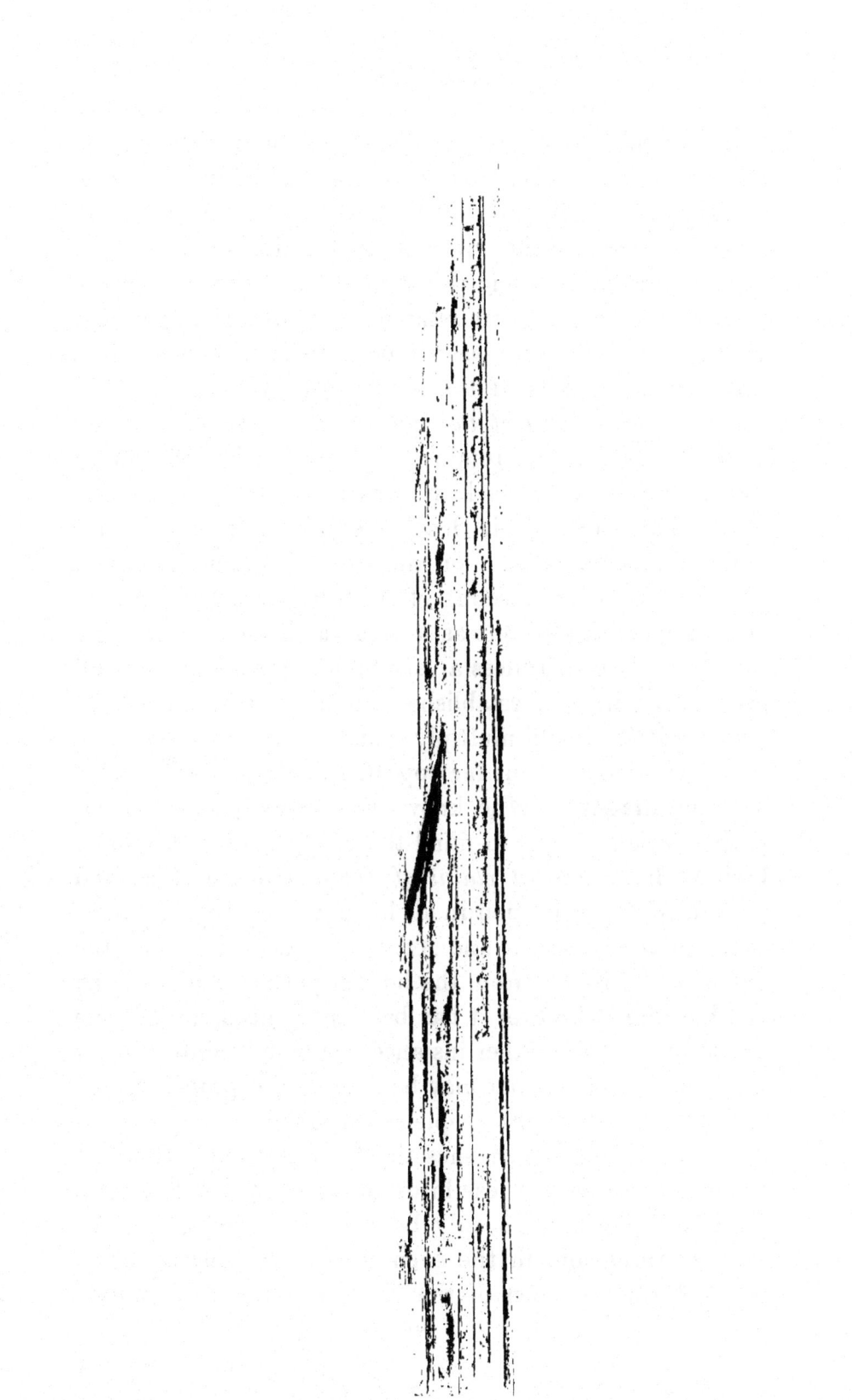

In size the *young Tragopan* equals a chick of the largest Cochin China fowl (when first hatched); its colour is rufous brown, slightly mottled on the back, the wings are marked much like the wings of the female Gold Pheasant. It is impossible to avoid thinking of the large tree-grouse (*Capercaillie*) when examining these birds; the eggs and young of both species, as before stated, are very similar, and also the habits of the adult birds, we are told; for instance, they *frequent the lofty trees in the pine forests* in the Himalayan mountains; they are capable of bearing any amount of cold, feed on berries and tender shoots of plants, etc., etc. Their flesh is excellent, therefore this bird appears to be one of the most desirable to introduce, not only on account of its brilliant colour and its charming markings, but as a great addition to our table luxuries. It is doubtless a very prolific breeder, and in all probability, if once established in the northern parts of Great Britain, would multiply rapidly.

The experiment thus far appears successful, and in every way encouraging. Who knows what may yet be accomplished when we call to mind the gaudy *peacock* originally brought from the *hot plains of India*, and now bred and kept in perfect condition in all his native beauty in almost every place in *Europe* and *America!* Look again at the *guinea-fowl*, brought from the hottest parts of Africa, living and breeding wherever it has been introduced, almost like a wild bird. Many other instances could be pointed out, if necessary, to show what may be done if the proper means are used, and the right people set about it.

Mr. T. W. Wood furnishes the following notes from his own observations of these birds in captivity:—" The male Horned Pheasants can only be seen to advantage in the early morning and in the evening, as they conceal themselves during the rest of the day; the females, however, are less retiring in their habits, one or two of them being generally visible at any hour of the day; this is also the case with two young males which have not yet assumed their adult plumage. I have no doubt that in thus concealing themselves during the bright daylight, the adult male birds, in their wild state, escape the attacks of enemies, to which they must be much more liable than their companions, on account of their attractive colours.

"Knowing the birds of this genus to be furnished with ornamental fleshy appendages to their heads, the form and colours of which cannot be preserved after death, I was very anxious to observe them in the living subject. The two horns are situated about half an inch behind each eye; they are about one inch in length, and of a very clear and beautiful light blue colour, with a slight tinge of green in one of the specimens. When the bird is not excited, these horns lie perfectly concealed under two triangular patches of red feathers, their points meeting at the occiput. In addition to the horns, there is a large wattle, which is also concealed or displayed at the will of the bird; it is almost exactly of the shape and size of the human tongue, thin and free at the sides and end, the central part being capable of inflation. This portion and the naked skin round the eyes, are of a pure ultramarine blue colour; the outer part on each side is deep red, of a tint between carmine and vermilion, upon which, proceeding from the central blue, are five pointed stripes of pure light blue, their points being directed outwards and slightly downwards; one of these stripes forms an edging to the basal portion of the wattle, the end of which is also broadly edged with the same light blue, which colour extends upwards for a short distance along the margin, and unites with the two lower blue bands at their ends.

"The male bird had three distinct modes of 'showing

168

off' (if I may be allowed the expression), the most characteristic of which I have endeavoured to portray in the plate. When this attitude is assumed, the bird, after walking about rather excitedly, places himself in front of the female in the next cage; the body is slightly crouching upon the legs, the tail bent downwards; the head is kept violently jerking downwards. and this causes the horns and wattle immediately to appear. The wings have a flapping motion, and the bright red patch on them is fully displayed. On one occasion I heard a loud tapping noise, as if a person near were knocking the railings with a small stick; it, however, proceeded from the bird, each movement of the wing being accompanied by a tap. I could not understand how this noise could have been produced, as the wings did not touch the ground, except, perhaps, at their extreme ends, which would not be sufficiently stiff to cause such a loud noise; this sound therefore is, no doubt, vocal. The whole of the neck appears to be larger than usual during this action, and also the horns, which vibrate with every movement. This wonderful display is concluded by the bird suddenly drawing himself up to his full height, with the wings expanded and quivering, the horns erect, and the wattle fully displayed.

"The bird courts the 'ladye love' in his own cage, very much after the same manner as the Common Pheasant (*Phasianus colchicus*), by simply erecting all his feathers and elevating one shoulder, thereby exposing a greater surface to view, without, however, showing his head-dress.

"The third mode of display is by simply standing boldly erect on an elevated perch, and giving the head one or two sudden shakes, when the horns and wattle appear for a few moments.

"The male Horned Pheasants have two or three distinct

call-notes; the one most frequently heard is much like the quacking of a duck; another is a loud and somewhat hoarse and plaintive cry, which is repeated at intervals of a few seconds, louder and louder each time. A third note is the 'crowing,' very different from that of the Common Pheasant, but accompanied by the same sudden and rapid fluttering of the wings as in that bird.

" I may add that the wattle is ordinarily contracted, and concealed by the feathers, no sign of it appearing. The display takes place chiefly, if not exclusively, during the

after J.W. Wood
1866

HORNED TRAGOPAN—LOVE.

breeding season, and even then it occurs but rarely; and a person who really means to see it must often wait an hour or two, and have a large stock of patience in store. The females are at least one quarter less in size than the opposite sex, and, although quietly and soberly coloured, the markings of their plumage are exceedingly neat and beautiful. Their quiet browns and other tints must be necessary to their very existence when engaged in incubation and the rearing of their young brood. Both sexes have a habit of crouching close to the ground when alarmed, and in this position even the gorgeously-coloured male has a good chance of escaping observation, the colour of his upper parts being chiefly brown, mottled with black, with a few dashes of red, and having a round white spot at

after J.W. Wood
1868

HORNED TRAGOPAN—COURTSHIP.

the tip of each feather. The tail is somewhat roof-like in shape, and consists of twenty blackish feathers, which are mottled with yellowish on their basal half. These, as well as the largest of the tail-coverts, are remarkably plain when compared with the rest of his plumage; the largest coverts are brown, edged at the end with a lighter tint of the same, inside of which is a blackish line. These feathers are somewhat squared at their ends, which circumstance, together with their edging, reminds one strongly of the plumage of the turkey, to which bird the Horned Pheasants are nearly related.

"The breadth of the light blue stripes on the wattle varies considerably in individual specimens. The plumage also varies much in depth of colour."

CHAPTER VII.

POULTRY.

THE FIRST POULTRY SHOW.

In June 1845 the Zoological Society held the first poultry show in the Gardens in the Regent's Park. I was an exhibitor of the following:—

Class 1.—Domestic Fowls bred in 1844.
  B. Surrey. Second prize.
Class 4.—Geese.
  P. Half-bred Wild and Domestic. Second prize.
  P. A fine Grey-lag Goose, *Anser palustris*, Fleming, from India. Second prize.
Class 1.—Turkeys.
  A A. Spangled Male. First prize.

At a recent Exhibition (September 12, 1889 ?) the *Daily Telegraph*, in giving an account of the show, added many funny stories. "Forty-five years ago the Zoological Society opened in its grounds in Regent's Park the first poultry show ever held in the United Kingdom, and its chief promoter was the highly-esteemed Superintendent of the Gardens, who, by the way, tells a capital story in connection with that early Exhibition. He himself was the exhibitor of a silver-crested turkey, for which he was awarded the Society's bronze medal. There were three or four judges, and among them a prominent poulterer of the day. It was a fine spring morning, and the Turkey-cock was in excellent spirits. He spread his tail and fluttered his feathers, and

173

dropped down his crimson wattles, and strutted up to the judges probably conscious that he deserved a medal.

"'Good heavens! What's that?' exclaimed the poulterer. The worthy man had been selling turkeys all his days, but he had never before seen one alive.

"Looking back to that early show, my interviewer asks, 'What do you take to be the most noticeable fact in poultry-rearing during the forty-five years?'

"'Well, I think the most astonishing thing, is the wonderful extent to which it has been found possible to develop by careful selection and crossing almost any characteristic that may be desired.'"

ELLIOT'S GUINEA-FOWL.

DESCRIPTION OF A NEW SPECIES OF *NUMIDA*.
(*NUMIDA ELLIOTI*, BART.)

Having had some correspondence with the owner, Mr. Gerald Waller, of some Guinea-fowl that were on their way to this country from East Africa, and having offered to take charge of them on their arrival, in order to restore them from the effects of the voyage, on June 4[1] I received five living birds, three Crested (*Numida cristata*) and two Vulturine (*N. vulturina*). Mr. Waller informed me that a sixth bird, which he believed to be a male, had died on the passage, and that the skin in a mutilated condition was then in his possession; and he kindly gave it to me upon my telling him it might prove to be a very interesting specimen.

On examining the skin, it struck me at once to be unlike anything I had seen. I, therefore, examined the splendid work by Mr. Elliot, and came to the conclusion that I had found a new and hitherto undescribed species of *Numida*.

[1] *Proceedings of Zoological Society*, 1877.

After a careful examination of Mr. Elliot's work, I wrote to Colonel Grant to ask if the figure of *Numida granti*, which came nearest to my bird, quite agreed with his original drawing. Colonel Grant has kindly shown me the original coloured drawing, and convinced me that the bird originally figured belonged to a species easily distinguished from the bird now before you, which, I have been informed by Mr. Waller, was obtained at Mombassa on the east coast of Africa.

This bird differs from *Numida granti* (to which species it appears most nearly allied) by the entire absence of the *black ring* or *collar* and *black patch on front of the neck*. The whole of the *neck, breast, belly, back, upper* and *under tail-coverts* are finely and minutely *spotted with white on a black ground*. I may state that the blue wattles differ considerably from the same parts in *N. cristata*, being *much longer* and falling *lower down ;* the bird appears smaller than the last-named species.

It may be interesting to know that the three Crested birds that came, as Mr. Waller tells me, from Mozambique, differ from all the figures of *N. cristata* in having the throat up to the edge of the under mandible *covered with black feathers*. I consider them to be young birds, and that the throat will (as the birds become adult) lose these feathers and exhibit the naked red skin, so well marked in the figure in Mr. Elliot's work.

I propose the name of *Numida ellioti* for this new bird, after Mr. D. G. Elliot, F.Z.S., who has devoted so much time and attention to this interesting family.

THE DOMESTICATION OF CURASSOWS.

The domestication, or acclimatization, of the Curassows or Guans in England is a failure, and may be looked upon as hopeless, because these birds cannot endure exposure to the climate of this country, even in the mildest winter; that some of them have lived through the cold season is quite true, but the loss of toes and attacks of general debility have been the result of the experiment, therefore further attempts to render them hardy would appear to be futile. That they can be kept and bred in this country is quite possible, but during the cold season they must be housed. They are naturally of a wild nature and much disposed to wander or stray from their habitation, consequently if the tame imported birds were allowed to be at liberty and bred in the open air, the young birds would be most difficult to capture, and would be probably lost. Domestication and acclimatization are two very different things. Animals may be acclimatized without, in the least degree, being domesticated, and the animals already domesticated may become acclimatized, that is to say we may transport the domesticated animals to a new country, and with proper attention to their wants we may succeed in establishing them, and they would in time become adapted to the changed condition and thrive. Instances of this kind are common enough; for example, sheep, cattle, pigs and poultry have been introduced into Australia; horses, cattle and pigs into America and elsewhere.

The introduction of animals from one country into another is common, and the success attending such introduction is well known, but when the question is asked, "Have any wild species that have been introduced into a country become domesticated within the time of recorded events?" an answer in the negative must be given. On the other hand, there are no end of instances of domestic animals having been introduced to new countries where, for want of attention and care, they have attained a perfectly wild state, and, nevertheless, exhibit the stamp of domestic variation and tendency to return, under proper treatment, to their former condition.

It is only necessary to point to the horse of South America, to the sheep and cattle in Australia, and to the pigs and cats in New Zealand in support of what is herein advanced. The Chinese must be regarded as the only people who have succeeded in obtaining and breeding domestic animals, as an article of food, far in advance of any other nation. They have prolific sheep that produce four or five lambs at birth, geese that lay and hatch all the year round, and pigs that produce from four to five and twenty young at a time, most of which, under the watchful care of these thrifty and careful people, are reared.

It may naturally be inferred that the animals most subject to variation and most capable of conforming to changed conditions were in the first instance selected, and that, as a probable result, the wild kinds belonging to the species that were taken under the protection of man became amalgamated with the semi-domesticated individuals until they ceased to exist as wild animals, hence the present difficulty of fixing, or determining upon, the wild origin of nearly all domestic animals. The reindeer is the only species that has shown a capability of being domesticated; in a wild state it exhibits a wonderful amount of variation, not only in size, but in colour and habits.

The success in domestication that has been attributed to the Laplanders is, in all probability, far more ancient than this present race of people; witness the very numerous remains of the reindeer's bones found in the ancient caverns and gravels of river-beds of Mid-Europe and associated with traces of man. The fallow deer makes a near approach to the condition of a domestic animal, but fails to become perfectly so. Many species of deer are brought from Asia, Africa and America, and thrive in Europe and Australia; antelopes from Africa and Asia thrive in Europe and Australia, and many birds from Asia have been introduced into Europe and acclimatized, such as peafowl, pheasants, ducks and geese of many species, but not one known case is on record of either of the above-mentioned mammals or birds ever having been domesticated. We may import wild animals and acclimatize them, breed from them and rear their progeny without the slightest chance of bringing them under domestication. Animals to become domesticated must be of those kinds which are easily changed, and which are subject to great variety amongst themselves, in fact of a plastic nature.

What has been done towards domesticating either the peacock or the guinea-fowl in this country amounts to little or, in reality, to nothing; it is true that they are acclimatized and breed freely in this country, yet they are anything but what may fairly be called domesticated birds; certainly they are not so wild as pheasants, and although these latter birds will, when bred tame, feed from the hands like common fowls, they nevertheless cannot be called domesticated. Efforts are made all over the world to tame and domesticate wild animals, and doubtless our own species always did aim at that object. There is every reason to believe that the larger number of the domestic animals now known were domesticated animals long before our race became, in any way, civilized.

Have not the various races of men, whom *we* please to call savages at the present time, pets and domestic animals about them, and do they not, in many countries, keep large numbers of them as a means of supporting life and of trading? Animals, such as deer or antelopes, that are bred in confinement are, of all creatures, the wildest

178

should anything cause them to be alarmed. It is a well-known and authenticated fact, a fact known to all who have had experience in the breeding and rearing of animals not domesticated, that they are when in their houses or paddocks perfectly tame, and that they will come even to a call, feed out of a person's hand, and will probably allow themselves to be stroked by those whom they know; should, however, anything new or strange be placed near one of them, or an attempt be made to remove one to another locality, the animal in an instant becomes alarmed, its fear knows no bounds, its whole strength and determination are displayed, and its wild disposition at once returns; in a word it is transformed from, apparently, a perfectly tame beast into one of the most uncontrollable of wild animals.

The difficulties and danger resulting in the catching and transporting wild animals of this class are known to few persons only, and the cause is by no means beyond comprehension. We will take, as an example, the case of a pair of antelopes which are imported from Africa; before they were shipped for this country they had been caught and tamed; large numbers die during the process, and it is only occasionally that the people who attempt or undertake to tame them succeed. The animals are then confined in a small space and sent on board ship. Out of a large number shipped but few survive the voyage, and those that reach England are so completely tamed and subdued that their original wildness and determination never return; so thoroughly subdued are they, so used to almost any kind of noise, of seeing various objects, and of change of condition, that they continue manageable all the rest of their lives. It is not so, however, with their offspring, which are produced in what we please to call domestication. In most instances the breeding, in captivity, of wild animals is attended with considerable difficulty and risk; consequently the young are regarded and treated in the most gentle and kind manner, not the slightest thing is done to frighten or annoy them; you look at them, talk to them kindly, pet them, and feed them with the best and most tempting food, and they appear perfectly tame, and fond of being fed and caressed; but only let something strange, trifling in itself, happen; at times the appearance of an umbrella, or anything moving in the bushes, or a boy's kite in the air, and away goes all the tameness at a moment's notice; the creature rushes at the fence, and, if possible, breaks its neck or legs, or, in its frantic effort to escape, breaks loose by either smashing the fence or leaping over it, and not unfrequently is so injured that it either kills itself or has to be killed. The simple truth is that the wild and vigorous natures of these animals manifest themselves only under the influence of fear. Endless instances in support of this have occurred in this country and on the Continent; in fact, wherever wild animals have been bred in captivity.

The vexatious losses to those persons who, after years of trouble, in an instant meet with them, are trying and disheartening.

MOUND-BUILDING BIRDS.

AUSTRALIAN WATTLE-BIRD.

(*TALEGALLA LATHAMI.*)

NOTES ON THE REPRODUCTION OF THE AUSTRALIAN WATTLE-BIRD (*TALEGALLA LATHAMI*) IN THE SOCIETY'S GARDENS.

The pair of *Talegallas* kept in the Gardens of the Society, during the spring and summer of the year 1860, formed a large mound composed of leaves, grass, earth and other materials. Within this mound the female deposited twenty eggs. The *time of laying*, the *interval of time between each egg*, and the *period of incubation* were at the time unknown to me.

But on the morning of the 26th of August, 1860, a young talegalla crept out of the mound, and, quite regardless of its parent, ran about searching for worms and other insects, upon which it fed with as much adroitness and apparent knowledge as the chick of a common fowl would exhibit at a month old.

Towards night this young bird flew about among the branches of the trees and shrubs in search of a safe roosting-place, and, having selected one about 6 ft. from the ground, settled down and appeared as comfortable and unconcerned as an adult bird,—the female taking no notice whatever of her offspring.

Upon carefully looking into the mound two days afterwards (on the 28th), I observed a second young bird moving about and busily engaged cleaning its feathers with its bill, the wing-feathers at this time being encased in quill-sheaths. This young bird remained in the mound enabled to fly immediately upon quitting the mound, which it did on the morning of the 29th. This second young bird conducted himself in the same manner as his predecessor. The two young birds took no notice whatever of each other, or of the old female, the three birds appearing perfectly independent of each other, *eating*, *drinking*, and *roosting separately*; and although an occasional small voice was heard from the young birds, it did not appear to indicate or excite any notice among them. These young birds grew amazingly—so rapidly, that at the age of three months they could scarcely be distinguished from the adult birds.

The foregoing observations lead me to believe that two or three days may elapse between the laying of each egg. The young birds will consequently come out of the mound in the order in which the eggs were laid, as it is evident that incubation must commence immediately the egg is laid. If, therefore, twenty eggs are laid in forty or sixty days, there must be this number of days difference in the age between the first and the last of the brood, and no two of the young birds could possibly be of the same age.

Perhaps the most remarkable feature connected with this bird is the very perfect development of the young, reminding us strongly of the next division of the vertebrate animals (the *Reptiles*),—not that I can see any connecting links between the great divisions of the Vertebrata.

But although it is only in the Mammalia that the young are fed by the fluid secreted in the mammary glands, yet in the highest order of the class *Aves* (the Parrots) the young are fed partly by the fluid secreted in the œsophagus, mixed with the softened and partially digested food from the crop of the parent birds.

Now in the *Talegalla* we seem to approach the reptilian character not only in the form and general appearance of the eggs, but in the manner in which they are deposited and the absence of care bestowed upon the young.

I believe I am correct in saying that, with this exception, all birds feed or provide food for their young, while, on the other hand, I am not aware that any reptile is known to do so, and that all the reptiles that lay eggs leave them to hatch, and the young to provide for themselves,—their young, as in the *Talegalla*, coming forth in a very perfect and well-developed condition, and being enabled to seek and obtain their food without the aid of the parents. I therefore cannot avoid considering the *Talegalla* and its allies as exhibiting in this respect the lowest form in birds.

In August 1869 a brush turkey (*Talegalla lathami*, Gray) and a pair of sun bitterns, or sun birds (*Eurypyga helias*, Pall.), were bred in the Gardens. Although this is not the first time these curious avine forms have been reared in this country, they nevertheless deserve a passing notice. In a part of the Gardens, by no means secluded (close to the small carnivora house), but nicely screened by shrubs, so as not to attract the attention of the careless passer-by, is a somewhat semi-circular enclosure within which is a dome-shaped nest, which, for size, might vie with that of the far-famed "roc" of the *Arabian Nights*. The grassy mound, for nest it at first sight seems not to be, is indeed the hatching-place of the wattled talegallas or "Wee-lah" of the Australian aborigines. Mr. Gould has the honour of first making known the remarkable non-incubating habits of this bird (*Tasmanian Journal*, 1840), but since then (1860) recorded facts have been published relative to their breeding in confinement. In the present instance but one young live bird has made its appearance, and, as noticed by previous observers, its parents take no interest whatsoever in its welfare. Chicky talegalla, though, seems quite lively and full of worldly knowledge. That the fermentation or heat developed from the rubbish heap, and not the warmth of its mother's breast, has been the means of bringing it forth is equally a matter of indifference to it.

As regards the affinities of the talegalla, Mr. Parker[1] believes it related not only to the curassows and palamedeas, but also to the wingless rails, and through them to the kagu (*Rhinochetus*). Apart from anatomical reasons, so graphically entered into by the above author, there is no doubt that the external characters most interesting to the public generally would lead to the talegalla being classed with the *Cracidæ* rather than alongside the *Vulturidæ*, as Latham and Swainson placed it.

After the above notes were published, my son Edward, upon his return from Peru, told me that the curassows and guans build their nests in palm trees many feet above the ground, and lay white eggs, the young being able to help themselves soon after they are hatched. This confirms us in placing the talegalla and crax together, the great difference being that talegalla lays perhaps twenty eggs, whereas crax lays only two.

[1] See *Trans. Zool. Soc.*, 1866.

CRANES AND PLOVERS.

CHINESE CRANES.

(*GRUS MONTIGNESIA.*)

NOTES ON THE BREEDING AND REARING OF THE CHINESE CRANE IN THE SOCIETY'S GARDENS.

Near the middle of May 1861, a pair of these birds formed a rude nest of dry rushes on the ground, and soon afterwards two eggs were laid. The parent birds took turns upon these eggs during the time of incubation. On June 24 a young Crane was hatched, the period of incubation having been thirty days.

The young bird was well covered with down of a light brown or fawn colour, with darker markings on the back; it was short on its legs, and the bill also appeared short, in fact, it appeared less like a Crane than I expected to see it. It was able to walk about as soon as it was hatched, but appeared feeble, and now and then fell or rolled over in its attempts to follow its parents.

The old birds attended to the young one with much care, and furiously attacked everything that came near the place; they collected worms and beetles, etc., from all parts of their enclosure, which they brought in their bills towards the young bird, and after mutilating all living food, they would hold it near the young bird, who would advance and pick it from their bills, or from the ground as soon as it was dropped by them. The young Crane never opens its mouth and cries for food like the Storks or Herons and many other young birds, but utters a rather loud note, like *peep, peep, peep*, not unlike the chick of a common fowl; it is not, however, as adroit and able to

185

obtain its food as the young of the Gallinaceous birds generally are; and consequently the parent birds are far more attentive, and watch every opportunity of obtaining food and preparing it for the young one. I have frequently seen the old birds offer a piece of biscuit (that the young bird found was too large to swallow), and they then would place it upon the ground, and by repeated blows break it up in small pieces, and then drop these close to the young bird, who would pick them up and swallow them. From these observations I am induced to consider that the Cranes (*Grus*) occupy an intermediate position between those birds that feed their young like the Herons and Storks, and those groups, like the Bustards and Plovers, whose young are at once able to run about and seek their food.

Perhaps the most remarkable thing is the rapid growth of the young Crane, which is very surprising. As I have before stated, at first the legs are short; in fact, as compared with the parents, the bird is remarkably small, and few persons would guess what it possibly could be; in a few days, however, the legs begin to grow rapidly, and the neck and bill become elongated, and the bird quickly appears a Crane in shape.

From the time of hatching the female alone broods upon or nestles the bird, although the male takes turn in the task of incubation; and I notice the female does not squat down on the young one to brood, but sits down on the ground near it, and the young bird immediately walks behind her; she then raises her long black plumes, between which he creeps, and passes forward under one of her wings, until quite out of sight; her plumes are then lowered into their ordinary position.

There is a beautiful example of the progressive growth from the first down to the perfect feathers to be seen on the young of this bird. I have in many birds observed this, but not to so great an extent. It appears that the first down is not thrown off, but continues to grow longer, until the perfect feather is developed, having the early down attached at its point: this condition is to be seen not only on the points of the primaries, but also on the ends of the feathers of the entire plumage. Thus the bird for some time carries his early dress on the outside of his second plumage. The rapid growth of the plumage can be best understood from the fact that on September 27 it was found necessary to catch the young bird in order to cut the primaries of one of its wings, to prevent its flying away. The bird by this time almost equalled its parents in size, and now is assuming the colour of the adult.

REMARKS ON CRANES.

The Cape crowned crane (*Balearica regulorum*) is one of the beautiful species of a family of birds of which the following genera are represented in the Society's Gardens by several species, viz. *Grus, Tetrapteryx, Balearica,* and *Anthropoides.* The species are not very numerous, but are widely distributed in Europe, Asia, Africa, America and Australia. By their structure, habits and economy they are easily distinguished from all other Grallatorial birds. They are cheerful and lively, and their sportive activity renders them great favourites in captivity. Nothing can exceed the graceful movements of a group of these delightful birds as they dance and skip about, raising and lowering their graceful heads and necks, and, with out-stretched wings, waltzing round each other with evident enjoyment and pleasure; occasionally they give chase to each other, and on the runaway being overtaken, skip and scamper off for another dance. A feather, a piece of paper, or a dead leaf is sometimes thrown up by them, and as it is carried about by the wind they jump after it and repeat the performance in great glee. Now, in all this is discernible a wide separation of this family from that of the storks or herons, the habits of which are slow, dull, stealthy and sulky. The grave and stately walk of that mangy, hump-backed scavenger, the adjutant, is well known to most Eastern travellers, but notwithstanding his ill looks he furnishes our ladies with the beautiful and delicate marabou feathers, which are in fact his under tail-coverts. The crane feeds upon grain, vegetable substances, and insects ; of the latter it destroys a great number, and as it is not tempted to live upon any kind of carrion or animal food we must regard it as a clean feeder; on the other hand, the stork will live on, and search for, any kind of garbage, and the heron will seek for living fish, frogs and other small living creatures for food.

The crane generally lays, in a nest of rushes on the ground, two eggs about the size of the egg of a goose, and of a reddish-cream or olive colour, covered with brown blotches; the parent birds take part in the incubation. When the young bird is hatched it walks slowly about, and the old birds collect food for it, which it picks from their bills. The youthful crane much resembles the young of plovers or bustards.

It is a very sociable bird, large numbers being found congregating upon the same spot; its flight is powerful, and it is able to continue on the wing for a considerable time, and thus fly to long distances. One species only (*Grus cinerea*) can be considered to belong to this country. Consequent, doubtless, on the cultivation of the land and the increase of gunnery, that species may now be regarded as an extinct race, and should an occasional unfortunate straggler find its way here from the Continent of Europe, it is at once shot down and destroyed, like the once famous great bustard.

Singularly enough, one species only is found in Australia (*Grus australasiana*), which is well known to the colonist as the "native companion," a name doubtless bestowed upon this sociable bird by the early settlers in that distant region. At the time that Europeans visited that country this harmless bird had not been taught the lesson it had soon to learn, viz. that of the destructiveness of firearms. An instance is related by Mr. Gould (vol. ii. p. 290) of a pair that not only became perfectly tame, but attracted a pair of wild birds to the residence of Mr. McArthur at Camden; would follow the servants about, enter the kitchen, feed from their hands, and exhibit all the signs of domesticated birds.

The lovely demoiselle (*Anthropoides virgo*) for beauty of form and gracefulness of manner cannot be surpassed by any of the feathered race; her bright eyes and pearly grey plumage, with the white ear tufts, give her an air of sprightliness and vivacity beyond description.

The voice of the crane is generally loud and harsh, and the remarkable structure in the windpipe of some of the species is singularly like that in some species of swan, such as the wild swan or hooper, and Bewick's swan.

The windpipe or trachea is lengthened in a wonderful manner by passing into the keel of the breastbone, the keel being expanded and open in front to receive it, and having a space, several inches in length, in which the windpipe bends round and returns before it reaches the lungs; by this arrangement the windpipe is much lengthened in several of the species, but not all the species possess this remarkable conformation. The same peculiarity in regard to the breastbone is observable in the swans. The mute or tame swan and the black swan of

189

Australia have the breastbone formed simple and single, like the breastbone of the common duck, while the hooper, trumpeter, and Bewick's swans have the double keel to the breastbone or sternum, and the hollow cavity into which the windpipe enters and returns before reaching the lungs.

It must not, however, be too hastily concluded that this arrangement of the vocal organs is sufficient to account for the loud "crank, crank, crank" so often repeated by the crane family, because the "crowned crane" is without this complicated structure, having only the single breastbone, without any opening in which the trachea could be elongated, and yet has a loud and powerful voice. In this respect we may instance the voice of the common duck, the female only gives out the loud quack, quack, the male being nearly mute; but, strange to say, the trachea or windpipe of the female is simple, and has none of the remarkable bony appendages found at the termination of the trachea or windpipe of the drake or male bird. This fact is not generally known, and likewise another one connected with the common and wild duck, which is, that the males all assume the plumage of the female soon after the young birds are hatched.

An amusing instance of the want of knowledge of these two facts occurred at a farmhouse where a large number of ducks were bred. The owner declared that the males had disappeared altogether, and nothing but females remained with the young birds; he was soon, however, convinced, on all the birds being caught, that he was mistaken, as by holding a bird up by one wing the loud quacking of the females contrasted forcibly with the inward and feeble "weese, weese" of the males, although by the plumage they were not distinguishable. It is necessary, therefore, to be careful in attributing the powerful and loud notes to the singular conformation of the windpipe.

The flesh of the crane is excellent food, more especially the young birds, being little inferior to that of the ever-memorable bustard ; and with respect to the edibility of the flesh of the crane we give the following extract :[1]—"Sir Thomas Browne of Norwich, who wrote in the time of Charles the Second, says in his works : 'Cranes are often seen here in hard winters especially about the champain and fieldy part. It seems they have been more plentiful, for in a bill of fare, when the Mayor entertained the Duke of Norfolk, I met with cranes in a dish. In the *Norfolk Household Book*, already quoted under the articles on the pheasant and great bustard, I find three separate notices of cranes : the first for a crane and six plovers, 20*d.* ; the second, four mallards and a crane killed with the cross-bowe ; the third, item, on Thursday for a crane, 6*d.* ; while in Dugdale's *Origines Juridiciales*, as quoted at page 366, we find that the price of a crane in London was 10*s.* Leland, in his *Collectanea*, includes in the bill of fare at the feast of Archbishop Neville, two hundred and four cranes, and, according to Sir David Lindsay, cranes formed also part of the bill of fare at a grand hunting entertainment given by the Earl of Athol to James the Fifth of Scotland and the Queen Mother, on the bank of the Loghaine in Glen Tilt. Ray mentions the winter visits of this large bird ; and Willoughby, in an abridgment of some statutes relating to the preservation of fowl, refers at page 52 to a fine of twenty pence levied as a forfeit for every egg of a crane or a bustard taken or destroyed. Smith, in his *History of the County of Cork*, vol. ii. p. 342, says the crane was seen in that county during the remarkable frost of 1739 ; though the editor of *Pennant's British Zoology* mentions four instances of the occurrence of the crane within his memory.'"

[1] *Yarrell's British Birds*, vol. viii. p. 438.

THE KAGU.

(*RHINOCHETUS JUBATUS.*)

NOTE ON THE HABITS AND AFFINITIES OF THE KAGU.

At the first sight of this bird, one is struck with its resemblance to several different genera, and at once calls to mind *Eurypyga, Œdicnemus, Cariama, Psophia, Nycticorax,* and *Scopus;* one and all appear more or less represented in its singular combination of characters.

The actions and movements of the Kagu are, generally, quick and lively, so opposite to the slow and chameleon-like movements of the true herons that one can hardly suspect it to be an Ardeine bird. This, however, it doubtless will prove to be, but so modified and adapted to a different kind of diet and mode of life, that its real affinities are difficult to recognize.

With its crest erect and wings spread out, the Kagu runs or skips about, sometimes pursuing and driving before him all the birds that are confined with him in the same aviary [among these are several Blue Waterhens (*Porphyrio*)], evidently enjoying the fun of seeing them frightened; at other times he will seize the end of his wing or tail and run round, holding it in his bill; from a piece of paper or dry leaf he derives amusement by tossing it about and running after it. During his frolic he will thrust his bill into the ground and spread out his wings, kick his legs in the air, and then tumble about as if in a fit. At other times he appears intent upon catching worms. He steps slowly, his neck close to his body, his crest flat on his back, all his feathers smooth and close, he raises one foot, and with two or three gentle strokes he paws the ground, swiftly he darts his bill into the earth and draws forth a worm, a sudden shake and it is swallowed; again he runs, stopping suddenly, he makes another dart; and thus he continues to capture this kind of food. With respect to feeding, this bird differs much from the heron family, seeking out, in every hole and corner, worms, snails and other living things, whenever they are not in motion; as soon as a snail is found, he breaks its shell by repeated knocks upon the ground, and, after shaking the fragments of the broken shell off, the animal is swallowed. In no instance, however, that I have observed, does this bird eat bread, seed, or any kind of vegetable, but he strictly confines himself to insects and other animal substances.

The skeleton and internal anatomy of the Kagu being entirely unknown to me, I can only form an opinion of the affinities of this bird by its external characters, habits, etc.; and I find that the remarkable powder-down tufts, which are well developed in all the Ardeines, are carried to a greater extent in this bird; for above and around the wings, on the breast beneath the wings, and on the back and belly, this structure exists, and the enormous quantity of the white powder given off is surprising. I have seen the bird enter the small pond and attempt to wash, and, upon dipping partly under water, the whole surface of the water was covered with a white film, like French chalk. The strong resemblance between this bird and *Eurypyga*, even in the markings upon the wing- and tail-feathers, the mode of spreading out the wings, and other resemblances, convinces me that I am right in considering the Kagu to be more closely allied to *Eurypyga* than to any other bird that has come within my notice.

THE PRATINCOLE.

(*GLAREOLA PRATINCOLA.*)

The following notice appeared in a paper, the name and date of which I was not able at the time to ascertain :—

'The Pratincoles (*Glareola pratincola*) in the fish-house at the Zoological Gardens have brought off their clutch—the first instance on record of these birds breeding in captivity, at any rate in this country. During the period of incubation they have been under close observation, and the notes taken by Mr. Bartlett, the superintendent, will form the subject of a communication to the Zoological Society, and find a place in the *Proceedings.* The results of the observations are important, for they are opposed in some essential points to much that has been written on the nesting habits of these birds. This, the common species, is a native of the warmer parts of the Old World, and has its breeding-places on both shores of the Mediterranean, along the valley of the Danube, and in Asia Minor. Mr. Howard Saunders found them abundant in the Marisma, near Cadiz, depositing their eggs—which, he says, were never more than three, and generally two—near the water. He is also the authority for the statement that the young run immediately on emerging from the egg. These statements have naturally been accepted, and are quoted, with one acknowledgment, in Dresser's *Birds of Europe.* There is, however, no doubt that they need considerable modification and revision. Four eggs have been laid by the birds in the Gardens, of these, one was eaten by the whimbrel, and three have been hatched, so that it is probable that the normal number is four.

194

Indeed, Gould, in his *Birds of Europe*, says that the Pratincole lays 'three or four eggs.' The last two birds of the clutch died on Saturday morning, having only lived a couple of days. It seems likely that they were crushed by the parent in her efforts to protect them from the other birds in the aviary. They lived long enough, however, to make it clear that they are not able to run about as soon as they are hatched, and they were fed by the old birds. All three have been skinned and preserved by Mr. Bartlett, and will form interesting practical illustrations of his promised paper."

I here append my notes, which are incomplete :—

" September 1894. A large number of Pratincoles arrived from Spain for the late Lord Lilford. For a time I had charge of them, and his Lordship presented two pairs to the Society, at the same time making me a present of a pair, which I kept in my room in order to become acquainted with their habits, and to determine the best kinds of food for them in captivity. During the last winter I transferred them to the fish-house, to associate with the waders there. At the beginning of June the birds laid the first egg, and the following morning the keeper informed me that a whimbrel in the aviary had destroyed it.

" I had the whimbrel removed at once, and shortly afterwards three more eggs were laid, and the male and female were observed to take turns upon the nest.

" On June 20 the young birds could be seen, and on the keeper's approach to the aviary the female would rush forward with wings and tail spread out and with open mouth, apparently craving for food, which she would peck or take from his hands and return to the young; brooding over them like a common fowl, she commenced the up-and-down movement of her head, and the food being regurgitated was taken from her mouth by the young. The young never left the nest.

"I have no doubt they died for want of proper food, and the observations, I am sorry to say, were stopped."

CHAPTER VIII.

SEA-BIRDS.

HERRING GULL.

(*LARUS ARGENTATUS.*)

REMARKS ON THE HABITS OF A HERRING GULL.

IN calling attention to the singular and remarkable habits of a bird of this species, permit me to give an extract from the *Garden Guide* of 1852, in order that the origin of this individual specimen may be perfectly known.

" In the beginning of June 1850, a Herring Gull (*Larus argentatus*) hatched out her young ones in the enclosure (No. 17), which is overshadowed by two weeping ash trees. The male bird had assisted her so constantly in the incubation that his strength gave way, and he died just as the young birds were chipping out of the shell. The female then became restless, left the eggs, and was only induced to resume her place for the few hours which were necessary to complete the hatch by the keeper having arranged the dead body of her mate in counterfeit presentment of the position he generally took up near her when not himself upon the eggs."

It will, I hope, be understood that the birds so hatched in 1850 were the parents of the individual whose habits I now wish to record.

This bird was one of two hatched about the latter end of May 1857, and was reared by its parents in the Gardens, where it remained during the summer and autumn of that year. At the commencement of the winter, he was in the habit of flying about (not having been pinioned), and occasionally staying away a *day* or *two*, then *for a week or more*, returning again generally about feeding-time, and alighting among the other gulls and feeding with them. This continued till the end of March 1858, at which time he disappeared. Nothing more was seen or heard of him until the middle of November 1858, when, to the delight and astonishment of all who knew him, he returned one afternoon at the usual time. *Meeting the keeper with the box of food, he followed him* to the enclosure where he was hatched, and settled down among the other gulls to his dinner as though he had never been away, not appearing the least shy or wild. Here he remained with his parents and the other gulls, occasionally flying off for a *day* or *two*, until the beginning of February 1859.

He again departed, and by many was given up for lost; others, however, thought he might again return, and one *Saturday morning* (Nov. 19, 1859), *between eight and nine o'clock*, we were gratified to behold the long-lost gull making his way to his old quarters much improved in his appearance, having nearly completed his adult plumage. He immediately came down and was greeted by his old friends, who evidently recognized him. He *appeared fatigued and hungry*. I sent for some food, and he came boldly towards us and fed almost from the hand. As soon as his appetite was satisfied he walked about, quite at home among the other gulls. Since Saturday, I have seen him flying now and then over the Gardens and Park, but returning after a short flight.

In conclusion, I beg to say I am indebted to one of the Society's most careful and very intelligent keepers (B. Misselbrook) for some of the facts which have enabled me to bring before you these very interesting particulars.

THE GREAT AUK.

(*ALCA IMPENNIS*, LINN.)

Notwithstanding the detailed and carefully compiled history of the Great Auk by Symington Grieve published in 1888, the following additional notes of this now extinct British bird may be interesting to naturalists and others.

As near as I am able to judge the date, it must have been about the year 1836, or perhaps a little later, that I saw in the shop of Mr. Tucker, who was then living under the Quadrant, Regent Street, a few doors from Air Street, the skins of ten or twelve good specimens of the Great Auk. I may remark that Mr. Tucker was a dealer in shells, minerals, bird-skins, and other specimens of Natural History. I secured one of these specimens, which I mounted for Mr. Edmund Maude, who then had chambers in the Inner Temple. In an old account-book of mine I found an entry :—"June 23, 1838. To supplying skin, stuffing, and grouping Great Auk £11 15s." Another entry was : "Sold to Edmund Maude (April 1842) egg of Great Auk, £2." The egg, if I recollect rightly, was furnished to me by Mr. Hoy, of Stoke Nayland, Suffolk. I am under the impression that the specimen of the Great Auk in the possession of Mrs. Lescher was also obtained from Mr. Hoy, who, if I am not mistaken, was related to her family. Mr. Maude unfortunately got into difficulties and was obliged to leave England. The specimens accordingly again came into my possession, and I disposed of them to Mr. Nathaniel Troughton for £26 5s., and they were afterwards purchased by Mr. Elliott. The egg and bird (or the stuffed bird only) are now in the Museum of Natural History in the Central Park, New York, America.

A second specimen of the Great Auk was possessed by me in a rather remarkable manner. One day a rough-looking sea-faring man came to my house in Little Russell Street to ask if I bought bird-skins (this was in the year 1844), saying that he had the skin of a great northern diver for sale. I told him that if it was a good specimen I would buy it, if the price asked was a fair one. The same, or the following day, the man came with the skin done up in paper, and upon unrolling it I found, to my astonishment, that it was the skin of the Great Auk, and for which he asked £1 6s. I at once gave him the money, and he left. I was so surprised that I did not think to ask him any questions about it, and although I immediately left the house to overtake him, thinking he might have more, I failed to find him. That specimen I sold to Mr. Henry Shaw, of Shrewsbury, in September 1844 for £9.

I believe this specimen is now, or was, in the collection of the late Lord Hill of Hawkstone.

HUMBOLDT'S PENGUIN.

(*SPHENISCUS HUMBOLDTI.*)

REMARKS UPON THE HABITS AND CHANGE OF PLUMAGE OF HUMBOLDT'S PENGUIN.

On January 24, 1878, a specimen of Humboldt's Penguin was purchased from a dealer in Liverpool. The bird was in poor condition when received, and very dirty, but perfectly tame, following one about, and seeming pleased to be taken on the lap and nursed like an infant. At first it required to be fed by hand, for if its food was placed on the ground the bird took no notice of it, although hungry. After a few days, if living fishes

Fig. 1.—*Spheniscus humboldti* (before moult).

were thrown to it, and the bird saw them jumping about on the floor, it began to pick up the fishes and swallow them. From the bird doing this, and from the colour and condition of its plumage, I have no doubt that it had been reared from the nest, and had never previously fed itself.

It was some days before the Penguin ventured into the water, but after the first wash the bird rapidly improved; the feathers became clean, its appetite increased, and it passed much time in the water, evidently gaining strength and weight. About this time it frequently uttered its loud braying jackass-like notes, and became fat and in full vigour. Figure 1 (p. 201) gives a very faithful representation of the bird at this time. About February 22, the bird appeared dull, and, with half-closed eyes, moped about; it became ill-tempered and spiteful, bit at any one who offered to touch it, and avoided going into the water. The bird looked larger than before, its feathers standing out from its body during this condition; but its appetite continued good, and it fed as freely as usual.

In a few days the feathers began to fall off from all parts of the bird, not, as birds usually moult, a few feathers at a time, but in large quantities; for instance, the bird generally remained stationary during the night, and in the morning there was left round it a circle of cast feathers that had been shed during the night. So rapidly did the process of moulting go on, that by March 7 the bird had entirely renewed its plumage, and appeared in the adult dress, as represented in Figure 2 (p. 203). The manner in which the flipper-like wings cast off the short scale-like feathers was remarkable, they flaked off like the shedding of the skin of a serpent; the new feathers being already plainly visible, the old feathers were pushed off by the new ones; this was very clearly noticeable, as many of the old feathers could be seen still attached to the tips of the

Fig. 2.—*Spheniscus humboldti* (after moult).

new feathers, so that the bird was entirely covered with its new plumage before the old feathers dropped off. The bird had by these means entirely changed its dress and appearance in certainly less than ten days. It looked thinner on account of the shortness of its new feathers, and doubtless from a decrease in bulk, consequent upon the rapid development of the entire plumage. The bird avoided the water for a few days before it began to moult, and also after it had renewed its feathers ; it soon, however, became lively, its eyes assumed their usual form and brightness, it took freely to the water, in which it passed the greater part of the day. Its movements in the water when swimming, diving, and pursuing fish were most extraordinary ; it seemed, as it were, to fly under water, using its flipper-like wings after the fashion of a seal.

The Penguin appears so much at home in the water, so perfectly adapted to an aquatic life, that one would conclude that, but for the necessity of breeding and moulting, this bird would be far more at home on the ocean than in passing even a short period on land, being so ill-adapted in form for travelling on shore.

PENGUINS.

ANTARCTIC EXPLORATION.

In 1895, and during the time that an Antarctic Expedition was talked about, I looked up all the information I could find respecting the bird life in those regions, and among my notes I find this extract :—" *Ross's Voyage to the Antarctic Regions,* January 5, 1841, p. 178 : several Penguins follow the ship and play about like porpoises ; p. 179, saw many Penguins of a different species from those we met with at Kerguelen and Auckland Islands ; p. 181, new species of seal differing from all the others in the total absence of ears; p. 189, landed on Possession Island, South Victorialand, met with inconceivable myriads of Penguins, completely and densely covering the ledges, the precipices and even to the summits of the hills, loaded the boats with geological specimens and Penguins; this was in lat. 71° 56' and long. 171° 7' E. January 12, 1841."

" Discovery of Mount Erebus, January 28, 1841." These notes refer to the Emperor Penguin (*Aptenodytes forsterii*) and King Penguin (*Aptenodytes pennantii*). After having collected other materials on the subject, I wrote the subjoined letter to the *Standard*, November 25, 1895.

" In the variety of notices that have from time to time appeared with reference to the Exploration of the Antarctic Regions, I have not seen any attention called to a remarkable fact concerning the bird life, which I think of considerable importance. In the Arctic Regions the birds are migratory, or, at any rate, have the power of flight, and during the winter months leave these inhospitable regions. Not so with most of the birds in the Antarctic. The large family of Penguins are unable to fly. Their rudimentary wings are only serviceable when in the water. The largest of this family, the Emperor Penguin, is found only within the Antarctic Circle, and must therefore remain in that part of the world throughout the whole year, where the species, no doubt, exist by thousands. It may be said they have the power of swimming, but they have never been found away from their natural habitat. The question is how they manage to exist during the long winter months, their food consisting of fish and other marine animals. There must be shallow landing-places, enabling them to come on land to lay their eggs and rear their young. They must also come on land during the moulting season. These feeble birds, with rudimentary wings and short legs, must inevitably find some landing-place where they are sheltered from the severity of the winter season, in which they are able to obtain food. As I have before mentioned, they must have easy access to the water on account of their food. It appears, therefore, to me that there must exist in this unknown land, probably near the volcanoes, warm lakes, teeming with food, and, for all we know, the darkness may be relieved by the burning volcanoes in the neighbourhood. So little is known of this vast region that one is tempted to imagine the existence of something marvellous."

I enclosed a cutting of this notice to my son Edward, who was in Sarawak at the time, stating that, in consequence of the efforts now being made for exploring the Antarctic region, I thought every little helps science. His answer was as follows :—

Sarawak, January 6, 1896.

" I must say you have opened my eyes with regard to the Antarctic. I never dreamt so much, although I often wondered how all those birds lived, but thought they left the South Pole and came to the islands nearer to the Equator ; but, as you say that they are not found outside the Antarctic Circle, then they must be there by millions, nearest the Polar Lakes."

On November 26, 1895, the following letter appeared—

TO THE EDITOR OF *The Standard.*

" Sir,—In *The Standard* of to-day one of your correspondents, speaking of bird life in the Arctic and Antarctic regions, seems surprised that no notice has been taken of the latter. He instances the Emperor Penguin, and asserts that it is found only in the Antarctic Circle. His supposition is certainly a plausible one—namely, that there must exist in that unknown part, probably near the volcanoes, warm lakes teeming with food, etc.

"Now, although the penguin has only a rudimentary wing, and, therefore, is deprived of the ability to soar aloft like the rest of the feathered tribe, it has, nevertheless, a powerful substitute, in its ability not only to swim and dive with incredible swiftness, but also to live for a very long time on and under the sea without any inconvenience whatever.

"I have for over three years lived both in the Falkland Islands and Tierra del Fuego, the natural homes of these eccentric amphibia, where I have seen them in their thousands, and I have studied their habits and mode of life. It has been found that this bird has travelled all the way across the South Atlantic (and why not from the Pacific?) to the Argentine Republic, and not far from Monte Video. The immense uninhabited tract of land and water included in that portion between Cape Horn and the Antarctic Circle must be taken into consideration when we speak of the Emperor Penguin and its habitat.

"It is not absolutely necessary for us to suppose that this special bird is found only within the Antarctic, and must remain there throughout the year. We do not know sufficient of bird life in those regions to pronounce definitely on the subject. Taking my foregoing remarks into consideration, it is quite possible that the Emperor Penguin does migrate northward during at least part of the winter, just as its northern congener does. And I believe that this statement will be borne out by the results of the contemplated Expedition to the South Pole.

"I am, Sir, your obedient servant,

"J. E. R. POLAK.

" Batley, Yorks, November 26."

WILD BEASTS IN THE 'ZOO'

From time to time many species of this interesting family have been exhibited in the Gardens. These quaint, harmless and innocent-looking birds are much to be pitied, for on shore they are quite at the mercy of rough and brutal men, who, it is to be deplored, frequently in the most wanton and cruel manner destroy them simply out of pure mischief, because, unable to fly, their mode of progression is necessarily slow. They are easily overtaken and are then ruthlessly killed; the only chance they apparently have of escaping annihilation is by breeding upon inaccessible rocky islands.

CHAPTER IX.

OSTRICHES, RHEAS AND EMUS.

EGGS OF STRUTHIOUS BIRDS.

I MADE the following notes which may be useful for future reference, viz. :—

Ostriches hatched in France 1861, in the open air, were forty-four days incubating.

Rheas the same as the Emus; male sits five weeks; the young break out, not by the usual chipping with the bill, but by hard and determined struggling with the feet, kicking.

Emus do not pick their way out of the shell like most birds, but, by a few hard kicks, or thrusts of the legs, endeavour to burst open the shell of the egg. As soon as the shell cracks, the young bird kicks with great energy and breaks out; the shell breaks in all directions.

At an evening meeting I exhibited a series of the eggs of struthious birds, including those of the Northern and Southern Ostrich, and American and Darwin's Rhea, the Common and Spotted Emu (*Dromœus novœ-hollandiœ* and *D. irroratus*), the Common Cassowary, and the Mooruk (*Casuarius bennettii*). The latter had been laid in the Society's Gardens on April 21, by the bird received from Dr. Bennett in May 1858, which was thus proved to be a female. This egg (see Aves, Pl. clxii.)[1] was of a pale grass-green colour, closely freckled with paler colouring, and

---

[1] *Proceedings of Zoological Society*, 1860.

much smoother and more finely granulated than that of the Common Cassowary. It measured 6·0 by 3·45 in. and weighed 22½ ounces. Its shape was more elongated and pyriform than that of the Cassowary or Emu.

SPOTTED EMU.
(*DROMÆUS IRRORATUS.*)

The specimen of *Dromæus* exhibited was obtained in 1858, with others, far in the interior of South Australia, several hundred miles from Port Phillip.

It differs from *Dromæus novæ-hollandiæ* in having the whole of the feathers of the body distinctly marked with narrow transverse bars of light grey and dark brownish-black. The feathers of the back and sides of the bird are broader and longer and less silky in texture than those of the common species : that this is so, is quite evident to the touch. The upper part of the neck and head is nearly black, and the feathers appear thicker than those on these parts in the common bird.

The specimen from which these remarks are taken was one of three examined by me, two of which were adult, and one a young bird about one-third grown. This young bird exhibited the transverse bars on its plumage as distinctly as the adult bird ; at the same time the broad longitudinal stripes were clearly to be seen. Judging from the skins, I am inclined to consider this bird to be smaller than the common species. As I hope before long that more information respecting these birds, together with other and more perfect specimens, may come to hand, therefore I beg to propose provisionally the name of *Dromæus irroratus* for this supposed new species.

"*Brockham Lodge, January* 15, 1862.

" A. BARTLETT, *Zoological Gardens.*

" I am much obliged by thy kind note of the 10th.

"The Emus continue to lay quite satisfactorily. We have now six fine eggs, one larger and heavier than any last year. The two first were laid in a corner they much resort to, down by our river, and liable to be flooded. They have since been induced to lay in the house. The eggs are not allowed to be touched by any one but myself. I take the earliest opportunity of removing them, always replacing them by some artificial ones I have had made ; they are brought into the house and kept in one proper store-room, through which runs a warming-pipe lighted only in very cold weather like the present. The birds do not seem to be at all suffering at present. I should be exceedingly glad if it suited thee at any time to run down, and give me any hints as to arrangements against when the time for sitting approaches. Should there be more than ten or twelve eggs laid, of which I think there is every probability, what had best be done with them ?

"Have you another Bird to which they could be entruded ? I should much prefer dividing the rest.

"Of course the poor crippled young one was doomed to die, and it is only surprising it has lived so long. I am glad to hear it will make a specimen. I am very respectfully and obliged,

"THOS. BENNETT."

" *Brockham Lodge, near Reigate,*
" *March* 25, 1863.

" MY DEAR FRIEND,—I was again not so fortunate as to meet with thee at the Gardens yesterday ; and found Misselbrook likewise absent on *Scotch duty.* I thought it would be interesting to thee to know how my birds are going on this season.

" The batch of eggs has been much larger than heretofore, and is, in fact, only just finished. The male bird did not show decided signs of brooding till after the twentieth egg was laid this time ; and he was finally settled on the 5th inst. with thirteen eggs.

" The bird, as usual, has sat exceedingly close, so that we have twice only got a good view of the nest since ; and the last time there were seventeen eggs in it, so that the total is twenty-four. I thought it best to take three away, reducing the number to fourteen, which the bird seems to cover well. I have sent a mem. of these

211

particulars to the Editor of the *Zoologist*, but do not know whether it would be in time for this next month.

"I have started an 'Incubator' for the surplus eggs, and though not at all expecting to succeed, I thought it worth trying, as the eggs are just as good for specimens afterwards. My special object yesterday was to gain any practical hints respecting its management. I remember Misselbrook told me 108°-110° for the (external) heat of the water; say 94°-96° or up to 100° for the internal (of the drawers). I should very much esteem the favour of any information or suggestions; also to know how the laying, etc., of your Emus are going on, as the man whom I saw could not tell me; but was very civil in showing me the incubator, and telling me all he knew about it. I am, very sincerely,

"W. BENNETT."

MANTELL'S APTERYX.

(*APTERYX MANTELLI*, BART.)

In calling attention at a meeting of the Zoological Society one evening to a large collection of specimens of the genus *Apteryx* on the table, I stated that I had been led to make a careful examination of all the individuals I could find in the Collections of the British Museum, the Museums of the Zoological Society, the Royal College of Surgeons, and elsewhere, in consequence of an *Apteryx* belonging to Dr. Mantell having been placed in my hands by that gentleman a few days since, which appeared to me to differ from all that I had before seen. As a careful comparison of this bird with the specimens in the collections before mentioned fully justified me in considering it as a distinct species, I was about to describe it as a new one; but most fortunately, I heard that the original specimen figured and described by Dr. Shaw (to which he applied the name *Apteryx australis*) was in the collection of the Earl of Derby at Knowsley. It is with much pleasure I have to acknowledge the kindness of his lordship in honouring me with the loan of this bird, which has

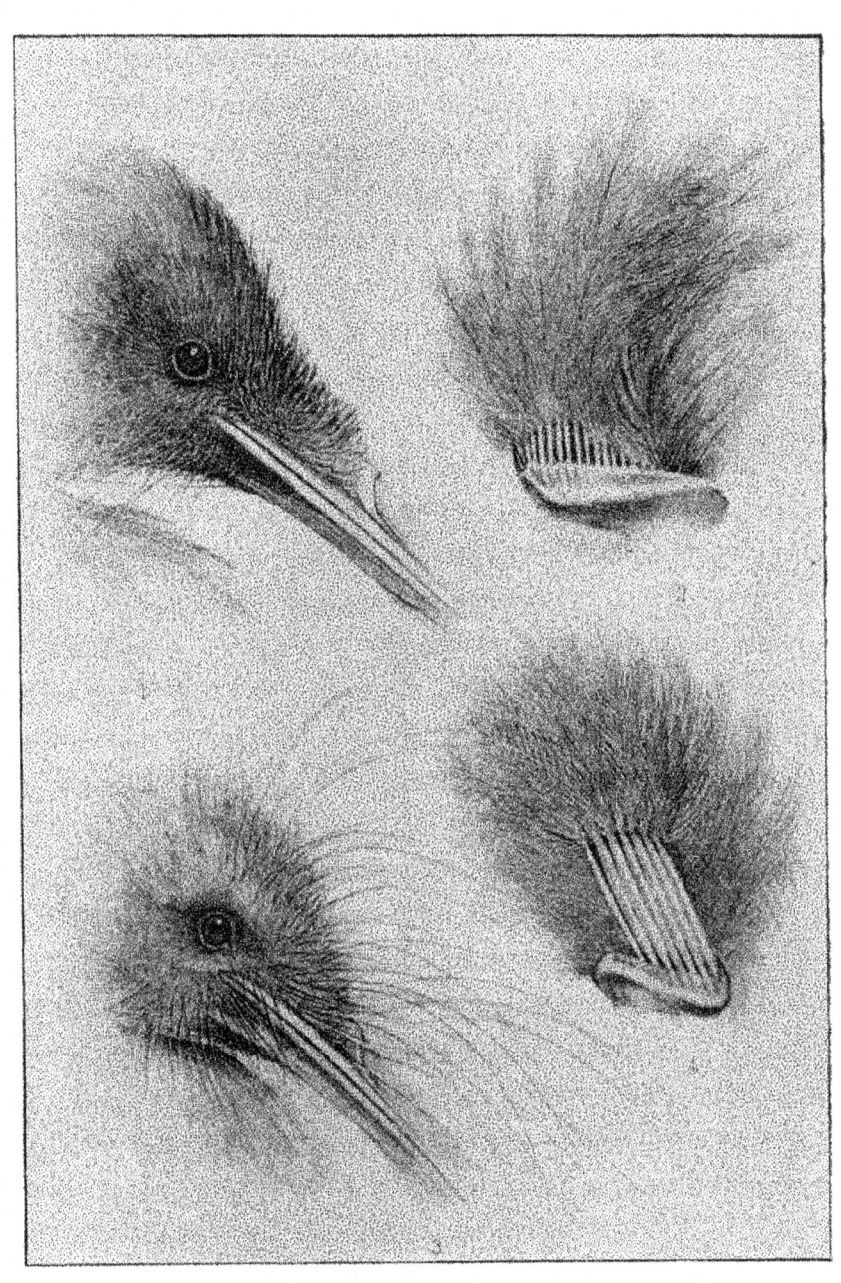

1, 2. HEAD AND WING OF APTERYX AUSTRALIS.
3, 4. HEAD AND WING OF APTERYX MANTELLI.

enabled me to identify the large *Apteryx* placed in my hands by Dr. Mantell as belonging to this species, and also to determine most satisfactorily the distinctive characteristics of the common species, which is considerably smaller, and to which the name of *Apteryx australis* has long been erroneously applied. This bird differs from the original *Apteryx australis* of Dr. Shaw in its smaller size, its darker and more rufous colour, its *longer tarsus which is scutellated in front*, its shorter toes and claws, which are dark horn-coloured, its smaller wings, which have much stronger and thicker quills, and also in having long straggling hairs on the face. I may however remark, that although individuals of this species differ much in size, depending probably on age, sex, etc., I have found no exception to the distinctive characters above given. I therefore propose the name of *Apteryx mantelli* for this smaller and more common species,—a humble effort to commemorate the exertions of Walter Mantell, Esq., to whom we are indebted for so many valuable discoveries in the natural history of New Zealand.

I subjoin a short description of the two species, together with figures of their legs and wings, in order that they may be more readily distinguished.

1, 2. APTERYX AUSTRALIS.	3, 4. APTERYX MANTELLI.
Colour pale greyish-brown, darkest on the back.	Colour dark rufous brown, darkest on the back.
Entire length . . . . . . 30 inches.[1]	Entire length . . . . . . 23 inches.[1]
Bill from forehead . . 6 ,,	Bill from forehead . . 4 ,,
Tarsus (reticulated) . . 2¼ ,,	Tarsus (scutellated) . 2¾ ,,
Middle toe and claw . 3⅝ ,,	Middle toe and claw. 2½ ,,
Claws nearly equal in length, and white.	Middle claw longest, all the claws dark horn-colour.
Wings with soft slender quills; face with short hairs.	Wings with strong thick quills; face with long straggling hairs.

[1] The entire length, being taken from skins, I consider of little value; the entire length of the bird ought always to be taken before the bird is skinned.

In conclusion, I would remark that the specimen of *Apteryx australis* belonging to Dr. Mantell was collected by his son in *Dusky Bay* ; and I have been informed by J. E. Gray, Esq., that the original bird described by Dr. Shaw was brought from the same locality. As far as I am able to ascertain, all the specimens of *Apteryx mantelli* are from the North Island.[1]

ON THE INCUBATION OF THE APTERYX.

In the second volume of Mr. Gould's book upon the *Birds of Australia*, at page 570, will be found several statements made with reference to the mode of reproduction of the *Apteryx*. As these strange stories are most of them derived from the natives of New Zealand, and do not appear to have been verified by any one upon whom we can place much reliance, it may be as well to record a few facts that have occurred under my own observation in the Society's Gardens.

In 1851 Lieut.-Governor Eyre presented to the Society an *Apteryx*. This bird proved to be a female of *Apteryx mantelli*. In the year 1859 she laid her first egg, and has continued to lay one or two eggs every year since that time. In 1865 a male bird was presented by Henry Slade, Esq. During the last year these birds showed symptoms of a desire to pair. This was known by the loud calling of the male, which was answered by the female in a much lower and shorter note. They were particularly noisy during the night, but altogether silent in the daytime. On January 2 the first egg was laid, and for a day or more the female remained on the egg ; but as soon as she quitted the nest the male bird

[1] An extract from this paper appeared in *Wild Animals in Captivity.*

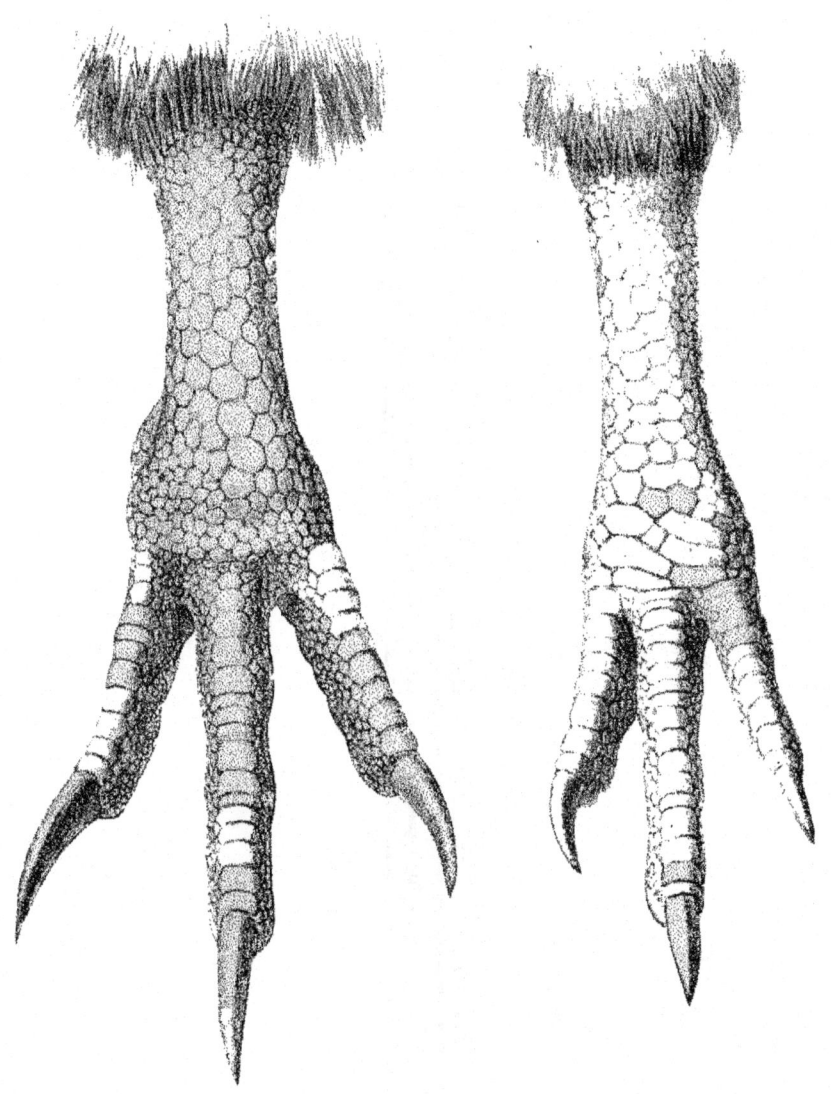

1. FOOT OF A. AUSTRALIS.   2. FOOT OF A. MANTELLI.

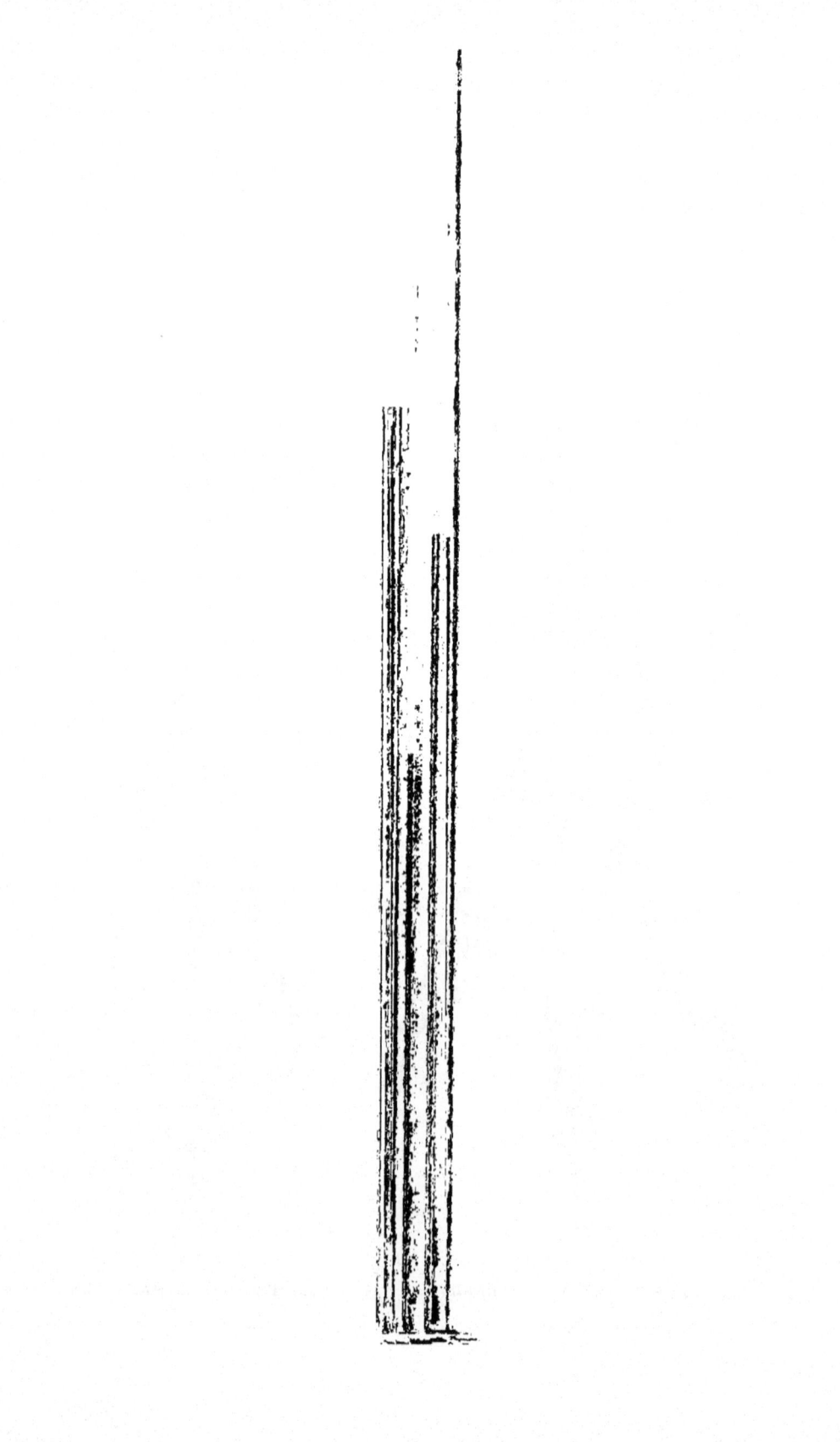

took to it, and remained constantly sitting. On the 7th of February the second egg was laid, the female leaving the nest as soon as the egg was deposited. The two birds now occupied the two opposite corners of the room in which they were kept, the male on the two eggs in the nest under the straw, the female concealed in her corner, also under a bundle of straw placed against the wall. During the time of incubation they ceased to call at night, in fact were perfectly silent, and kept apart. I found the eggs in a hollow formed on the ground in the earth and straw, and placed lengthwise side by side. The male bird lay across them, his narrow body appearing not sufficiently broad to cover them in any other way ; the ends of the eggs could be seen projecting from the side of the bird. The male continued to sit in the most persevering manner until April 25, at which time he was much exhausted, and left the nest. On examining the eggs I found no traces of young birds. An egg deposited June 9, 1859, weighed 14½ ounces. The weight of the bird was 3½ lbs.

Notwithstanding the failure of reproducing the *Apteryx*, I think sufficient has been witnessed to show that this bird's mode of reproduction does not differ essentially from that of the allied struthious birds, in all cases of which that have come under my observation the male bird only sits. I have witnessed the breeding of the mooruk, the cassowary, the emu, and the rhea; and the mode of proceeding of the *Apteryx* fully justifies me in believing the habits of this bird to be in no way materially different from those of its allies.

CHAPTER X.

ROOKS.

ROOKS FOR NEW ZEALAND.

"Sir,—In your last number of *Land and Water* a letter appeared from my friend Captain Salvin, seeking assistance in forming a collection of rooks for the above destination ; permit me to offer my most sincere thanks for the prompt and very kind response that I received, in the shape of a most abundant supply of fine, strong, and healthy young birds, and I hope, under the care and management of my son, Edward Bartlett (to whom also I beg to refer your correspondent 'C. M.,' for information upon this subject), they may live to reach and prosper in New Zealand, where, from the accounts that reach us, they are likely to prove of inestimable value.

"I trust I may be allowed to mention the names of Captain Salvin, Jonathan King, Esq., Mr. and Miss Onslow, and Lord Lilford, by whose kind aid I have a sufficient number of specimens for the present season.

"A. D. Bartlett."

ROOKS IN NEW ZEALAND.

"Sir,—As many of the readers of *Land and Water* already know that I undertook in the early part of last year (1870) to obtain and rear from the nest one hundred rooks, and prepare them for shipment to New Zealand, you will be pleased to know the great success that has attended the first lot of fifty, shipped on board the *Countess of Kintore*, in care of Captain Petherbridge. Forty-eight of these birds were landed in good health and condition, only two birds having died on the voyage. I hope soon to hear of the second shipment, and trust they may be equally fortunate. I herewith enclose the particulars of the mode of obtaining, feeding, and managing these birds, thinking these may be interesting to some of your readers, and perhaps useful to any one who may feel inclined to repeat the experiment—I must admit, a task I did not contemplate at the time I entered upon it ; but having had four years' experience in collecting and bird-nesting in Peru and on the banks of the Amazon, I thought it would not be attended with any very great difficulty, and I readily undertook the job. My father wrote to our kind friend Captain Salvin, informing him of his wish to obtain a collection of these birds. The Captain, with that ready goodwill and prompt mode of action, not only replied at once to offer his valuable assistance, but at the same time forwarded a letter to the Editor of *Land and Water*, asking the assistance of those persons able to aid us in this work, and inviting us to come down to Guildford and try our fortune in climbing some of the high fir-trees in that neighbourhood. In this invitation my father accompanied me, and notwithstanding a very unfavourable and excessively windy day, I succeeded in bagging twenty-five strong and well-fledged birds, not taking any that were not well fledged. In the course of a few days, by the kind assistance of Jonathan King, Esq., Mr. and Miss Onslow, Lord Lilford, and Captain Salvin, I received a sufficient supply to render my stock over one hundred birds, and I here again beg to offer my very sincere thanks for this kind assistance, and which has enabled me to lend consider-able aid towards that very much desired object of establishing the Rooks in New Zealand.

"EDWARD BARTLETT."

REARING ROOKS FOR SEA VOYAGES.

In rearing a large number of rooks, you must be pre-pared to be subject to a vast amount of trouble and vexatious annoyance. In the first place, many of them will close their mouths as firmly as the well-known American oysters, and unless they are carefully opened and the birds fed they will surely die from starvation ; others will be constantly gaping with open mouth as though they intended to swallow all creation. There is as much difference in their appetites as between an Alder-man and a starved apothecary.

Now those that sulk and you have to cram, you must be very careful not to overcram them; for in this case all is soon thrown up again, and in a few hours they die for want of food. In the next place the gaping and greedy birds will also take a larger quantity at once than they can retain, and when a bird casts up its food among a multitude of others, it is utterly impossible to say which has its stomach full or otherwise; great care is therefore necessary to make sure of each bird having food regularly, and with so large a number, first have a good lot of baskets or hampers, each to contain six or eight birds of about the same size, and select from them all those that are sulky or refuse to open their mouths for food when offered, for these sulky birds must be taken in hand and the bill opened, and the food slipped into the throat, holding the bird quite still until the food is fairly swallowed; then quietly and carefully put each bird aside until they are all fed; in a few days these birds will become tame and less sulky, and take the food without trouble.

In the early state, that is while in the nest, the food consists almost entirely of animal substances, viz. grubs, worms, and insects of various kinds. It is therefore necessary that the food be assimilated as far as possible to the natural diet, as each bird should be fed by hand every two hours from daylight till near sunset, and at each meal each bird will take from one to two ounces of food; thus they take from six to eight meals per day. You will find that the weight of each bird's food per day will average about twelve ounces. By far the larger portion of this quantity must be *raw lean beef*, rendered fine by grinding in a sausage machine; with this you may mix scalded bread, boiled carrots, boiled potatoes, and hard-boiled eggs. The quantity will vary for each bird from time to time, and in mixing it is always advisable to vary the quantities of each ingredient daily, carefully watching if any marked change takes place in the condition of the birds by the slight change of diet.

As soon as possible give them liberty to hop and try to fly, by letting the basket remain open at top. They begin to sit upon the edge at first, and in a few days hop on sticks you can place within easy reach. If the weather is warm and dry, give the oldest, as soon as they begin to hop about, a slight bath with a fine garden syringe. Great care must be taken in this, for an overdose will give them the cramp, and probably render the bird a cripple for life. The more space they have, with branches of trees and sticks to perch upon, the better, and a little food, such as bits of meat, worms, etc., thrown on the ground to tempt them to feed themselves, is a great help to them. But it must not be taken for granted that they can be trusted to feed themselves entirely for a long time after they begin to do so, for this is a most critical period, and requires all the perseverance and care you can bestow upon them, for they now begin to get sulky again; some of them will get quite wild, and although they pick a little food on the ground and about, do not take sufficient, and the want of food causes them to feel unwell, and unwilling to come near you; they appear sulky and die, unless carefully watched and attended. One more important matter upon which the success entirely depends—viz. cleanliness. Not only must the birds be kept clean, but the places in which they are kept, and the food always fresh and sweet, for if the birds' feathers get dirty and sticky, the birds pine and become inactive, while if the birds are clean, they delight in pruning their feathers to keep them so. Therefore, as soon as they begin to feed themselves freely, the food may be given much dryer; as water is always allowed to stand by them, they can drink when they require it. But in spite of all that you can do, or I can say, you must expect to be troubled and annoyed by certain parasitic attendants, always found among rookeries, and particularly abundant some seasons about the young birds; it is utterly impossible to avoid them, and dangerous to attempt entirely to rid the birds of them, for the means usually employed would probably destroy the birds; but as these very disagreeable and troublesome pests will not exist long upon any other animal except its own dear rook, you must do your best to keep their numbers in check as much as possible by extreme cleanliness. With reference to the food, the greater the variety the better, on account of using these birds to eat almost any kinds that come to hand on board ship; and if accustomed to a mixed food composed of animal and vegetable substances, they will be able to live for a considerable time, and do well upon one or two kinds out of a considerable number, without suffering from the change. The birds keep cleaner the drier the food, as they are apt to throw the moist food about and thus mess each other. The following are the kinds and quantity of food that was required for one hundred birds daily, just before they were shipped :—Raw beef 18 lbs., bread 7½ lbs., potatoes 3 lbs., carrots 3½ lbs., rice 2½ lbs., peameal 3 lbs., oatmeal 2 lbs., Indian corn flour 3 lbs., eggs 1½ lbs.—together 44 lbs., mixed according to instructions sent; as it is impossible to obtain a fresh supply of raw flesh on board ship, and animal substances being very desirable, beetles, cockroaches, rats, and mice may be caught and given to the rooks, or the entrails of fowls, ducks, sheep, pigs, etc., or bits of fat and scraps from the table will help as change of food.

In order, however, to ensure an occasional change of fresh animal food, a good stock of guinea-pigs and rabbits were shipped together with their fodder, and instructions for the mode of using them were as follows :—When a guinea-pig or rabbit is killed, it should be scalded to remove as much of the hair and fur as possible ; it can then be cut up. The skin and bones should be chopped up small, as the crushed bones are particularly good for these birds.

For some years past some rooks have selected one or two plane trees growing in the garden of a house situated at the foot of Haverstock Hill, Chalk Farm Road, in which to build their nests, of which there are generally from five to seven in the trees. The last two seasons there were seven, and each year two were blown out by gales of wind.

The parent birds are very familiar with and favour the Zoological Gardens to an extent that is not appreciated, because they not only rob the various beasts and birds of their food, but also steal the eggs of the water-fowl and other birds. Upon one occasion one of these rooks invaded a swan's nest, and thrust his beak with such force into an egg which was within a day or two of being hatched, that he carried it off a distance of over a hundred yards, when he dropped it, and it fell at the back of the small bird aviary ; Travis, the keeper of the aviary, saw and heard it fall, and on picking it up found the young cygnet still alive, but it was too much injured to recover.

When eggs are about to be hatched they are much lighter than when newly laid, and no doubt when the rook thrust his bill into the egg some fluid escaped, thus rendering it lighter still.

CHAPTER XI.

SUPPLEMENTARY NOTES.

THE BREEDING OF SEVERAL SPECIES OF BIRDS.

NOTES ON THE BREEDING OF SEVERAL SPECIES OF BIRDS
IN THE SOCIETY'S GARDENS DURING THE YEAR 1865.

THE year 1865 was somewhat remarkable, from the
long continuance during the summer and autumn of dry
hot weather; and this probably much influenced the
breeding, and the tendency to breed, among many animals
that have not before reproduced, or shown signs of reproducing, in the Society's Gardens.

Among the birds, perhaps, the most interesting to notice
will be the Sun-Bittern (*Eurypyga helias*). A pair of these
birds were purchased in September 1862, and have always
appeared in good health and condition. Early in the
month of May last they began to show signs of breeding,
by carrying bits of stick, roots of grass, and other materials
about; they were constantly walking round the pond,
evidently in search of materials to compose a nest, and
appeared to try and mix wet dirt with bits of moss, etc.
This suggested the idea of supplying them with wet clay
and mud, which they at once commenced to use. After a
short time they settled to make a nest on the top of a pole
or tree about ten feet from the ground, on which was fixed
an old straw nest. Both birds carried up mud and clay
mixed with bits of straw, roots of grass, etc. The sides of
the nest were raised, and thickly plastered inside with

mud. One morning the keeper Travis came to me with the fragments of a broken egg, which he found on the ground under the place where the nest was, telling me he believed the egg had been dropped by the Sun-Bittern. Upon looking at the fragments I observed that the egg was spotted at the broad end, and that it resembled the egg of a Moor-hen, or perhaps rather the egg of a Wood-cock than any other bird. I felt doubtful of the correctness of Travis's information, the more so as there was in the same aviary a Blue Water-hen, which I strongly suspected to have been the producer of the egg in question. I therefore removed this bird, to prevent any mistake; and in the early part of June Travis again called my attention to the Sun-Bitterns, the female having laid an egg in the nest. I at once went up a ladder to look at it, and found it agree in every respect with the egg already spoken of. The two birds were very attentive, and took turns at incubation, and in twenty-seven days the young bird was hatched (July 9th). On the following day I ventured to look at the young bird, and in a few seconds made a rough sketch of it, as I was fearful that the inspection of a stranger might interfere with and perhaps cause the old birds to desert the young one. It is certainly one of the prettiest young birds I ever saw. It is thickly covered with fine short tufts of down, and much resembles the young of the Plovers and Snipes, with this addition, that the head and body was thinly covered with rather longer hairs than are to be seen in the former-mentioned birds. The young bird remained in the nest and was fed regularly by both parents, the food consisting principally of small live fish, a few insects, etc. The mode of taking its food was somewhat peculiar: it did not gape and call or utter any cry like most nestlings; but as soon as the old birds flew upon the nest with the food in their bills, the young one snapped or pecked it from them and swallowed it at once. The young bird remained in the nest twenty-one days, by which time its wings were sufficiently grown to enable it to fly to the ground. It was there fed as before, and never afterwards returned to the nest; it grew quickly, and at the end of two months was indistinguishable from the old birds. Early in August the old birds began to repair the nest, and added a fresh lining of mud and clay, and at the end of August laid another egg. The male bird now appeared to attend to the duties of incubation with much greater care than his partner, who fed the now nearly full-grown young one; they, however, managed to hatch this second young bird on September 28. But as both the old birds were seen feeding the *first* young one more frequently than the *second*, the keeper Travis was afraid the little fellow might starve from their neglect; so he frequently went up the ladder to the nest and fed the young one. It readily took food from his hand; and in this way both the young birds have arrived at maturity, and now appear perfectly adult.

In remarking upon these interesting facts, I may observe that the egg differs considerably from the eggs of any true Ardeine bird with which I am acquainted in its spotted and blotched markings, and in this character bears a strong resemblance to those of the Plovers and Snipes; nor are these the only resemblances, its downy covering, colour, and markings leading one to regard it as allied to these forms. The great difference, however, in habit is remarkable, as in all the Plovers and Snipes the young birds run about as soon as they are hatched or a few hours afterwards, and, as far as I know, find their own food. We have, therefore, in the inactivity of this bird in the nest, and in its being fed by the parent bird, an Ardeine character. I must not omit to call attention to another form, the

228

genus *Rhynchœa*, or Painted Snipe. I am inclined to believe, from some of the habits of this genus, that it may have affinities with *Eurypyga;* but I have not been able to determine this, not having the materials (perfect specimens) to examine. That *Eurypyga* is less of a Heron than has generally been thought must now be admitted, and the spotted egg, together with the downy young one, abundantly shows. I feel, however, certain that this bird has its nearest ally in the Kagu (*Rhinochetus jubatus*), as has been already stated.[1]

Since writing the foregoing, Mr. Bates has called my attention to his account of the habits of this bird, published in vol. i. p. 82 of the *Naturalist on the River Amazon,* from which I copy the following :—

" I was told by the Indians that it (the Sun-Bittern) builds in trees, and that the nest, which is made of clay, is beautifully constructed." [2]

The Pin-tailed Sand-Grouse (*Pterocles alchata*) have repeatedly laid eggs in the aviary and made frequent attempts to hatch them without success until the last summer, when two eggs were laid about the 4th of August, in a small depression in the sand in the aviary, and on the 29th of August one young bird was hatched, from which the figure [3] was taken a day or two afterwards. The young bird was tolerably active, but much less so than the young of a fowl, pheasant, or partridge, probably owing to the shortness of its legs; it was at the same time strong and vigorous, and grew to a considerable size, but died before it reached maturity.

[1] See *Proceedings of Zoological Society,* 1862, p. 218.
[2] Consult also the notes on the nidification of this bird by the well-known French naturalist Goudot, in the *Revue Zoologique,* 1843, p. 1 ; and the figure of the egg given in the *Magasin de Zoologie,* 1843.—ED.
[3] See *Proceedings of Zoological Society,* 1866, p. 68.

Of other birds that have laid eggs, and some of which have hatched for the first time, I may mention the following :—

Hatched.

Nicobar Pigeon (*Calœnas nicobarica*).
Lineated Pheasant (*Euplocamus lineatus*).
Spotted-sided Finch (*Amadina lathami*).
Variegated Sheldrake (*Tadorna variegata*).

Laid eggs.

Scarlet Ibis (*Ibis rubra*).
Saras Crane (*Grus antigone*).
Hardwick's Francolin (*Galloperdix lunulosa*).
Red-headed Pigeon (*Erythyœnas pulcherrima*).
Guira Cuckoo (*Guira piririgua*).
Sœmmering's Pheasant (*Phasianus sœmmeringii*).
Cinereous Vulture (*Vultur monachus*).
Long-billed Butcherbird (*Barita destructor*).
Wattled Fruit-Pigeon (*Carpophaga microcera*).

THE NICOBAR PIGEON.
(*CALŒNAS NICOBARICA.*)

A pair of these birds took possession, in the early part of June, of an artificial nest made of straw and sticks, and laid one white egg; the nest was ten or twelve feet from the ground. The period of incubation was twenty-eight days. The young bird when hatched was black, or nearly so, and naked; the down-feathers grew slowly; and the tail-feathers, which are white in the adult birds, are black in the young one, and still continue so. This led to the young bird being described a few years ago as a second species.[1]

[1] *Columba gouldiæ*, Gray, *Ind. Zool.*, pl. 37 ; *Calœnas gouldiæ*, auct.

GUIRA CUCKOO.

(GUIRA PIRIRIGUA.)

One of these birds during the early part of the summer dropped or laid an egg on the ground in the aviary; but unfortunately the specimen was broken by the fall, or by the birds themselves or their companions. Sufficient pieces, however, were saved to enable a good drawing to be made; and it is interesting to find this bird lays an egg that agrees completely with the egg of the Anis (*Crotophaga*), to which it is doubtless closely allied.

SCARLET IBIS.

(IBIS RUBRA.)

A female of this bird has been in the aviary with other birds since March 1864; and notwithstanding that there were three of her own species in the same aviary, she paired with a white Ibis in June last. These two birds built a nest upon the ground, composed principally of twigs, pieces of birch-broom, sticks, etc., upon which was laid an egg of a pale green, thickly spotted and blotched with a dirty-brown colour. The egg was constantly attended by both birds, and the nest was raised considerably under the egg by the constant addition of materials, the egg being rolled from side to side as the sticks, etc., were placed under it. This raising the nest continued for about ten days, after which time the birds began to incubate, taking turns on the egg. After sitting four weeks, the egg was found to be addled, and was removed in order to save the specimen.

231

NOTES ON THE BREEDING OF SEVERAL SPECIES OF BIRDS
IN THE SOCIETY'S GARDENS DURING THE YEAR 1867.

The following list of species of birds bred during the
year 1867 will be found to contain several that I believe
have never been before recorded as having reproduced in
the Society's Gardens; and some of the facts noted are of
considerable importance with reference to the habits and
affinities of the species to which they belong :—

Impeyan Pheasant.	Rufous Tinamou.*
Pallas' Eared Pheasant.	Common Cassowary.*
Japanese Pheasant.	Black Kite.*
Barred-tailed Pheasant.*	Black-crested Cardinal.*
Cheer Pheasant.	Turquoisine Parrakeet.
Swinhoe's Pheasant.*	Dusky Duck.
Lineated Pheasant.	Bahama Duck.
Purple Kaleege.	Carolina Duck.
Black-backed Kaleege.	Ruddy Sheldrake.
Bankiva Jungle-fowl.	New Zealand Sheldrake.
Talegalla lathami.	Ruddy-headed Goose.
Sun-Bittern (*Eurypyga*).	Ashy-headed Goose.

Those marked thus (*) have bred for the first time.

RUFOUS TINAMOU.

(*RHYNCHOTIS RUFESCENS.*)

I made some further remarks in 1867 on the breeding
of the Rufous Tinamou in the Society's aviaries, which
had taken place for the first time this year. I believed
this to be the first instance recorded of any species of
this genus breeding in captivity; the interesting fact of
the male bird performing the office of incubation was
supposed to be likewise hitherto unrecorded.

A more detailed account of the number of eggs laid, period of incubation, and particulars of other birds which have bred in the Society's Gardens during the present year was promised at a later meeting.

The most remarkable of these is perhaps the Rufous Tinamou (*Rhynchotis rufescens*), of which species I am able to state that the male bird incubates, and that one male will attend to two or more females.[1] The number of eggs laid by two birds between May 20 and September 24 was eighty-five; out of this number, upwards of twenty birds were hatched. Many more would have been hatched had it not been for the parent birds, who were guilty of frequently eating the eggs before the young birds had arrived at a perfect state. It was only by removing the eggs to the care of common hens that we succeeded in hatching and rearing sixteen or eighteen young birds.

The male bird would take to the eggs when ten or twelve were laid, and after about fifteen days' incubation was found breaking them up and eating the contents, which in many instances were imperfectly developed young. In no instance did the female attempt to incubate. The period of incubation was twenty-one days. The chick much resembles the young of a rhea, and, from its small size, looks and walks about like a little *Apteryx*; in fact, the keepers and others who saw Tinamous for the first time thought they were the young of the former bird. They fed upon worms, chopped meat, boiled eggs, etc.

Of the several species above mentioned some have bred in the Gardens many times; but as a few of them have bred for the first time, I beg leave to call particular attention to these.

Perhaps the most valuable addition to the list is the

---

[1] The eggs are laid on the ground in a hollow formed by the male bird in the sand or mould. No other nest is made.

breeding of the Barred-tailed Pheasant (*Phasianus reevesii*). It is most remarkable that the birds arrived on June 22 and commenced laying immediately, and four birds were hatched on August 10. Another singular instance of late breeding occurred with a fine pair of imported Versicolor Pheasants, which arrived from Japan on July 27, and three young birds were produced on September 20. These birds were considered useless and not likely to live; but two of them (hens) are now strong and healthy birds, having perfectly got over their moult during the coldest part of this winter.

Of the *Crossoptilon* or Eared Pheasant of Pallas we have reared nine fine birds, the second hatch, having lost by the gapes the first brood of seven. With reference to this species, I may remark that these birds breed when only one year old. At the first moult the young birds assume the adult plumage, the male and female being exactly alike. They are remarkably hardy, and extremely tame.

In concluding, I beg to call attention to my paper published in the Society's *Proceedings* for 1862, on the habits and affinities of the Kagu (*Rhinochetus jubatus*). I there gave it as my opinion that this bird was more nearly allied to *Eurypyga* than to any other bird. Again, in the Society's *Proceedings* in January 1866, at pp. 77, 78, I stated, after speaking of the egg and young bird :—

"That *Eurypyga* is less a heron than has generally been thought must now be admitted, and the spotted egg and downy young one abundantly shows. I feel, however, certain that this bird has its nearest ally in the Kagu (*Rhinochetus jubatus*), as already stated." [1] Having stated this so long since, it is with great pleasure I have this opportunity to offer a most striking proof of the correctness of these views, one of the kagus at the Gardens

[1] See *Proceedings of Zoological Society*, 1862, p. 218.

having had the kindness to lay a very fine egg, which I placed before the meeting. This egg was rendered useless for hatching immediately after it was laid, by being pecked by the bird that laid it, or by some other bird in the aviary. It is, however, a very fine and well-marked specimen, and in many particulars closely resembles the egg of *Eurypyga*, but perhaps exhibits rather more of the form of the eggs of the Cranes (*Grus*) than of the rails and plovers. Moreover the lively movements of the bird as described by me in 1862 fully support its affinities with the cranes, and show, I think, that it has less affinity to the Ardeine group.

SUN-BIRD.

(*EURYPYGA HELIAS.*)

In August 1869 the Sun-bird produced two young; they are very prettily marked, its quaint downy plumage begirt with so much frill and lacework, for the stripes and spottings give it quite this character. A curious circumstance in the nidification of the Sun-bird is that a considerable interval elapses between the laying of the eggs. The keeper states a single egg was hatched before the second was laid, and that the old birds then left the incubating process to be performed by the heat of the youngster. This fact, however, may require further observation. A good figure of the chick of this bird is given in the *Proceedings of Zoological Society*, 1866, with notes.

BIRDS LIVING WITHOUT WATER.

A few words about doves, who are generally regarded
as the emblem of love, devotion, and affection. I know
the danger of approaching or offering to disturb this
long-cherished belief, for who that has heard the mournful,
melancholy, and plaintive *Who-who-who*, or *Coo-coo-coo*, can
doubt the sincerity of the utterer, and not be led to
believe that the disconsolate bird had lost its partner and
was inconsolable ? From early dawn till dusk this monotonous and dismal sound disturbs our rest, and produces
in many persons a feeling of painful distress.

We sympathize with this apparently forlorn, distressed,
and beautiful bird, whose voice and soft wailing so resembles the lamentations so well known to *our* species,
that it seems impossible such sounds can represent
anything but the most acute mental suffering.

I am almost afraid to say that the great amount of
kind feeling, sympathy, and regard bestowed upon doves
in general is wasted upon the undeserving. To all keepers
of doves and pigeons the pugnacious disposition exhibited
by birds of this class is well known, although the means
of inflicting injury upon each other is somewhat limited
in consequence of the comparative want of weapons. Not
being armed with claws, spurs, and a powerful beak
like most gallinaceous birds, they not only do battle with
a somewhat weak bill, but strike each other with the wing
joint. The heavy blows thus inflicted by the aid of the
powerful pectoral muscles would perfectly astonish any
one who received it, and although they seldom kill each
other, they are prone to quarrel, fight, and keep up a very
determined disagreement. Doves and pigeons form a very
well-defined family. Naturalists have no difficulty in

saying at a glance that any individual specimen that may be brought forward belongs to this family, for, like the parrots and parrakeets, they do not appear to run by slow digressions into other families, but are by such unmistakable characters distinguished from every other family of birds.

I am again tempted to say a few words about the remarkable condition and power of many species of birds living and thriving without water. With regard to the parrots, all the known species can be kept for years without water, and continue in the most robust health and beautiful feather condition. At the present moment may be seen in the parrot house of the Zoological Gardens, a Greater Vasa Parrakeet, presented by the late Mr. Charles Telfair, July 25, 1830, therefore this bird has lived in the Society's possession fifty-one years [1] without being supplied with water. As the bird was quite adult when received, it is impossible to say what was the age of this individual. It must be borne in mind that the food supplied to birds of this kind is pretty moist, such as boiled Indian corn and scalded bread, fruit, vegetables, etc. But the little parrakeets that are brought by thousands from Australia can and do live and thrive without water or moist food, for it has been found they are stronger, and arrive in splendid condition, if kept upon good canary seed only.

I have lately seen a large collection of Indian quails in the very finest state of health and plumage, that have had no water or moist food of any kind since they left India; the only food supplied to this lot of birds for months has been dry millet seed, upon which they have become fat and in beautiful plumage. No greater proof is required to show the healthy state of a bird than its plumage, for a bird that is weak or sickly grows its

[1] This was written in 1881.—ED.

feathers badly. Falconers know this better than most
people, for a falcon with badly-grown wing-feathers is useless to the falconers, and at the time the primary feathers
of the wings of falcons are growing, should the bird be sick
or refuse to feed, a distinct mark or bar is produced across
the feather, and these defects in the feathers are called by
falconers *hunger traces*, and the feathers are apt to break
off at this point, rendering the flight of the bird weak and
consequently useless for the purpose of the chase. A very
similar case is observable in the nails of persons who have
suffered from fever ; the nails cease to grow, or grow so
imperfectly for a time, that upon recovery the patient
finds a distinct line or ridge across the nails, showing that
some obstruction had occurred and arrested the proper
development of these parts.

I am quite at a loss to account for certain peculiarity
of habits in many of that numerous class of animals
known as rodents, or gnawing animals, to which the rats,
mice, rabbits, hares, squirrels, etc., belong.

Why some of these animals are so harmless, and, when
caught wild, if handled carefully, do not bite, such as the
dormouse, short-tailed field-mouse, most of the cavies, and
others, while, on the contrary, the hamsters, the squirrels,
rats, etc., never fail to make a lasting impression upon the
hands of their captors, if they only have the chance, for a
bite from a full-grown hamster or rat is about as painful
a wound for its size as can be well imagined, I fail to
understand.

Another very remarkable thing connected with the
Rodentia is the extraordinary difference or conditions of
their young at birth. Many are born naked and blind,
and remain in this condition in the nest for twelve or
fourteen days, such as rabbits, rats, mice, etc.

At the same time, we find that many other rodents are

born in the most perfect state, covered with fur, their eyes
open, and able to run about and feed almost as soon as
born. The common hare and guinea-pig, for example,
are in perfectly developed condition at birth.

PRESERVING EGGS OF BIRDS.

I believe there are but few persons who are quite
satisfied by seeing and examining the dried skins and
feathers of birds.

The great desire, therefore, to see, or to possess, in a
living state, these wonderful and generally beautiful creatures, has led me to consider the possibility of preserving
their eggs for a sufficiently long period to allow of their
being brought from distant places and afterwards hatched.
We might thus be able to obtain some of the more
delicate species, and many perhaps that a long sea-voyage
would prevent our obtaining by any other means.

The mere keeping fresh and sweet the eggs of birds has
been accomplished in many ways, for instance, they will
keep, for a long period, imbedded in lime and water, or in
fat or salt; but by these means the vitality is destroyed.
It appears to me, therefore, to be essentially necessary,
not only to prevent evaporation, but also to keep the
texture and surface of the shell in its pure and perfect
condition. To accomplish this object the eggs must be
newly laid, or nearly so, and the following is the best
method of preserving them.

Obtain the gut of any animal whose intestine is large
enough to admit the egg intended to be preserved, and
having carefully cleaned the gut and rendered it free from
fat, dry it as much as possible in powdered chalk or other
earthy matter. Pass the egg into the gut, tying it close

to the shell at both ends of the egg, and hang it up in a *cool, dry place* until it is quite dry. Two, three, or more eggs can be tied in the same gut like a string of beads, or they can be tied separately. When thoroughly dry, they may be packed up in a box with oats, wheat, or any *other dry grain or seeds*, until the box is quite full. The object in having the box full is for the greater convenience of turning the eggs. This is accomplished by turning the box bottom upwards, which should be done occasionally. Thus the whole of the eggs may be effectually turned with very little trouble. The eggs thus packed must be kept in a dry, cool place, and ought not to be taken out or unpacked before the means are at hand for hatching them. Upon wishing to place them under a hen, or otherwise, if the dry gut be cut with a sharp knife, it will peel off without in any way injuring the shell of the egg.

I was successful in hatching and rearing the young from some eggs kept three months in this manner, and I have no doubt that, under favourable circumstances, they may be kept for a longer period.

"Among the numerous subjects of importance now engaging the attention of the English farmers may be particularly instanced those of poultry rearing and production of eggs.

"In a recent article in the *Scientific American* the subject of the preservation of eggs is alluded to as follows :—

"The question, 'How can eggs be preserved for market ?' just now engages the attention of many of our readers. The following will prove of timely interest to many :—

"In the common 'liming' process a tight barrel is half filled with cold water, into which is stirred slacked lime and salt in the proportion of about one half-pound each for every pail or bucket of water. Some dealers use no

salt, and others add a small quantity of nitre—one quarter-
pound to the half-barrel of pickle. Into this the eggs,
which must be perfectly fresh and sound, are let down
with a dish, when they settle to the bottom, small end
down. The eggs displace the liquid, so that when the
barrel is full of eggs it is also full of the pickle. Eggs
thus pickled, if kept in a cool place, will ordinarily keep
good for several months. Long storage in this liquid, however, is apt to make the shells brittle, and impart a limy
taste to their contents. This may be in a great measure
avoided by anointing the egg all over with lard before
putting in the pickle. Eggs thus prepared are said to
keep perfectly for six months or more when stored in a
cool cellar.

"A much better method of storing eggs is the following:—Having selected perfectly fresh eggs, put them, a
dozen or more at a time, into a small willow basket, and
immerse this for five seconds in boiling water containing
about 5 lbs. of common brown sugar per gallon of
water. Place the eggs immediately after on trays to dry.
The scalding water causes the formation of a thin skin of
hard albumen next the inner surface of the shell, the
sugar effectually closing all the pores of the latter.

"The cool eggs are then packed, small end down, in
a suitable mixture of one measure of good charcoal,
finely powdered, and two measures of dry bran. Eggs thus
stored have been found perfectly fresh and unaltered after
six months.

"A French authority gives the following:—' Melt four
ounces of clear beeswax in a porcelain dish over a gentle
fire, and stir in eight ounces of olive oil. Let the resulting
solution of wax in oil cool somewhat, then dip the fresh
eggs one by one into it so as to coat every part of the
shell. A momentary dip is sufficient, all excess of the

mixture being wiped off with a cotton cloth. The oil is absorbed in the shell, the wax hermetically closing all the pores. It is claimed that eggs thus treated and packed away in powdered charcoal in a cool place have been found after two years as fresh and palatable as when newly laid.'

"Paraffin, which melts to a thin liquid at a temperature below the boiling of water, and has the advantage of being odourless, tasteless, harmless, and cheap, can be advantageously substituted for the wax and oil, and used in a similar manner.

"Thus coated and put into the lime pickle the eggs may be safely stored for many months; in charcoal, under favourable circumstances, for a year or more.

"Dry salt is frequently recommended as a good preservative packing for stored eggs, but practical experience has shown that salt alone is but little better than dry bran, especially if stored in a damp place or exposed to humid air.

"A mixture of eight measures of bran with one of powdered quicklime makes an excellent packing for eggs in transportation.

'Water glass—silicate of soda—has recently been used in Germany for rendering the shells of eggs non-porous. A small quantity of the clear syrupy solution is smeared over the entire surface of the shell. On drying a thin, hard, glassy film remains, which serves as an admirable protection and substitute for wax, oil, gums, etc. Eggs thus coated and stored in charcoal powder, or a mixture of charcoal and bran, would keep a very long time.

"In storing eggs in charcoal the latter should be fresh and perfectly dry. If the eggs are not stored when quite fresh they will not keep under any circumstances. A broken egg stored with sound ones will sometimes endanger the whole lot. In packing the small end of the egg should be placed downward ; if in charcoal or other powder they must be packed so that the shell of one egg does not touch that of another, the interspaces being filled with the powder.

" Under all circumstances stored eggs should be kept in as cool a place as possible. Frequent change of temperature must also be avoided."—*Land and Water*, July 1881.

PART III.—REPTILES AND FISHES.

CHAPTER I.

THE HABITS OF SNAKES.

REPRODUCTION OF SNAKES.

IT has been generally stated that the mode of reproduction of serpents was of two kinds.

The viperine serpents were supposed to produce the young alive, and all the harmless species to deposit their eggs, afterwards to be hatched by the warmth of their surroundings. These suppositions were at variance with facts, of which we have now proof by breeding various serpents in the new reptile-house. Some of the harmless ones have produced their young alive, and, on the other hand, some of the poisonous species have deposited eggs. The following are good examples illustrating the above facts :—

Among the harmless serpents that produce young alive may be mentioned—

Boa constrictor (South America) produced, on June 30, 1877, between twenty and thirty living young ones in the Zoological Society's reptile-house.

Also hybrids between a male pale-headed tree boa (*Epicrates angulifer*) and the yellow snake (*Chilobothrus inornatus*). These snakes bred twice, August 30, 1878, having three living, and September 9, 1871, two only.

The Moccasin snakes (*Tripodonotus fasciatus*) bred repeatedly, having living young in large numbers.

247

The seven-banded snake, *Tripodonotus lebris,* produced living young many times also.

The poisonous serpents, puff-adder and rattlesnakes, always produce their young alive, as does also the British viper. The poisonous Egyptian cobra (*Naia haje*) and the great snake-eating snake (*Ophiophagus elaps*), or great cobra, always, so far as I know, lay eggs.

The common English grass snake always lays eggs, and most commonly in heated manure-heaps.

I have never heard of any species of snake that bring forth young and produce eggs also.

POISONOUS SNAKES AND SNAKE POISON.

EGYPTIAN COBRA (*Naia haje*) AND PUFF-ADDERS (*Clotho arietans*).

About these reptiles, and in fact all snakes, poisonous or otherwise, there always hang a great dread and mystery. This is natural, and will ever continue to be so, in spite of all the teaching, the advance of knowledge, and of anything that can be said to the contrary.

It must be admitted that the first record of our species contains the earliest indication of the evil and bad consequences that followed the track of the serpent, and wisely should we take the lesson thus set before us that the infant be taught to dread those animals, for the danger of death would be constantly attendant upon children not so warned and not taught to avoid handling or catching creatures that they would be sure to meet with in all warm climates during their childhood. If, at an early period, they become aware of the danger, the fear, once thoroughly implanted, will continue with more or less intensity during their lives. It may seem unwise to those who have made the subject a study, or have become acquainted with the serpents that are perfectly harmless, that the rest of the world should have a constant and a perpetual fear of all serpents, but it is quite out of the power of such persons to overcome the terror and dread they have felt during a lifetime, at the thought of meeting this supposed enemy of mankind. Moreover, it would be injudicious to attempt to alter a natural law; it is far safer to teach the avoiding of all serpents, as the difficulty of knowing the poisonous from the harmless kinds is far beyond our power of teaching to the mass of the human race.

It is, however, consoling to know how few people are injured or killed by these creatures, and that they are not to be looked upon as anything like so great a plague as most persons are apt to think; and, unless great carelessness or wilful folly is displayed, the danger of travelling or living in countries that abound in poisonous snakes is not great. These animals generally endeavour to retreat and hide themselves, or lie perfectly still, on the approach of man; so that it is only when an accidental injury is done to the snake that the animal defends or strikes at its opponent. In no instance will a poisonous serpent come forth to attack a man or an animal of equal size; all the poisonous snakes are of small size, in no case has any poisonous serpent been found large enough to swallow a full-grown hare, and therefore it is unlikely these creatures would seize or bite, except in defence, an animal much larger than one suited for their food, which is always swallowed whole.

From long experience I find that poisonous viperine serpents are, as a rule, sluggish. The cobra and the more slender species alone are active, and most frequently escape rapidly on the approach of man. The old stories of fascination are pretty nearly exploded, and the marvellous swindling of snake-charmers is slowly giving way, but so firmly do many hold to the belief in the power of the snake-charmer, that it is quite dangerous to throw out a too positive statement. Nevertheless it is known to the writer that serpents in his possession, well armed with their perfect fangs and deadly poison, were offered to several of the professed snake-charmers of Egypt, who would only consent to perform with them after removing their fangs, or by a careful sewing up of the mouths of the serpents, a practice common among these people. Few persons dare to touch or interfere with these charmers or their snakes, but I have been present during the performance of a great variety of tricks, and afterwards examined the unfortunate snakes. I found some of them with their mouths closely stitched up, and others without fangs, these having been carefully removed by their captors, this being done before they commence the exhibition of the so-called charming.

But there is this to be said, that snake-charmers are doubtless taught the art of handling and managing snakes from their early childhood, and are sometimes, in so doing, slightly wounded and suffer from the poison. May not this be a kind of inoculation that happens from time to time until the poison takes less effect, and thus renders the person accustomed to it almost proof against it? This is known to be the case with many other poisons. The bites of mosquitoes poison those long used to them less than fresh comers, who, after a year or two, care but little about them, although at first they were driven almost mad by the pain and annoyance.

Much has been written and said about the cure of snake poison, but great misapprehension exists respecting the subject. In the first place the difficulty of knowing if the individual wounded is really poisoned at all, and, if so, the amount of poison received in the wound. The terror with which most persons would be seized on being wounded by a serpent is almost sufficient to cause death by the shock to the nerves, and supposing a said remedy to be at hand, the person who used it and did not feel any bad symptoms afterwards would naturally believe he had been cured. Now it happens that a full-grown rabbit is killed by the poison of a cobra in seven seconds after being struck. The chance of finding a remedy in such a case is perfectly ridiculous.

A fact not generally known or believed is that the bite of one poisonous serpent will destroy another of its own species. This has been observed more than once, the injured animal died after many days' suffering from convulsions and tetanic twitchings. Although they frequently bite each other, if kept and fed together, it rarely happens that they are poisoned. Another common mistake is to suppose that the food is always killed by poisoning, as these animals sometimes catch and swallow their prey alive, apparently without a wound. No doubt, however, the most frequent or general mode is to kill by wounding with the poison fangs the animals before they feed upon them.

FEEDING SNAKES WITH LIVING ANIMALS.

The lack of arrivals has afforded a short respite, and taking advantage of the opportunity we beg to remark upon a recent investigation that has taken place at the Liverpool Police-court before Mr. Mansfield.[1] The charge was against Mr. Edmonds, proprietor of Wombwell's menagerie, for cruelty to rabbits given as food to the serpents in the collection of wild animals. Considering the amount of

[1] See *Morning Post*, December 30, 1869.

trash brought forward day after day upon the subject of cruelty we are induced to say a few words upon this subject.

What is cruelty? Acts of cruelty are committed in various forms: a single harsh or untimed word uttered under some circumstances oftentimes inflicts a wound far more painful and more difficult to heal than gaping sabre-cuts, and thus a cruel word may be a death-blow. Yet we must kill to live, and ask in all humanity to kill quickly with the least amount of suffering and pain, but with ourselves are we not shocked when cruel death strikes without warning those we love, which we imagine an act of cruelty?

One of the witnesses upon the occasion referred to above was Mr. Dobie, whose experience and knowledge of feeding snakes seem on a par with the ploughboy's knowledge of chemistry. The idea of distinguishing a tame from a wild rabbit is rather amusing, and the reason why it is more cruel to one than the other very obscure. That the valuable time of a justice of the peace should be taken up by such a useless inquiry, to the neglect of more important and pressing duties, is not to be commented upon. The following is a letter which appeared in a contemporary:—

"SERPENT FEEDING AT A MENAGERIE.

" To the Editor of the *Manchester Examiner and Times.*

" SIR,—In your paper of to-day I noticed an account of the prosecution, before the Liverpool magistrate, of a small menagerie proprietor for giving live rabbits to serpents. Part of the defence was that it is the customary practice in all zoological collections. As proprietor of the largest travelling collection in the world, in which there are more snakes and reptiles exhibited than are to be found in all the other travelling collections put together, I never resort to this barbarous practice, but feed them on fresh meat—it must be fresh—and not only do they live but thrive wonderfully, as can be seen in the case of the large *Boa constrictor*, which is now thicker than an ordinary man's arm.

"Wm. MANDERS, Proprietor of the Grand National Star Menagerie.
"*Huddersfield Fair, December* 29, 1869."

This statement is unworthy of credit, and so utterly contemptible that it is only noticed to be condemned.

It may be called to mind that some time since a paragraph appeared in the papers emanating from the same establishment, announcing the escape of rattlesnakes said to have killed the bison and other animals in the collection, etc., etc., the whole of which was a vile fabrication intended as a sensational puff.

The natural food of all serpents is living animals, and if we are to have and keep these creatures for the advancement of knowledge we must comply with their natural habits.

It is true that serpents will by chance take a dead animal, or a part of one, and swallow it, but as a rule they would die of starvation if it were attempted to keep them upon flesh. There are many serpents in captivity that would not take any food other than living animals, be they rats, mice, sparrows, frogs, rabbits, guinea-pigs, pigeons, or ducks; and that is about the extent of animals used for the purpose. Accidents will happen to men and other animals; *we* take our chance in the struggle for life; the serpent kills its prey, as a rule—quickly, as such it is evident was intended by the means provided in its structure, and should it by accident fail to accomplish this act perfectly, who shall we dare to blame? The strength of some animals can only be supported by the destruction of other animals, and with appetites and desire for animal food which render them fierce and savage, they with fiendish teeth and claws tear down and devour without mercy; yet who can say this is not right?

Then let us notice the wisdom, in all creation, of the means provided for taking life; the largest of our animal destroyers, lions and tigers, etc., kill quickly by attacking with their powerful weapons the most vital parts, and the animals destroyed are those most easily captured.

Wild beasts, like tame or domesticated animals, grow old and weak, and the old lion, like the old stag, must fall when he can no longer defend himself and drive off others of his species that trespass upon the ground he once was proud to claim; far better so to die than linger on a miserable object and slowly perish. Witness the weasel tribe biting at the neck and throat to find out the blood-vessels and spinal cord, the eagle, falcon, and other birds of prey that clutch their victims in the grasp of their powerful claws, pierce through the heart or other vital organs and thus destroy life. We thereby learn a lesson from nature that we cannot improve upon. The falcon swoops upon the harmless dove, which faints and dies without a struggle, and from its warm and bleeding breast the falcon makes his morning meal.

> Sometimes he strikes upon the pointed bill
> Of one who, like himself, can kill,
> Thus striving hard to live, he dies;
> Sad fate for fools and men most wise.

In the whole series of living creatures the everlasting destruction of one form of life for the support of another is discernible.

Now, as to the cruelty of one animal taking the life of another, we have not to answer for the nature of the animals that prey upon others—they follow a law stronger and more perfect than all the laws made by Acts of Parliament put together, a law that it is wrong on our part to complain against; we must therefore receive and abide by that which is unalterable. Let us avoid cruelty

in whatever form it may be found, but if the use can be
shown to exist of having serpents brought before us as a
means of advancing knowledge, let us avoid inflicting
upon them the most cruel death that is known, viz. that
of starvation, by withholding from them that food most
suited and most natural for their existence. We assuredly
should be guilty of this most cruel and unnecessary act,
by attempting to force them to live upon food unnatural,
and consequently unwholesome and unfitted to their
existence. No wild beast can be compared for cruelty to
animals with the human savage; the acts of torture to
which the animal creation is sometimes subjected by him,
would surely be incredible except to those who have had
to witness the ferocious treatment animals receive in
countries far removed from civilization. To relate any
one of the acts of atrocity which are known to us would
be to shock and disgust our readers; suffice it to say that
things are done without the slightest thought or the
least idea of their being wrong, the little care for life or
for the sense of pain, the total want of sympathy or kindly
feeling, are akin to other wants and deficiencies that
render a hard and precarious existence callous and quite
indifferent to almost every kind of suffering.

The love for animals of all kinds, and the very laudable
anxiety to prevent them being cruelly treated should be
encouraged by all; at the same time let us not forget the
helpless and suffering of our own species. At the present
moment in this country the alarming increase of human
misery demands of all thinking persons, that they should
come forward and assist by the most untiring energy and
devotion, in aiding the suffering thousands which are to
be found in this metropolis, nor can we forget that the
whole country, unhappily, abounds with the most frightful
and almost universal state of want among the poorer

classes, whose sufferings we are called upon to lessen, and attending to which will not prevent our good aid being at the same time bestowed upon the wrongs inflicted upon the lower animals.

Let all cases of wanton and unnecessary cruelty be visited upon their perpetrators with due severity; do not let us descend to trifling and paltry attempts to show our zeal in any case.

There is no doubt but that the people who are cruel to the lower animals are, as a rule, the greatest cowards in existence.

CONVULSIONS IN SNAKES.

Convulsions occur not only in animate but also in inanimate bodies, in the earth, in the air and in the water. These disturbances are not common in the lower animals, at least I have but rarely witnessed them in reptiles, but serpents have suffered, the result sometimes of bites from the venomous species. I have seen some of the non-venomous kinds in convulsions which have lasted for some days, the twisting, twirling and twitching of the body accompanied by strong contortions have been quite distressing to witness. Although the reptile sometimes recovers from the attacks it more often dies. I am quite unable to account for the reptile being so afflicted, as previous to the attack the snake had fed well and was apparently in good health and condition.

Poisonous and other serpents when startled move suddenly and set the end of the tail in rapid motion, exactly in the same manner as is done by the Rattle-snake, therefore, if provided with the rattle the same vibratory sound would be produced. I have observed

[1] *Land and Water*, January 8, 1870, p. 25.

this motion in the Black Water-Viper and also in Say's harmless snake, both found in North America. Now these creatures could not have learnt the habit from Rattlesnakes notwithstanding they live in the same country. This is a matter for further scientific research.

THE NEW BRITISH SNAKE.

SMALL CROWNED SMOOTH SNAKE.

(CORONELLA LÆVIS.)

A minute description of the size and colour of this snake would fail to distinguish it from the viper, as both these species vary greatly in size and colour. The markings, the general appearance, and form and size of the head are the best characters to attend to; in general appearance it much more closely resembles the viper than the common ringed snake (*Natrix torquata*), but may at once be known from the viper by the imperfect V on the top of the head, and instead of a single dark zigzag line down the centre of the back, as in the viper, there are two rows of dark spots down the back; the head is also much shorter, smaller, and rounder than the head of the viper.

It was on the morning of August 24, 1862, I saw, for the first time, one of these reptiles, Mr. Fenton having stopped me as I was driving along the road in the Regent's Park, and, taking from his pocket what I then thought was a viper, asked me if I would accept it for the Zoological Gardens. I confess I felt in fear of its bite, until Mr. Fenton held it in his hand, and allowed it to bite his finger several times. I then examined its mouth, and saw that its teeth were like the teeth of the harmless snakes, the poison fangs not being present. Having perfectly satisfied myself upon this point, I handled it, but could not help observing that this snake was much more fierce than any common snake; it bit me several times, but without any injury to the skin, in consequence of the shortness of its teeth. Mr. Fenton's opinion of the origin of this snake was at that time stated to me; he said he believed it to be a *hybrid* between a *viper* and a *common snake.* This led me to call the attention of Dr. Gunther, Mr. Buckland, and others to the subject, which soon proved our new animal to be a well-known continental species, and Mr. Buckland at once set to work to learn all that was known, or could be ascertained, respecting its occurrence in England. The result of Mr. Buckland's energetic action has brought to light no less than fourteen individuals of this reptile that may fairly be considered British specimens. And, doubtless, many more will follow, now that the subject has been brought to notice. It is by no means surprising that this snake has so long passed unnoticed, considering its near resemblance to the viper, and considering also how few persons are inclined closely to examine such creatures.

To say that serpents, large and small, have at all times, and in all countries, been regarded with fear, is not sufficient to account for the almost universal dislike and abhorrence in which they are held. The true cause of this instinctive dread doubtless arises from the real danger that attends the too near approach to these reptiles, many of them being provided with the most deadly of poisons. And the knowledge required to distinguish these from those which are harmless, will at all times prevent their becoming commonly or universally understood. To distinguish the poisonous species from the innoxious is not so easy a matter as sometimes stated, and considerable danger attends examinations to determine to which they belong; the poisonous snakes of Australia fully bear out this point, as their external form and general appearance would indicate that they belong to the snakes that are without poison. In the early-recorded history of our species, the serpent is held up as the symbol of evil; in the hands of the cunning and skilful they become powerful agents to deceive, and impose upon the credulous. Snake-charming, as it is called, is still practised in many countries, and it is quite impossible to remove the superstition that exists in the minds of many intelligent persons upon this subject; the artful and crafty manner in which these designing persons have studied the habits and nature of these reptiles almost exceeds belief. The opportunities I have had of testing the power of some of them (the so-called snake-charmers), convince me that they do not dare handle a freshly-caught cobra, or other poisonous serpent, except in their own peculiar way, and they fear the poisonous bite as much as other people. The rapid action of the poison, in many cases, must satisfy any one who may have the opportunity or desire to investigate the subject, of the danger attending the experiments. It frequently happens that an animal, struck and wounded by the poisonous fangs of a serpent, say, a *puff adder*, *cobra*, or *rattlesnake*, will die in six or seven seconds; with a knowledge of this power, it cannot be a matter of surprise that these animals are regarded with feelings of horror and disgust; the dread of death from such a cause would call forth a natural repugnance towards the whole race; the larger ones are feared on account of their great strength and power, the smaller, from the danger of their poison fangs. Again, the habits of these creatures are not likely to decrease our fear. Many of the most deadly lie concealed just below the surface of the sand, ready to strike a death-blow to the incautious traveller; others lurk and hide in the branches of trees and bushes, from which they dart upon the unwary. The wonderful resemblance in colour they bear to the places in which they are found, renders them difficult to be seen by the unpractised eye. Many species are aquatic, and among these there is reason to believe that many are highly poisonous. This point has been warmly disputed, but doubtless the best authorities assert such to be the case. The power of fascination attributed to these creatures appears quite unfounded, having for many years paid considerable attention to this subject, and having almost unequalled opportunities of forming a correct opinion, I have arrived at this conclusion, not hastily, but with, I trust, a fair and impartial consideration.

CHAPTER II.

SNAKE STORIES.

RETICULATED PYTHON.

(*PYTHON RETICULATA.*)

SOME few years since I was invited to the house of a surgeon, who had just returned from Ceylon, to see a freshly-imported serpent of this species. Upon arriving at the house I found that the doctor was absent and that his wife and maidservant were the only inmates.

Upon mentioning the nature of my visit, I was told that the serpent was in a large box in the greenhouse. I was handed the key of the box and informed that there was no danger in opening it, because the serpent was below wire-netting, and therefore I should be able to see it without the chance of it making its escape.

I accordingly proceeded to the greenhouse, unlocked the box and opened the lid. To my utter astonishment the snake was coiled up on the top of the wire-netting, and with the quickness of lightning darted at me; I had just time enough to seize it by the neck, when it instantly wound itself round my right arm, and I had not the power to disengage myself from the grip this serpent had made upon me. The two women were horrified, and nothing would induce them to come to my assistance. My only chance of getting rid of this powerful brute was by trying to strangle him, to do which, with both hands, I strove my utmost. It appeared to me, at the time, that I should not be able to accomplish my efforts to squeeze his life out.

The constant increase of the pressure he put upon my arm caused me to fear that I should entirely lose the power of my right hand, as I was grasping the brute just below the head with all my strength.

The time appeared to pass very slowly without any visible diminution of its extraordinary grip. However, I felt some relief on finding, after a time, that it was slowly relaxing the pressure, and presently it gradually slid off my arm until its tail touched the ground. So soon as I found the snake sufficiently disengaged from my arm I dropped it into the box apparently more dead than alive. After this I did not consider it worth while to purchase the reptile, although I heard from the owner that it was none the worse for the squeezing I had given it.

This snake was between 8 and 9 ft. long, and about 12 in. in circumference. Since that time I have carefully avoided the embrace of a lively python.

In removing the large serpents in the Society's reptile-house, we have always endeavoured to drive them into a large strong sack, or bag, where they are powerless, and have no chance of getting hold of any one. I should consider a man as lost if he were alone with a large python which could but put one coil only round his neck. He would certainly be strangled if this happened. Many serpents exhibit a great amount of intelligence to those who pet and perfectly understand the mode of handling them, more than most people imagine they are capable of possessing, apart from all tricks of snake-charming.

Many serpents that have been tamed recognize the call of the individual who has been in the habit of feeding and handling them. The reticulated python is, I may say, a semi-domestic serpent which (whilst young) can, when in a wild state, be taken up quietly by any one without the slightest danger to the person handling it, so long as it is not frightened or annoyed.

A wild reticulated python nearly 5 ft. long was carefully picked up in the jungle and placed in the lower part of a bungalow (the dining-room) in which were several water-holes round the floor, and at night it used to wait at these holes and catch the rats or mice which came in. In the day-time it wandered about the garden and house to the annoyance of the cook and boys; at times it was found, to the consternation of the cook, winding its way among the plates, dishes, glasses and crockery on the shelves; but, so long as no one touched it, no mischief occurred.

THE POWER OF CONSTRICTING SERPENTS.

Much sensational nonsense has been written about the strength of serpents and their movements, such as leaping off the ground, their power to fascinate other animals, their crushing and swallowing large animals and going through other marvellous performances. All these supposititious tales can be easily accounted for, when we for a moment consider the fear and terror which overcomes most persons who meet with creatures so much dreaded; their imagination and alarm may easily lead them to magnify everything that happens, hence we have most extraordinary stories told of narrow escapes and sad disasters.

Some of these tales are very amusing, especially when related by persons who have, in imagination, escaped death, they having been frightened by perfectly harmless serpents only.

It is indeed necessary that all serpents should be avoided by every one, except by those persons who are perfectly well acquainted with them, as fatal accidents have happened through the folly of careless people who were not familiar with the poisonous kinds. The tradition of the viper swallowing its young, the power of fascination, and many other old fables have been told, and have become too strongly rooted among equally erroneous superstitions for any one to attempt, with any reasonable hope, to remove them from the minds of those persons whose early teaching has stamped them there for ever. It therefore appears useless to endeavour to contradict them.

> " He who consents against his will
> Is of the same opinion still."

The following is a specimen of the conviction which is instilled into some people's minds :—

" *November* 13, 1894.

"DEAR SIR,—I should take it as a favour if you would be good enough to settle a wager, by letting me know by return if there be any serpent that can swallow a horse. Thanking you in anticipation and apologizing for the trouble,

"Truly yours,
"S. M."

Answer :—

' *November* 14, 1894.

"SIR,—There is no serpent living capable of swallowing a horse, or an ass.

" Yours faithfully,
"A. D. B."

ON A SINGULAR CASE OF ONE SNAKE SWALLOWING ANOTHER IN THE SOCIETY'S REPTILE-HOUSE.

Since January 1894, two fine examples of the common boa (*Boa constrictor*) have lived together on friendly terms

264

in one of the large compartments in the reptile-house. One of these, rather the larger, was presented by Messrs. Mole and Urich, October 12, 1892, the other, rather smaller one, was purchased on January 9, 1894.

The snakes are usually fed at dusk once a week, and on the evening of October 5, 1894, Tyrrell, the keeper of the reptile-house, placed two pigeons in the den of the two boa constrictors. The larger one seized one of the pigeons, and no doubt swallowed it, after which the keeper closed the house and left. On his return the next morning he was astonished to find only one boa in the compartment instead of two, and from the enormously increased size of the remaining one, he concluded at once that the larger boa had swallowed its companion. That this was so was evident to all who visited the house. The enormous enlargement of the creature's body was most remarkable. It had no longer the power of curling itself round, as snakes usually do, but remained extended nearly its full length in a straight line, and appeared to be at least three times its normal size in circumference. It was almost painful to see the distended skin, which had separated the scales all over the middle of the body. After examining the snake, my expectation was that it would ultimately disgorge its companion. I have, however, been disappointed. Recalling to mind a former and very similar case, in which the decomposing body of the snake swallowed caused the death of its destroyer, I had much doubt about the digestive powers of this animal. But in the present instance the snake has not only digested its companion, but has regained its appetite as well as its normal size. On Friday, November 2, the keeper finding the creature moving about as if in search of food, placed a pigeon in its den, which was seized and swallowed immediately.

I have had this voracious serpent measured, and find

it to be 11 ft. in length. The one which it swallowed was about 9 ft. in length. It will be seen by this that a serpent 11 ft. in length can not only swallow and digest another serpent only about two feet shorter, but is ready to feed again twenty-eight days afterwards.

THE SOUTH AMERICAN SNAKE.

I have found the following extract, and shall comment upon it, but unfortunately it is without date :—

"SIR,—I agree with your correspondent 'Dooker,' that there are some matters which, though unconnected with sport, are sufficiently strange, or, at all events, amusing, to be recorded. They might, perhaps, better be described as 'Travellers' Tales.' During the cruise of the *Ruby* on the S.E. coast of South America we visited the port of Santos, and whilst at this place I heard a wonderful snake story, and as it was sworn to by every one in Santos, it must be true. A woman was nursing her child in bed, and fell asleep with the babe at her breast, when a snake came in, and, taking in the situation, gently removed the child and sucked the milk from the mother, and to keep the child quiet the snake gave it its tail to suck. The poor woman woke up, and was so horrified that she cleared out of the country by the next packet. In confirmation of this story, it is an undoubted fact that snakes have been known to draw human milk from the breast.

"W. R. KENNEDY."

What kind of a snake was it ? Had it arms and legs ? The absurd story of the serpent removing the babe from its mother's breast and inserting its tail in the infant's mouth is certainly sufficiently comic, so much so as to make the former part of the statement appear a strange kind of joke.

But the concluding remark by your correspondent, W. R. Kennedy, deserves to be treated with ridicule, as it must be by any one who has the most remote knowledge of the habits of serpents.

RATTLESNAKES AND AN OLD WOMAN.

A friend of mine, a gentleman living in chambers in Lincoln's Inn, once gave me an account of some rattlesnakes he kept as pets.

These snakes were confined in a cage which was so constructed that the wire-work was placed some considerable distance away from the front, so that any persons looking at and examining them were out of danger if they were struck at, which occasionally happened. My friend's occupation taking him away from home, he had the snakes properly secured and covered up in green baize, and bought a new padlock which he put on the cage, and of which he took the key with him. He had previously fed them well, and knew, from experience, that they could go without food for weeks without injury, but he forgot to say anything to the old charwoman who cleaned up and took charge of his rooms. Some time after he had left, the old lady noticed these snakes; "Poor things," said she, " he has forgotten them—and, bless me, locked them up too." Not having a key to fit the lock, she fetched a locksmith who picked the same; she then deliberately opened the cage and placed a saucer of *bread and milk* amongst them without receiving any injury. When her master returned and he discovered what she had done, his wonder and amazement may be imagined.

SNAKE-CHARMING.

When in London, Dr. Lynn had under his management
some Indian snake-charmers. In consequence of the
cruel treatment the serpents received from these Indians
they generally very soon died, and consequently Dr. Lynn
applied to me to supply him with serpents for the use of
the performers. I need hardly say that, previously to
their being exhibited, the fangs were extracted. I have
received from him from time to time cobras from India
that only survived a few weeks, never having fed after
they came into my possession.

Before examining these dead cobras I was rather surprised to find that their mouths had been very carefully
and neatly sewn up, and consequently they were unable
to feed or bite. When Dr. Lynn received a box of living
cobras from India for the use of the snake-charmers, he
applied to me to take charge of them and have their
fangs removed, before handing them over to the performers. He told me that the most skilful man in
removing the fangs having left him, the remaining performers refused or declined to undertake the operation.
With the assistance of our man Holland, who was at that
time in charge of the reptile-house, I removed the fangs
of six or seven cobras, for which Dr. Lynn paid something
like ten shillings each.

CHAPTER III.

THE GREAT SEA SERPENT.

I was asked by Mr. F. Buckland to give my opinion on the report of the large marine animal seen off Cape St. Vito, Sicily, June 2, 1877, by the officers of the Royal Yacht *Osborne*, and placed in the Admiralty by the above officers.

In undertaking to write my opinion upon the statements in this report, I must endeavour, as far as possible, to divest myself of the knowledge of all previous accounts that have, from time to time, been published upon this subject.

Firstly, I think few men holding an honourable and trustworthy position in Her Majesty's Service would risk their reputation by concocting any false or fabricated story of this nature. I will, therefore, take it for granted that they have described to the best of their ability what they saw.

Secondly, I have now to consider what appears to me to be a very simple matter.

All persons, by continual practice in the use of their eyes on land and at sea, acquire great facility in distinguishing and recognizing the objects which they have constantly under observation, and persons accustomed to the sea are very expert in this, to them, most important matter. Men who are always on the look-out notice the smallest, as well as more important objects, and during the long periods which they pass in watching "for something to turn up," they are not likely to mistake the ordinary and common occurrence of the appearance of seals, porpoises, sharks or whales, for some previously unseen or unknown monster of the deep.

I am, therefore, willing to admit and believe that some large animal has come within sight of the officers of the *Osborne*.

My difficulty does not lie in being unable to offer some explanation of the phenomenon and to ascribe to what class or species of animal the one whose description is laid before me is likely to be affixed, or is probably allied. It is evidently not a serpent, according to all known species of serpent; none of them has fins or flippers or any external organs which could be used for swimming; nor does its description agree with any of the seals or sea-lions, as no animal of this kind has fins on its back, nor does it use the flippers in front while swimming.

Sketch *B* at first sight looks like a monster turtle, but sketch *A* at once dispels this idea.[1]

I have now to consider in what respect it resembles the whales and porpoises, and I find it quite impossible to believe that men who must be well acquainted with the movements and frequent appearance of these creatures could so distort and magnify any of the known kinds into the object they report as having been seen by them.

Lastly, I come to the sharks. The largest specimens known fail, however, to give me any hope of satisfying myself or any one else that any number of sharks could have deceived the officers of the *Osborne*.

The description given of the sea serpent is wanting

[1] See *Land and Water*, September 8, 1877.

entirely in so many important points, that one cannot help being struck with the dissimilar appearance it presented to the animals referred to.

I may remark that the fins said to have been seen upon the back of the sea serpent give strength to the idea that sharks bear the nearest resemblance to the creature, while on the other hand the description of the head and neck at once dispels the thought that any kind of shark could, by any possibility, have been mistaken for what was seen.

The sketch *A* represents a number of fins like the back fins of sharks, and, supposing two or three sharks to be in company, it would easily be conjectured that they, at a distance, represented a single animal. The great height (six or eight feet) out of the water, however, at once settles this hypothesis, because no known shark has fins of these dimensions. I now feel called upon to answer the question—

What was it?

From the dimensions given, it is most conclusive, in fact, proof positive, that no known species of animal was seen, and that, the dimensions being so extraordinary, no other decision can be arrived at than that the creature is entirely unknown to naturalists.

I must admit that I am unable to identify the figures and description with any known animal, but I fully believe in the existence, in the deep, of animals at present unknown either by specimens or by perfect descriptions; not only do I accept, as true, the statements made to the best of the judgments and belief of the parties who have made them, but I do not doubt that, from time to time, these wonderful sights have presented themselves to the observer, and have remained unrecorded by him simply through fear of his statements being derided and discredited.

When we consider the vast extent of the ocean, its great

271

depth, and the rocky, cavernous nature of the bottom— of many parts of which we know really nothing—who can say what may have been hidden for ages, and may still remain a mystery for generations yet to come ; for have we not evidence on land that there still exist some of the largest mammals, probably in thousands, of which only one solitary individual has been caught or brought to notice ? I allude to the hairy-eared, two-horned Rhinoceros (*Rhinoceros lasiotis*), captured in 1868, at Chittagong (where it was found stranded in the mud), and now known as an inhabitant of the Zoological Gardens.

I could quote other instances, but I will content myself by stating that the animal to which I have just referred remains unique, and that no part or portion of any speci- men was previously known to exist in any museum at home or abroad.

We have here an instance of the existence of a species of Rhinoceros—as large, or nearly so, as the Hippopota- mus—found on the continent of India, of which country we, in England, are supposed to know so much—where for many years collectors and naturalists have worked, and published lists of all the animals met with, and have hitherto failed to meet with or obtain any knowledge of this great beast. May I not, therefore, presume that, in the vast and mighty ocean, animals, perhaps of nocturnal habits, and therefore never, except by some extraordinary accident, forced into sight, may exist, the forms of which resemble the extinct reptiles whose fossil remains we find in such abundance ?

The form indicated and described strongly resembles some of the extinct reptilian characters, and reminds me of the models of fish-like lizards and other animals repre- sented and constructed by Waterhouse Hawkins under the direction of Professor Owen, and exhibited in the grounds of the Crystal Palace at Sydenham. As far as I am able to judge, from the evidence before me, I have reason to believe that aquatic reptiles of vast size have been seen and described by the persons who have endeavoured to explain what they have witnessed. One thing is certain, that many well-known reptiles have the power of remaining for long periods (months in fact) at the bottom, under water or imbedded in soft mud, being so provided with organs of circulation and respiration that they need not come to the surface to breathe. The large crocodiles, alligators, and turtles have this power, and I see no valid reason to doubt but that there may and do exist, in the unknown regions of the ocean, creatures so constructed.

It may be argued that, if such animals still live, they must, from time to time, die; that their bodies would float, and that their carcases would be found, or part of them, washed on shore. To this I say, however reasonable such arguments may appear, it is well known that most animals that die or are killed in the water sink at first to the bottom, where they are likely to have the flesh and soft parts devoured by other animals, such as crustacea, fishes, etc., etc., and sinking in the deep, the bones being heavier than the parts, may soon become imbedded and be thus concealed from sight.

In conclusion, I cannot shut my eyes to the many reports and statements made from time immemorial by persons far above suspicion of fraud or deception, whose lives have been, for the most part, spent at sea, and whose knowledge of the appearances of all marine animals which are commonly seen, entitles them to our most serious consideration.

These more recent instances recorded by honest and trustworthy persons, satisfy me that it is not only unfair, but unwise and a great mistake, to disregard and throw overboard, as it were, the evidence brought by these different observers, simply because we cannot, at present, define exactly, by specimens or otherwise, the exact nature of the creatures that have been observed.[1]

[1] This, with the opinion of Professor Owen, F. Buckland, H. Lee, and others, appeared in *Land and Water*, September 8, 1887.

CHAPTER IV.

LIZARDS AND TOADS.

THE MARBLED POLYCHRUS.

(*POLYCHRUS MARMORATUS.*)

A SPECIMEN of this rare and curious lizard was presented
to the Society on August 28, 1891. It is the second
specimen exhibited in the Society's Gardens; the first was
received from Dr. Stradling, March 17, 1880. This reptile
is a native of Trinidad, it inhabits trees, and feeds principally on insects, is one of the most active of the family of
lizards, and one of its remarkable features is the tail, which
is three times the length of its body.

GIGANTIC SALAMANDER.

One of the Salamanders which is now (March 3, 1876)
in the Gardens is 4 ft. 6 in. long, and weighs 48 lbs
I am unable to distinguish the sex. This perhaps
accounts for its dastardly act of murder, for that charge
must be brought against him, or her, whichever it be, for
having cut his or her companion's throat, an act so cleanly
executed that had any one performed it with a razor, it
could not have been better done. This ugly monster, no
doubt, was out of temper, or wanted to devour the other,
and having, with its mouth, seized its friend by the head,
as far back as the neck, the teeth in the lower jaw acted

like a knife on the throat, while the victim wriggled to extricate itself from the grip of its assailant. It feeds upon live fish and a little raw flesh; the fish are fresh-water species, and live in the pond with the Salamander. These reptiles are not injured by the cold; those which have been in the Gardens lived in the open air all the winter; the water is changed only when dirty. No sand, gravel, or pebbles are used, and the bottom of the tank is slate. When a large stone is placed in this tank, the creatures will sometimes lie on it out of the water. They can swim well, and have not been kept in the dark.

The shape of the pond or tank to keep them in might be oblong or square, it is of little importance, with a depth of 18 to 20 in., and 4 or 5 ft. long, and width 2 or 3 ft.

THE SURINAM WATER-TOAD.
(*PIPA AMERICANA*.)

NOTES ON THE BREEDING OF THE SURINAM WATER-TOAD (*Pipa americana*) IN THE SOCIETY'S GARDENS.

In the early part of 1895 we were surprised to find one of the females of the Surinam Water-Toad in the warm tank at the reptile-house with her back covered with eggs, the uniform and regular arrangement of which caused us a considerable amount of speculation as to how they had been placed there.[1] The old story of the female depositing her eggs on land and afterwards having them arranged on her back by the male was at once dismissed as a fable, as we now know that these animals do not voluntarily leave the water. Along with Mr. A. Thomson, the head keeper, and the two keepers at the reptile-house

---

[1] See Mr. Sclater's remarks on this subject, *Proceedings of Zoological Society*, 1895, p. 86.

(Tyrrell and Tennant), I therefore determined, should the opportunity again occur, to watch constantly with the hope

SURINAM WATER-TOAD (♀) AFTER DEPOSITION OF EGGS

of being able to solve this unknown problem. About April 28 of the year 1896, the males of this species

277

became very lively, and were constantly heard uttering their most remarkable metallic, ticking call-notes. On examination, we then observed two of the males clasping tightly round the lower part of the bodies of the females, the hind parts of the males extending beyond those of the females. On the following morning Tennant, the keeper, arrived in time to witness the mode in which the eggs were deposited. The oviduct of the female protruded from her body more than an inch in length, and the bladder-like protrusion being retroverted passed under the belly of the male on to her own back. The male appeared to press tightly upon this protruded bag and to squeeze it from side to side, apparently pressing the eggs forward one by one on to the back of the female. By this movement the eggs were spread with nearly uniform smoothness over the whole surface of the back of the female, to which they became firmly adherent. On the operation being completed, the males left their places on the females, and the enlarged and projected oviduct gradually disappeared from one of the females. In the other female, the oviduct appears not to have discharged the whole of the eggs. At any rate it remains distended, as shown in the figure, but is gradually shrinking in size.[1]

[1] [May 22nd.—This specimen died, and was sent to the British Museum. Mr. Boulenger examined it, and kindly reports as follows :—" The uterus contained a good number of ripe ova, so that only a few could have been laid when the male abandoned the female. The ovipositor, formed by the cloaca, was still protruding and much inflamed. It may be deduced from the observation made by Tennant, that fecundation must take place before the extrusion of the eggs, and it is probable that the ovipositor serves in the first instance to collect the spermatozoa which would penetrate into the oviducts, the eggs being laid in the impregnated condition, as in tailed Batrachians."—P. L. S.]

CHAPTER V.

THE NATURAL HISTORY OF COMMERCIAL SEA FISHES.

THE observations and remarks I am about to make will be confined to the sea fishes of Great Britain and Ireland, excluding, as irrelevant to the subject, all other marine animals, such as whales, porpoises, seals, lobsters, crabs, oysters, etc., as these creatures are not recognized by naturalists as fishes, and any reference I may make to them will be simply to illustrate the subject. Having for many years had the opportunity of meeting with fishermen not only in England, but in other parts of the world, and having paid much attention to the natural history of fishes and other marine animals, and being practically well acquainted with this most interesting subject, I take the present opportunity of stating my views, with the hope and expectation that the following remarks may prove useful, and lead to the improvement of the present state of things in connection with the sea fisheries of Great Britain. I beg to state that I am in no way commercially interested in fish or fisheries. The productive power of fishes, generally, is too well known to require any lengthened statement from me; the care that has already been bestowed in weighing and counting the ova of a large number of the best-known species of sea fishes by the late Frank Buckland is a sufficient testimony upon this point,

as will be seen by the following statement, taken from the
last published work of that most distinguished observer:—

Cod-roe, weighing 7¾ lbs.,	contain	.	6,867,000 eggs
Plaice, weighing 4 lbs. 15 oz., roe 1¾ lbs. ,,		.	144,600 ,,
Sole ,, 1 lb.	,,	.	134,466 ,,
Turbot ,, 28 lbs., roe 5¾ lbs.	,,	.	14,311,200 ,,

The question of protection of the young in the early stages
of their existence is a matter that requires the greatest
care and attention, and it is my intention to call especial
notice to this part of the subject; but before doing so I
may remark that sea fishes are as abundant, or appear to
be so, as at any period known to fishermen. This will
not look so surprising when we consider the enormous
destruction waged by men upon the fish-eating animals in
the ocean. The annual slaughter of thousands of whales,
porpoises, seals, sharks, dog-fish, and other fish-eating
creatures, may, in my opinion, fully compensate for the
quantity of fish captured by man. For example, take a
single instance recorded by Jonathan Couch, a most trustworthy authority, who states that a young sperm whale
20 ft. long, captured on the coast of Cornwall, was found
to contain in its stomach 300 mackerel. This quantity
he considered a meal. A shoal, or, as they are called,
school of these monsters, say twenty or thirty of them
(not an uncommon number), feeding night and day, would
make a considerable reduction in a shoal of fishes, however large. It must be borne in mind that the destruction
of these ravenous monsters, which breed slowly, most of
them producing only one at a birth, must have added
greatly to the stock of fish. I am led by these considerations to believe it to be beyond the power of man to
exhaust the supply of fish by fair fishing, *i. e.* with nets or
lines, in the deep waters of the ocean. At the same time

the destruction of the fry in the breeding season upon the shallow, sandy banks of the river or estuaries requires especial notice, and to this part of the subject I beg to direct the attention of those in authority. The food of fishes consists principally of fish. Many species feed upon their young. It is not commonly known, but I have found the stomach of the herring filled with the fry of the herring. (In speaking of the herring I might mention that I have observed a large number of small sea-gulls and other birds hovering over a vast shoal of this fish, dipping from time to time into the water, but none of them captured a fish. This circumstance caused me to obtain specimens of the birds for examination, when I found their stomachs filled with a greenish oily substance which floated over the shoal of herrings and proved to be the excrement of the fish.) The food of all species of fishes depends much upon the age, size, and locality in which they are found ; as, for instance, the fry of most fishes at first feed upon very minute, in fact microscopic, objects. The fry of the sole, turbot, and fish of this class that hide in the sand, find their food among the young of shrimps and other marine productions, and it is in this early condition of their existence that they are so ruthlessly caught and destroyed by the trawlers engaged in shrimping. This I have no hesitation in saying is the most important part of the subject. The enormous quantities of the young sea fishes that find food and shelter on the sand-banks in the estuaries and mouths of rivers are, during the helpless condition of their early life, caught in the fine meshes of the shrimpers' nets and destroyed by millions. One district I will mention as an illustration of the fearful waste of the young fish, viz. from Liverpool south to East-ham, north up to Waterloo, and all intervening places to Southport, outside the port of Liverpool, distance fifteen miles, greater part of the river Dee, and the north Welsh coast as far as Rhyl. Upon this district I have ascertained that the number of families engaged in shrimping amounts to nearly 1000, the shrimping being carried on uninterruptedly all the year round by trawling and hand-nets.

In trawling for shrimps there are thousands of bushels of the young of soles, ray, turbot, brill, flerk, and other valuable fish (less than 2 in. long) caught and destroyed. The fishermen have to sort these from the shrimps, and throw them away. The greatest difficulty is experienced in obtaining reliable information from fishermen, and it is only by personally visiting the locality that this object can be obtained. The oldest fishermen show great ignorance when asked any questions. Many seem determined not to know anything, while others, from interested motives, will mislead the inquirer by denying and falsifying the facts. From all the evidence and the information I am able to obtain, and after a careful inspection of this neighbourhood, I have arrived at the conclusion that a "close" season for the protection of the fry of soles, ray, turbot, brill, flerk, and other fish of this class should embrace the months of February, March, April, and part of May. I would suggest that certain of these breeding-grounds should be marked out upon the estuaries, the rivers, or on the coast, and shrimping or whitebait fishing within such limits should be strictly prohibited during at least three months in the year, the time fixed as the "close" season to be determined upon after a careful inspection and full investigation of each and every locality.

The migratory habits of fishes have engaged the attention of naturalists for generations, but little has been positively done. The somewhat mysterious appearance and disappearance of fishes is most difficult to understand.

The migration of birds affords but little help in studying the movements of fishes. Birds are more easily observed, and their movements better understood. How difficult it is, when at sea, to be able to say what species of fish compose that vast shoal passing at a rapid rate; it is little more than guess-work to name them. That large shoals of fish traverse the ocean is well known. This is indicated by the thousands of sea birds that flutter over them, and by the whales and porpoises that follow and feed upon them. It is rarely that any competent person has a chance of determining the kind of fish or their destination. Taking into consideration the knowledge and care required to determine some species of fish after capture, how much more difficult it is to do so when seen only for a moment, and then in rapid motion. The differences of opinion among fishermen concerning the various kinds of herring are most perplexing. The collection of facts respecting the tides, temperature of the water, the electric state of the atmosphere, storms, and other conditions, if carefully recorded and observed in connection with the movements of fishes, might lead to the elucidation and give a fair and probable solution to this much-wanted information. Many attempts have been made to endeavour to account for the sudden arrival or departure of many kinds of fishes, but little can be adduced in proof of the various theories put forward on this subject. The great success that has attended the artificial propagation of fish, especially in the *Salmonidæ*, cannot for one moment be questioned; it, however, appears to me extremely doubtful if anything could be accomplished, under the most favourable circumstances, with sea fishes. No artificial propagation that it is possible to carry out could, in my opinion, replace or compensate for the destruction of the fry on the breeding-grounds before alluded to.

In conclusion I would state, that after giving the matter very careful consideration, I am of opinion that fishing in the open sea may be carried on at all seasons by every fair and legal means of catching fish, but that a "close" time for the helpless fry is of the most vital importance.

CHAPTER VI.

MUD-FISH OF THE RIVER GAMBIA.[1]

(*LEPIDOSIREN ANNECTENS.*)

MR. W. HAWKINS, in the *Illustrated News* (Supp. September 20, 1856), which gives a very good figure of the animal from life, observes—

"Three living specimens of this animal were brought to England from the Gambia, enclosed in balls of hard clay, where they had been for eight months without showing any signs of life, until those balls of hard clay were immersed in water, which caused the clay to crack and break up, discovering dark-coloured egg-like forms, which also presently burst, liberating their inmates, which briskly swam or rather dashed through the water, showing unmistakable signs of life by feeding voraciously upon very large worms, small frogs, and pieces of meat that were presented them."

The *Lepidosiren* uses its tail to propel itself forward and upward towards the surface of the water. The subulate limbs are very much elongated; the front ones are furnished with a narrow membranaceous margin of nearly equal width the whole length of the hinder edge; the hinder one has a narrow membrane on the middle of the outer side; they are exceedingly mobile and flexible, and are used by the animal to direct its motions, and are more

[1] J. E. Gray and Bartlett, *Proceedings Zool. Soc.*, Nov. 11, 1856.

like feet than fins, especially when they are within reach of some fixed body which the animal can use as a fulcrum.

There are two processes on each side over the base of the anterior members, which have been regarded as gills by some authors [1]; they are coloured like the rest of the body, and I could not discover, even when examined by a hand-magnifier of 1 in. focal length, that they were pervaded by any peculiar vascular structure, or furnished with any cirri or other processes usually found on the external gills of *Batrachia*. They scarcely moved during the time that I was examining the specimen, except when the animal was swimming, when they were used like the larger members, apparently to assist in directing its motions, and they evidently form part of the anterior members. They are placed rather close together somewhat above the base of the elongated finned filament. These limbs are used to support the animal some height above the surface of the gravel when it is at rest.

Indeed, all the motions of the animal much more resemble those of a *Triton* or *Lissotriton* than of an eel-shaped fish.

The upper and lower surfaces of the head are furnished with lines of mucous pores placed in a symmetrical manner on the two sides, similar to the pores observable on the head and chin of different kinds of fish, and of *Tritons* and *Lissotritons*: and there is a distinct continuous line of pores, like the lateral line of fish and *Tritons*, which is continued on the tail some distance behind the base of the hinder members, but becoming less distinct at the hinder part of the series.

The eyes are of moderate size, scarcely raised above the surface, round, without any eyelids; the pupil is black,

[1] See Peters, *Ann. and Mag. Nat. Hist.* xvi. 348.

small, circular, less than one-third the diameter of the globe, with a narrow golden iris.

The Mud-Fish is generally to be observed swimming about under the water, or resting at the bottom of the tank, supporting itself by its members, 1½ in. or 2 in. above the surface of the gravel, with its nose generally in the corner, bent down and partly hidden in the gravel.

The mouth is firmly closed by the overhanging upper lip, except in front, where there is a small oblong, transverse, horizontal opening on the outer edge of the lips, admitting the water to the small open external nostrils, which are on the middle of the under side of the upper lip. This opening does not extend to the hinder part of the lips, which are closed behind it, so that water cannot enter the mouth in that direction except through the nostrils.

In this quiescent state the lateral gill-opening is generally closed, but sometimes it is slightly elevated, and a small current appears to be emitted now and then from it, as if a small quantity of water were taken in by the nostrils and emitted by the gill-flap; but this action is not continuous nor very distinctly visible.

While remaining under the water the animal sometimes opens the mouth to its full extent, leaving it open for some time, dilating the throat by the action of the *os hyoides;* when fully dilated it closes its mouth, opens the gill-aperture, and contracting the throat emits a strong current of water through the lateral gill-aperture.

It occasionally, but at uncertain periods, rises perpendicularly to the top of the water, until the front part of the head and the whole mouth are exposed above the water; it then opens its mouth, which it retains open for a time, dilates its throat, as if taking in all the air it can contain, closes the mouth, descends under the surface and contracts its throat, as if it were forcing the air into the lungs (sometimes during this action one or two very small bubbles of air are emitted at the gill-aperture), and then the animal takes up its old position near the bottom of the vase.

I once saw the animal ascend and so take in air almost immediately after it had been passing a fresh supply of water to its gills. When I have been observing it, it appeared to take in air more frequently than water.[1] It often rises with its body perpendicular, as if it were going to take in free air, but descends again without reaching the surface of the water.

The organs of respiration of this animal are twofold :—

1. Well-organized gills on the inner edge of the branchial arches, as in fishes, and a regular gill-cover with a small oblong aperture in front of the base of the anterior members (see Owen, *Trans. Linn. Soc.* xviii. t. 25. f. 3, t. 26. f. 1).

2. Two well-developed cellular lungs of nearly equal size (see Owen, *Trans. Linn. Soc.* xviii. t. 25. f. 3, t. 26. f. 1, 2).

3. The nostrils are close together, situated on the under side of the inner lip, with their internal opening on the side of the mouth between the lips and the outer edge of the large inner series of teeth ; the passage is short, as a probe is easily passed from the one opening to the other,

---

[1] Mr. W. Hawkins in the *Illustrated News* observes—" It is seen habitually to rise to the surface of the water for a larger supply of atmospheric air, thrusting its mouth above the surface."

Dr. Holbrook appears to have observed the same habit in the *Necturus maculosus* (which is probably the larva of the hell-bender or *Protonopsis horrida*). He states that that animal in confinement " ascends to the surface (of the water), taking in a mouthful of air, and sinks again with it to the bottom."—*Amer. Herpet.* i. 113.

and the inner nostrils are very evident in the living animal when it opens its mouth to take in air.

M. Bischoff observed these interior nostrils also in the *Curamuru* or *Lepidosiren poradoxa* of the Brazils.

The animal is, therefore, provided with well-developed organs for both aërial and aquatic respiration, and its manner of breathing is perfectly conformable to this organization: it is consequently the most perfectly amphibious animal, equally adapted for living on land or in water, that has come under my observation.

The character which best separates the Batrachian—as the toad, frog and salamander—from the fish, is, that in both the larva and perfect state they are provided with an external and internal nostril, and it is through this nostril that these animals take in or emit the air which they respire; while in fish, the water which they respire is taken in by the mouth, and after passing over the gills is emitted by the lateral aperture of the gill-flap; the nostril being only a sac, without any communication with the cavity of the mouth.

When a Batrachian respires, the mouth is kept closed, the throat being used like a pair of bellows to force the air into the lungs; and if the mouth is kept open, the animal dies for want of the power of respiring. In fish, on the contrary, the mouth is always more or less open, the fish either constantly gulping in the water, then closing the mouth or lips, and emitting it by the lateral opening; or the mouth is partially open, and the animal uses its tongue and the hinder internal edge of the lip as a kind of valve, by which the cavity of the mouth is closed and the water is forced to pass through the gills.

The *Lepidosirens* appear to take in water by the nostrils, and at the same time to respire both air as Batrachians and water as fish.

The generality of the Amphibia, such as the toads, frogs, and efts or salamanders, are organized for aquatic respiration in their young and lower state, and for aërial respiration in their adult condition; but this animal has both kinds of organs in a state fit for perfect use at the same time, and the animal evidently uses them simultaneously.

It appears to me that the Mud-Fish is much more nearly related to the Amphibia than to any fish that I am acquainted with; at the same time it evidently forms a particular group in that class.

Dr. Daniel, who has lived for several years on the Gambia and on Macarthy's Islands, informs me that the *Lepidosiren*, like the mud-eel or true *Siren*, is only found in the rice-fields, which are for more than half the year under water, and that they are only procured by the natives towards the end of the dry season, when they are dug out of the nearly-dried mud. They are eaten fried, and like eels have a rich oily flavour.

The habit of living in the mud is common to several Amphibia; thus the mud-eel, or *Siren lacertina*, which has lungs and external gills, lives chiefly in mud, being dug out when the ditches of the rice-fields in Carolina are cleared. The hell-bender or mud-devil (*Protonopsis horrida*) and the Congo snake (*Amphiuma*), which have internal gills and lungs and a small lateral gill-opening, live sunk in the mud to the depth of 2 or 3 ft., especially in winter; and they and the *Siren lacertina* will live for some time out of water, and are said sometimes to leave it voluntarily.

Aquatic animals much more frequently bury themselves in the mud than is generally supposed. The common English frogs and the large efts bury themselves in the mud during the greater part of the winter, and this also is the case with *Dytisci* and other aquatic insects.

But some fish also, which have only gills adapted for aquatic respiration, have the same habit. Dr. Hancock observes, " When the water is leaving the pools in which they commonly reside, the yarrow (a species of *Esox*, Linn.), as well as the round-headed hassar (*Callichthys littoralis*), bury themselves in the mud, while all other fishes perish for want of their natural element, or are picked up by rapacious birds. The flat-headed hassar (*Doras costata*), on the contrary, simultaneously quits the place and marches overland in search of water, travelling for a whole night, as is asserted by the Indians, in search of their object. I have ascertained by trial that they will live many hours out of water even when exposed to the sun's rays. Their motion over land is described to be somewhat like that of a two-polled lizard : they project themselves forward on their bony arms by the elastic spring of the tail exerted sideways; their progress is nearly as fast as a man will leisurely walk." [1]

" The Indians say that these fishes carry water within them for a supply on their journey. There appears to be some truth in this statement, for I have observed that the bodies of the hassar do not get dry like those of other fishes when taken out of the water; and if the moisture be absorbed, or they are wiped dry with a cloth, they have such a power of secretion that they become instantly moist again ; indeed it is scarcely possible to dry the surface while the fish is living." [2]

Dr. Hancock further observes, that a fish which he thinks is *Loricaria pleistomus* " is not only furnished with the common appendages for swimming, but also with four strong bony supporters, one attached to each of the pectoral and belly fins (*i. e.* constituting the first ray of each), by

---

[1] *Zool. Journ.* iv. 243.   [2] *Loc. cit* 243.

which the animal creeps on the bottom of the river, and perhaps where there is little or no water, also being as it seems partly amphibious."[1]

From this account, it appears that the habits of these fish bear very little relation to those of the Mud-Fish.

It is well known that many fresh-water Mollusca which respire free air, and I believe some of those which are furnished with pectiniform gills for aquatic respiration, as *Paludinæ* and *Valvatæ*, in the warmer climates, such as

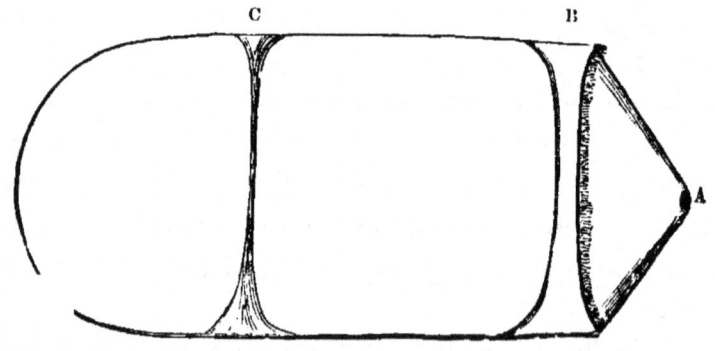

FIG. 1.—COCOON OF THE MUD-FISH (*Lepidosiren annectens*).

A. Breathing-hole at nose.   B. A thin partition.
c. An attaching band that passes through the space where the animal bends, as in *a*, Fig. 2.

India, where the waters of the streams or ponds are dried up, bury themselves in the mud to a considerable depth like the Mud-Fish, and like them remain in a torpid state until the return of the rainy season.

Sir William Jardine has described the kind of cocoon in the clay in which the Mud-Fish are brought to this country; but I am informed by Mr. Bartlett that the cavity is always furnished with a small aperture opposite to where the nose of the animal is placed.

In referring this animal to the class of Fishes, authors

[1] *Zool. Journ.* iv. 243.

have laid great stress on the fact of its being provided with a lateral line. Thus M. Duméril, in the last essay on the subject, notices the line, "which is ramified on the sides of the head as in *Chimera*," overlooking the fact that the *Triton cristatus*, the common eft, has similar lines on both the sides and head. He compares the gill-rays and branchial aperture to that of *Mormyrus* and *Cobitis*, but they are equally like those of *Protonopsis*; and he compares the nostrils to those of the lamprey, overlooking the fact that the animal is provided with nostrils communicating with the cavity of the mouth.[1]

I have been informed that this genus is found in other parts of Africa, as Senegal, where it is called *Tobal*, and

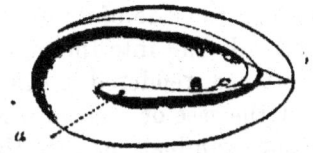

FIG. 2.—A SKETCH OF THE ANIMAL IN THE COCOON.

a. The position of the band c.   *b.* The head, nose and eyes.

the White Nile, from whence M. Armand sent specimens to the Paris Museum in 1843; and Dr. Peters found a species in Quillemanes, which Peters and J. Müller have called *Rhinocryptes amphibia*.

In reply to a note I had addressed to him, I have received the following interesting communication from Mr. Bartlett, who at the same time informed me that he intended to have communicated it to the next meeting of the Society :—

[1] See *Erp. Générale*, ix. 213.

"*Crystal Palace, Sydenham,*
"*November* 17, 1856.

"DEAR SIR,—In reply to your note respecting the living Mud-Fish, I beg to say that in the month of June last I received from Western Africa a case containing four specimens of this animal, each specimen was imbedded in a block of *dry hard muddy clay,* about the size of a quartern loaf; these blocks of clay were each sewn up in a piece of canvas to prevent the clay crumbling or falling to pieces. According to the instructions I received from Capt. Chamberlayne (the gentleman who sent them), I placed them in a tank of fresh water at the temperature of 83 degrees; in doing this a portion of the clay crumbled off one of them and partly exposed the case in which the animal was contained; I was watching the operation when suddenly the *case or cocoon* rose to the surface of the water. I at first thought the animal contained in it must be dead, but I shortly afterwards observed a slight motion, apparently the animal was endeavouring to extricate itself, and this it soon afterwards accomplished by breaking through the side of its tough covering; it swam about immediately, and by diving into the mud and clay, which by this time had become softened, rendered it difficult to make further observations; I removed the case or cocoon, which still floated, and which I now send for your examination. On the following morning I found that two more of the animals had made their appearance, their cases however were not to be seen—they evidently remained imbedded in the soft clay. In the course of the next day the fourth animal suddenly floated to the surface enveloped in its case; as it showed no signs of life I removed it, and found the animal had been dead some time, as it was much decomposed. At the time these animals first made their appearance they were very thin, and about 9 in. long; they began to feed immediately upon *earth-worms, small frogs, fish,* etc., occasionally taking raw flesh. I saw them sometimes attack each other, and one of them (I imagine in endeavouring to escape) leaped out of the tank into the large basin in the Crystal Palace in which the tank was standing (this specimen is still at large among the water-lilies, etc.). The remaining two lived together for some time, apparently on good terms, but in the month of August the one now remaining in the tank seized its companion and devoured nearly half of it, leaving only the head and about half the length of its body. In feeding, this creature masticates the food much, frequently putting it forward almost quite out of its mouth and then gradually chewing it back again, and often (when fed upon raw flesh), after having so chewed it for some time, it will throw it out altogether. The growth of these animals is most extraordinary. In June, as I have before stated, they were about 9 in. long ; in three months they attained their present size, which cannot be less than 18 in. in length. It rises frequently perpendicularly to the surface to breathe, and at other times it supports itself on its fin-like appendages, and with the aid of its tail raises its body from the ground, the fins being bent or curved backwards. The movement of this animal is generally very slow, and would give one an idea that it was very sluggish ; this however I have good reason to know is not the case, as in attempting to capture the one at liberty in the large basin it darted away with the rapidity of an arrow. I have reason also to believe the animal finds its food as much by *scent as sight*. With reference to the cocoon which I herewith send for your examination, the end covering the nose of the animal is rather pointed, and has an aperture about the size of a pin's head, through which I have no doubt the animal breathes during its state of torpor. The animal when in its case is coiled nearly twice round, and I observed in each of the blocks of clay a small hole about the size of a mouse-hole, which was quite smooth on the inside, as though the animal had crept through it.

> "I am, dear Sir,
> "Faithfully yours,
> "A. D. BARTLETT."

CHAPTER VII.

SUPPLEMENTARY NOTES.

PROPAGATION OF THE SALMON.

THE Committee of the Australian Association have been trying a series of experiments with a view of ascertaining the possibility of conveying Salmon to Australia, for the purpose of introducing this noble fish into the rivers of that country. The difficulty is to convey them across the tropics; and the object of these experiments, which have been carried on in the Crystal Palace under my supervision, has been—

1. To filter a sufficient quantity of water to supply a running stream for the spawn or young fish.

2. To ascertain the highest amount of temperature in which they would live.

3. To discover the best and most economical means of lowering the temperature, that they may be kept alive while passing the tropics.

In order to accomplish the first object, arrangements were made with the Charcoal Filter Company to fix filters to supply a running stream through long boxes, which were partly filled with gravel and small stones, upon which the Salmon ova were to be placed.

Mr. Ramsbottom being engaged to obtain the ova, to ensure their being perfectly impregnated, and to deposit them in the breeding-place in the Crystal Palace, proceeded to Wales, and on February 5, 1859, obtained from two female fish at least 20,000 ova, which, by the usual process adopted in the artificial propagation of fish, he rendered fertile, and then starting immediately for the Crystal Palace, arrived there February 7, and deposited the ova in the breeding-boxes, which had been duly prepared. Unfortunately, at this time the filters had ceased to act, and the water supplied by the Lambeth Water Company was obliged to be laid on in its usual state. In a few days the ova and the bottom of the breeding-boxes became covered with a dark deposit, from the impure condition of the water, and large numbers of the ova died daily in consequence. Another batch of filters was then fixed, and a fresh supply of filtered water obtained, and no more sediment was deposited upon the ova. Notwithstanding this, they continued to die for some days; but about the 20th the whole of the deposit, which had settled upon the bottom of the boxes and upon the ova, began to rise towards the surface in the form of Confervæ, the bottom of the boxes and the remaining ova appeared quite fresh and clean, the surviving ova rapidly assumed the perfect state of the young fish, and on March 7 the young fry began to move about (the outer covering being thrown off), endeavouring to hide themselves between the stones and gravel. The temperature of the water during this experiment was 57°. In order to ascertain if any advantage could be gained by placing some of these in filtered water at a lower temperature, a number of them were carefully removed to a glass tank, supplied with a fountain at the temperature of 54°. In this they appeared to be doing well, were evidently larger and more active, and exhibited great promise. Unfortunately, on the morning of the 13th, the workmen having been ordered to make some alteration in the water-pipes in the building, turned off the water, leaving the young salmon, together with the ova which had not yet been hatched, five or six hours without fresh water, in the tropical end of the building ; in consequence of this, they were all destroyed, and this interesting experiment delayed for a whole year, as it is impossible to obtain the ova until the next breeding-season.

There are, however, some important facts learned from this experiment, one of which is the early period of hatching. Previous experiments have shown that sixty days usually expire before the young come to life, sometimes 140 days have passed. This experiment has proved that the young fish can be hatched in thirty days; it yet remains to be tested whether this is an advantage. It is certain that in the case of more highly organized and warm-blooded animals, their production at an earlier period than the ordinary one is attended, if not with death, at least with great debility; while, on the other hand, it is not possible to retard the operations of nature beyond the ordinary period without destroying the mother or the offspring. There are many circumstances that induce the belief that the young fish would be stronger by the early development, but no positive conclusion can be arrived at without further experiments.

ELECTRIC FISH.

One morning a railway porter brought to my office a large glass jar containing an electric fish which had arrived from Liverpool. After the jar had been deposited on the floor I left the office for a few moments. I was rather startled at hearing my office boy scream, and I hastened back and found him on the floor struggling, kicking, and screaming, "Oh, I shall die!" I at once perceived that, in my absence, he had attempted to lift the fish out of the glass to have a look at it; the shock he received so terrified him that he fell down, and for an hour or two afterwards was unable to use his right arm, which he carried slung in his waistcoat.

For several years two fine electric eels have been exhibited in the Gardens. From time to time an inquisitive person has taken the liberty to reach over the tank and touch one of these fish; so far as my experience goes I never knew any one to do so a second time, as perfect satisfaction is expressed at the first experiment.

These creatures possess the power to kill, or disable, a fish without coming in contact with it, they being able to completely paralyze it.

One of these eels was lent to illustrate a lecture at the Royal Institution, being conveyed there in a large tub about half full of water.

Two men were carrying this tub up the staircase at the Institution, when both received most severe shocks, and so strong were these shocks, that it was with difficulty that they prevented themselves from letting the whole lot fall.

OUTSIDE THE FISHERIES EXHIBITION.

When writing this notice of the few living creatures deposited outside the building, the thought flashed upon my mind of the joy, amazement and delight that would have filled the heart of the late much-lamented Frank Buckland could he but behold within this vast pile of buildings the wonderful collections of specimens of the various subjects upon which he worked with such devoted and determined zeal. The public, the fishermen, and all concerned with fish or fisheries owe to him a deep debt of gratitude for the labour and care he bestowed upon this important subject.

The living birds and other animals outside the building are mainly intended as illustrations of the various forms of fish-eating creatures, and as some of the species exist in countless numbers, the destruction of fish by these enemies must be enormous.

Considerable interest is attached to the beavers sent for exhibition by the Marquis of Bute, from the fact that they are British born. Several years since the Marquis had a considerable portion of land at Rothsay walled round, enclosing a small stream. Into this enclosure were introduced some beavers imported from Canada. The beavers soon commenced gnawing down the trees and felling them across the stream, which they dammed up and formed a lake of considerable size; and in the lake they have established their dwellings, and their numbers have vastly increased. By this introduction we may now boast of the possession of British beavers.

It may be asked, however, by some one acquainted with the subject—What have the beavers to do with fish or fishing? as they eat not fish, but are, strictly speaking, vegetarians, feeding upon the leaves, tender branches, and the bark of trees, grass and roots. The answer to this inquiry may be, that the beavers perform and have performed many very important changes in the rivers in various parts of the world. By their habit of gnawing down trees and causing them to fall across the streams they inhabit, and thereby, like skilful engineers, dam up the rivers, lakes are formed and the overflow diverted to parts of the country previously dry, by which means both water and fish become distributed.

THE WATER-VOLE OR WATER-RAT.

Like the beaver, this little animal appears somewhat out of place in a fishery exhibition, as, until lately, it was supposed to be strictly a vegetable feeder. According to the account given in *Bell's British Quadrupeds*, its habit of feeding upon any kind of animal food is most positively denied. The individuals now exhibited show, however, a partiality to the spawn of fish, and must be classed among the numerous enemies of fish.

THE SEAL.

There is probably no animal of its size so destructive to fish as the seal, and when we consider the numerous species of seals and their numbers—for many species exist in countless thousands—and inhabiting, as they do, so many parts of the world, it may appear wonderful that a sufficient supply of fish could be found to maintain them ; and were it not for the amazing fertility of most fish, they would naturally become scarce, but fortunately for the fish, seals are much sought for by man, both for their skins and fat, and a constant slaughter is kept up, by which means their numbers are greatly reduced.

THE OTTER.

This is too well known as a most destructive and determined enemy of the finny tribe, and were it not for the various packs of hounds kept in this country for the purpose of otter hunting, by which their numbers are kept under, the rapid increase of these destructive animals would render some of our finest fishing rivers of but little value. The specimen exhibited is a somewhat remarkable one, inasmuch as it was bred in captivity by Mr. Cocks.

PELICANS.

Of the living birds exhibited, the largest and most powerful are the pelicans, whose capacious mouths appear capable of swallowing a bucketful of fish at once. Fortunately they inhabit regions remote from the habitations of men. Pelicans are abundant enough, and widely spread over dreary swamps and marsh land, feeding upon the inland lakes found in tropical climates.

THE CORMORANT.

This individual deserves especial notice, being probably the first of the species bred and reared in captivity. The parents, belonging to Captain Salvin, having been deposited in the Gull pond at the Zoological Gardens in 1881, built a nest of sticks, and hatched two young ones, the subject of this notice being one of them. This bird has been trained to fish after the fashion adopted by the Chinese.

THE FLAMINGOES.

Of this remarkable form among the aquatic birds there are several species. They are widely distributed over India, Africa, and America ; they feed upon small aquatic insects, seeds of aquatic plants, spawn of fish, and shrimp-like animals.

SEA-GULLS.

The large family of gulls are too well known from their being found upon every sea all over the globe to need description. They feed upon fish and other marine animals, and not infrequently upon grain and vegetable substances.

THE FISHES OUTSIDE THE BUILDING.

Unfortunately the ponds or tanks are very shallow, and consequently unfitted for the perfect display of fresh-water fish, especially during the warm weather, the water so rapidly becoming turbid. The fine supply of large pike, carp, and other fish that were introduced before the opening of the building, have not done so well as could be wished. The most noticeable among the collection are the splendid specimens of golden tench supplied by Lord Walsingham. One trifling omission appears to be that there are no labels to indicate to the visitors the names of the various kinds or species that are seen swimming about. This may seem of little importance, but the frequent inquiries made indicate the want of this information.

APPENDICES.

APPENDIX I.

ADDITIONAL
BIOGRAPHICAL NOTES AND ANECDOTES

BY

EDWARD BARTLETT.

MY first school-master, John Walker, was a man never, by me, to be forgotten. A descendant of a wealthy family, —at least he had a rich aunt who was extremely attached to him, and whose kindness and liberality were almost unbounded,—he was undoubtedly clever, and wrote several plays, one of which I well remember was performed with great success at the Olympic Theatre in Wych Street, Strand. It was entitled *The Wild Boy of Bohemia.* Mr. Walker, however, did not attend very regularly to the school, but entrusted the management to two tutors; nevertheless, whenever he came into the school-room he made up for his seeming neglect. It was a practice of his to have all the boys stand around him, and he would then deliver a short, concise lecture, giving all sorts of good advice; many of his remarks would no doubt be called to mind in after years by the boys who, like myself, listened to him with great attention. He had such an agreeable and pleasing manner, that it was considered a treat to see and hear him. I well recollect that, on one occasion, he endeavonred to impress upon us the desirability of avoiding any exhibition of ill-temper, "for," said he, "a teaspoonful of honey will catch more flies than a ton of vinegar;" this was one only of many of his remarks, and, if generally acted upon, would render the lives of many persons less uncomfortable than they now are.

NEWGATE.

Some years ago I was intimately acquainted with the then Governor of Newgate Prison, to whom I expressed a desire to see the interior of that old place, and he invited me to call upon him at any time most convenient to myself, have luncheon with him and look over the building.

It was late in the autumn, and being a dull day, and scarcely any one about the Gardens, I said to my daughter Julia and her husband that I was going to see the Governor at Newgate Jail (we had often promised to go). When they were ready we walked out of the house and called the first cab that was in sight; the man recognized me at once. "Where to, sir?" "Newgate Jail," I answered. The man looked at me with wide-open eyes and mouth. "Do you mean it, sir?" "Yes," I replied. He never said another word, but nodded his head and drove to Newgate. He watched me ring the bell, and when the door opened he stared harder than ever until the door closed upon us; he then went away, as we supposed.

After we had enjoyed a very pleasant luncheon the Governor conducted us all over the place, explaining and relating the histories of each department until we came to one of the padded dark cells. "Now, Mr. Bartlett, this is, perhaps, the darkest place on earth, step in and see for yourself." I did so, and the door closed upon me to convince me how utterly impossible it was to either see or be heard ; in a second or two I tried to find the door to get out, but this I could not do. I called and received no answer. I tried to knock, but it was useless to do anything, and it began to dawn upon me that I was trapped. The few minutes that I was in that pitch-black cell seemed longer than I liked.

When the door was opened they thought I looked scared, and I felt so. But I declared openly that I would never go inside again unless carried in. After a few jokes on the subject we returned to the Governor's apartments and refreshed ourselves, and then left for home much enlightened with regard to the home of criminals.

Some days later I met the same cabman. He pulled up. "Good-morning, sir. May I ask when you came out of Newgate ? Well, I waited so long for you I gave it up, and picked up a fare, and drove home. I suppose you left those friends of yours there safe enough ? " I then told him all about it, and didn't he laugh ! He thought I had trapped them when he saw me.

TRIP TO NORWAY.

It is not an uncommon occurrence for the remark to be made to me by persons whom I meet, " What a charming employment yours must be ! How delighted I should be to have such an occupation," etc. To a certain extent there is some truth in these remarks, but there is a limit to the pleasure to be derived from such an occupation as mine, and this I have on more than one occasion experienced. A great desire for a change from constant and unceasing anxiety by leaving the Gardens and all their interesting occupants and, for a time, to find some place of retirement where I should be unknown and unrecognized has come over me. To do this I have found always a difficult task. Some few years ago I made up my mind to go to Norway for a few weeks, and travelling by mail train to Hull, I went by the steamer to Christiania.

There were a number of passengers on board, and, to me, all were strangers. As usual, some of them were very chatty and pleasant, but I found their inquisitiveness rather made me somewhat uncomfortable.

Wishing at first to preserve my *incognito* I became reticent, as the Press reporters say of the police when they can get no information out of them, and this being observed by some of my fellow-passengers, they were induced to make remarks to the captain, who was one of the most genial, kind, and good-natured men I ever met. He, too, endeavoured to try to, what he good-humouredly called, " make me out," and when he tackled me I felt that I must give in. At the same time I determined to have some fun over this little affair. The captain chanced to speak about the purchase of Norwegian ponies, and I ventured the remark that " I bought a great number of horses and ponies during the year." This was an opening for the captain, who, on hearing what I said, and looking pleased, observed, " Ah ! I thought you were in that line." I replied, " I assure you, captain, I am not a dealer in horses ; and although I buy two or three hundred a year, I never sold a horse in my life." The captain looked very straight at me, evidently somewhat at a loss to keep up the conversation. By this time two or three of the passengers joined us, and when I left them he no doubt told them what had passed, because the next time I met him he laughingly said, " Your horse story is a caution." I now thought it time to speak more definitely, as I could plainly see from a remark I overheard, that I should be looked upon as "a hatchet-thrower." I then said, "Now, captain, I must tell you who I am, but before doing so, let me beg of you to believe what I am about to tell you. It is quite true I have bought at least three hundred horses a year for many years without selling one of them, and the highest price I pay is three pounds each, many I get for less than half that price." For a moment he seemed puzzied. "Ah, ah!" said he, "I have it—Maiden Lane, King's Cross, ah, ah!" "No, no, excuse me," I said, "I am not a horse-knacker. Here is my card, put it into your pocket and don't let these prying folks see it." However, the captain was not willing to allow me to go on shore with the passengers all under the impression that I was a "knacker," and he invited me on the last evening on board to sit next him at dinner. This I did, and he then informed them that all I said about horses was true, and he then told them who I was and where I came from. This fact pleased them all very much, and they were then quite satisfied. We had many trips together afterwards during my stay in Norway.

NIGHT EXPERIENCES OF ANIMALS IN THE ZOOLOGICAL GARDENS.

I feel that, in many respects, I resemble the ancient relative of man, Adam, living, as I do, in an extensive garden surrounded by wild beasts and birds, I may say in the midst of the largest collection of wild animals on record (except the first and renowned collection in Noah's Ark), and being exhibited at the present time, in the Gardens of the Zoological Society, Regent's Park.

Reader, for one moment kindly imagine that you are in

my place, and that you have retired for the night, exhausted and tired, the result of walking, talking, thinking, being worried by endless inquiries upon inquiries, and by other incidents which happen during eighteen hours a day, and also draw on your imagination to the extent that the time of the year is the middle of August.

You fancy everything has settled down and is at rest, and you try to sleep. All is as still as death; presently there is a soughing of the wind, the leaves begin to rustle, and this forebodes a storm.

As the wind begins to move in anger the low, soft howl of the wolf is heard, at first difficult to distinguish from the wind; it gradually deepens, and being joined by the more harsh and distinct whining howl of the jackal and the sharp bark of the fox, the overture begins. The wolves and other denizens of the Gardens, one by one, join in the woeful concert. The hyæna now and then utters a sharp laugh, while the Tasmanian devil lends his fiendish and dismal cry to render night hideous. These disturbers of the peace arouse the lions, who, no longer able to refrain, send forth their thunder, that seems like noisy smoke rolling on in volumes, and resounding in the distance renders obscure, for the moment, all other sounds.

As the lions' voices die away the lesser din becomes more clear, and now the Polar bear tunes up, with all his might, his hoarse and savage blare, which once heard is not easily forgotten.

Then comes a lull, and you are in hopes that they are tired now, as this band of savage vocalists has kept you on the listen for at least two hours. No! it's not over; you ask, "What horrid noise is that so close to where I lay? Have my quiet neighbours the hippopotami fallen out?" Indeed they have, and their voices seem more frightful than all the rest, because they are so unusual.

Another fearful bellow, roar or grunt, and then another, as if, with rage or pain, you know not which, these monsters seem determined not to rest till break of day. The laughing jackasses from the other side of the world begin to mock each other, often grinning, you would imagine by their voices, at you and all on this side of the globe; this provokes the feathered tribe to utter cries to stop the laughing chorus or to hoot it down.

The cranes then trumpet forth their loud alarm, and this is answered everywhere at once with notes of various keys that seem to unlock all their vocal powers, shrieking discordant sounds, which, mixing with mellow notes, require time to discern from whence they come. All this, dear reader, has fallen to my lot to experience. These are somewhat the sort of nights I sometimes pass, and I like them. About sunrise I hear the Birds of Paradise begin to call, which sound I know full well, and the great pleasure it affords me to know that, by their loud voice and utterance, they are in perfect health well repays me for my loss of sleep. As daylight broadens the shrill trumpet of the elephant is heard. I know well the strange antics of this beast, and, to enjoy the fun, I have frequently watched the movements of the female as she trots about her paddock; now playing with mud, scraping it up in small heaps, then, throwing it up, lets it fall on her head and neck or back; then she sits down and squashes it about until her appearance is most ludicrous. She comes to me, I hand her an old broom (minus the handle) with which she rubs and scrubs herself, holding the stump of the broom with her trunk; she then throws the broom high in the air, rushes into the water, has a good roll, dashes and splashes it about, blows and spouts, and comes out delighted at the mess she has made.

VISIT TO ROSCOFF.

During my short stay at Roscoff in August 1875, I daily frequented the laboratory of Professor de Lacaze Duthiers, and was much pleased to observe the very complete and excellent arrangements of this establishment for the study of the various forms of life. It is my opinion that the study of the early indications of animal life intensifies the sensitiveness and intelligence of the student and produces in him a profound and exalted idea of the wondrous creative power exhibited in minute and delicate structures, thus rendering important assistance in the future to those who become acquainted with this branch of scientific knowledge. I am certain also that such a laboratory in so suitable a locality must assist materially in the attainment of the object for which it was designed.

A FEW WORDS ABOUT THE MYSTIC NUMBER SEVEN TO BE OBSERVED IN NATURE.

The student of natural history must from time to time meet with some kind of uniformity in the operations that take place with unerring certainty or precision. Thus the doves and pigeons as a rule (to which, however, there are exceptions) lay two eggs, and the male and female take turns on the nest in the process of incubation, and at the end of fourteen days, if all be well, two young birds are produced. It will be seen, then, supposing that the parent birds had equally divided the time of incubation, each one had sat seven days, and this fourteen days is the earliest time known to me for hatching any bird.

I am reminded that this statement resembles the story of the two Irishmen who had to walk fourteen miles, but,

314

as they agreed to go together, fell into the strange notion that it would be only seven miles apiece.

But to proceed with my subject. I find that the time required for the incubation or hatching of a very numerous class of birds is three weeks, or, in other words, three sevens. Breeders of common fowls know this fact full well. We next come to other families of birds, such as ducks, geese, swans, etc., that require a longer time, but still the time is fairly divided by seven until we arrive at a class of birds that, as far as my knowledge extends, require the greatest length of time—seven weeks—seven times seven; this period of incubation is usual with the struthious birds such as ostriches, cassowaries, emus, etc.

That this mystical number is carried on, and appears among the class of animals known as mammalia, can be easily shown. Take man: the child at its seventh year losing its sucking-teeth, which are replaced by its permanent set; and its development continues to undergo a change at fourteen, and it may be considered adult at twenty-one—three sevens; and at the termination of ten sevens, the three-score and ten, the final. Shakespeare's seven ages forcibly call to mind these conditions of our species.

Another illustration is the important part played in nature by the seven days' incubation of some of the diseases to which we are liable, and the changes that take place in connection with many of these maladies; the seventh, fourteenth, or twenty-first are watched for often with the greatest anxiety.

In a large number of animals the period of gestation is fixed at the seventh month. One remarkable one is the hippopotamus. This extraordinary monster goes with young seven months and twenty-one days.

It appears to me that in the earliest dawn of humanity

the nature of these fixed periods suggested and caused to be created certain laws that have descended to our time, for we find that crimes are punished by imprisonment for seven, fourteen, or twenty-one years. The same fixture of time for the lease of a house, land, or other agreement, apprenticeship, and many other human laws are, as it were, based upon the same foundation.

The frequent reference in Holy Writ to the seventh day, the opening of the seventh seal, and endless repetitions of this number in every language in all parts of the world, cannot fail to produce and fix in our minds a profound belief in the natural laws that are with unerring certainty carried on throughout the universe, and which have from the beginning, and still continue to exercise, the power we witness, and which I, for one, fail to comprehend.

I have no doubt if your numerous readers would kindly contribute the different and widely spread facts upon this subject, a vast accumulation of very interesting matter would be collected upon this subject. For instance, say the origin of the seven champions of Christendom, the seventh charmed bullet in *Der Freischutz*, Sevenoaks in Kent, Seven Sisters-road, Holloway, or last, and perhaps least, Seven Dials, St. Giles.

The above led to a very long and interesting paper on " The Figure 7 used throughout Scripture," also another article in *Weldon's Ladies' Journal*, 1897.

THINGS NEW AT THE ZOO!

Go, people, and pay all
To see the she-gayal
　　That Bartlett has had brought from the Indies ;
And the wolves from Thibet,
Which mammals we bet
　　Will raise in their dens fearful shindies.

The arctonyx snout
Is the newest thing out,
  The first ever heard of in London ;
A Panolian deer,
Fresh to this hemisphere,
  Awaits you, your beer and your bun done.

There's a pigeon that sings,
And one with bronze wings,
  Polyplectrous and likewise a Loris ;
A monkey—men tell us
To call it Entellus—
  The charge but a bob at the door is.

There are demoiselle cranes
To be seen for your pains,
  With six or eight of the tortoise ;
And a Hemipode ends
This list of new friends
  The *Marian Moore* lately brought us :

No, stay, there are pelicans—
Rhyme to them Helicon's
  Verse-helping fount might supply us ;
But a New River draught,
Teetotally quaffed,
  Is all the liqueur we have by us.

So then Floreat "Zoo,"
Both old beasts and new ;
  And when you have seen all its treasures,
Take an ice or a tartlet,
And thank Mr. Bartlett
  For adding so much to your pleasures.

ANON.

This is supposed to have been written by Henry Lee.

LONGEVITY OF ANIMALS.

Doubtless certain animals attain to a great age. I have no doubt that fishes and reptiles have, in many instances, lived to be very old, and under the circumstances, from the nature of their porous bones and cartilages, they continue to grow for a much longer period than those animals having more solid and harder bones.

Instances of the great age reached by some birds have come under my notice, one of the most remarkable being the case of a bird that lived upwards of fifty years in the Society's Gardens. It was a Vasa Parrot (*Coracopsis vasa*) presented by a Mr. Telfair in 1830, and which died in 1880. It was fully adult when it came to the Gardens, but how old it then was it is impossible to say. Towards the latter part of its existence it became somewhat feeble, and many of the sooty-black feathers turned white, especially about the head. The next parrot of this same species was presented in 1866.

Many other birds are known to have lived to a great age, especially raptorial birds, including the eagles and vultures. Most of these birds take a number of years to put on the adult plumage, and it would be impossible to give any precise date as to the age to which they may attain in a wild state, but they live to a very great age in captivity. A vulture in the Society's Gardens was known to have been the property, for many years, of the celebrated anatomist Dr. Brooks. So far as I am able to judge, there is no hard and fast rule by which we can in any way calculate to what age some animals may arrive, but there can be no doubt that the larger cetaceous animals, such as the whales, have a very long life, and we know that many old whales are covered with barnacles, etc., which indicate

318

very clearly the great age to which they must have attained.

As a general rule all the larger species of animals were, in olden times, supposed to live to a great age, and as so few opportunities, probably, of watching their growth and development then existed, people believed that a great length of time was required for the attainment of their large size.

At the present time, however, these notions and suppositions have undergone a very decided change, and many of the large animals that were thought to live two or three hundred years, are found to be old, feeble, and quite worn out at thirty; the hippopotamus and rhinoceros are instances of this kind.

The male hippopotamus, which was presented by the late Viceroy of Egypt in 1850, died in 1877, an old worn-out animal, the teeth, bones, and all other parts exhibiting every sign of great age. The same condition is now manifest in the female presented in 1854, and the same may be said of the Indian rhinoceros that was purchased in 1850, and died in 1873.

All these great animals were quite young and small when received, and died within thirty years of their birth, apparently of old age.

It has often happened that visitors from a distance who had seen the first rhinoceros that was exhibited in the Zoological Society's Gardens in 1834, fancied, on re-visiting the menagerie, that they recognized their former acquaintance in the animal now living; mistakes of this kind have probably caused many animals to be considered much older than they are.

Many attempts have been made to discover some kind of rule or guide by which the length of life of different kinds of animals could be calculated.

The period of gestation has been suggested, but has utterly failed ; the length of time required for growth has been proposed, but is also useless. For instance, a goose is adult and full grown in one year, and if kept under favourable circumstances lives as long as an ordinary human being.

An old male swan that died some years since in St. James's Park was said to have been put there in the reign of Queen Anne.

The male African elephant (Jumbo) was, when received in 1865, about four years old, and he is, at the time of writing these lines, in his twentieth year, and no doubt full grown.

REMOVING AND PACKING WILD ANIMALS.

It may appear strange, but it is nevertheless true, that animals which have been bred from wild animals in captivity and reared are the wildest and most difficult of animals to pack up or remove. They are always regarded, by those who have to remove them, as liable to accident, and the cause of this is not difficult to understand. When we take into consideration that they have been accustomed to be treated kindly, being fed by the persons around them to whom they are attached, and are, seemingly, perfectly tame, generally coming to a call or feeding from the hand, etc., etc., it is not a matter for wonderment if, on the occasion of something strange occurring to which they are not accustomed, their naturally wild and timid nature suddenly comes to the front, and they make the most determined effort to escape from the strange treatment to which they are being subjected, and the new conditions under which they find themselves.

They are terrified at everything fresh that is happening,

and in their frantic madness sometimes injure themselves to such an extent that they die, or are perfectly useless.

Animals that have been captured in a wild state and have undergone the hardship of being confined, during a sea voyage, in a small space become tame. Such animals are afterwards much less troublesome to pack up and transport than those who have, as before mentioned, been produced by wild animals in captivity.

It is a well-known fact that a great many animals which are captured in a wild state either die or kill themselves by the determined resistance they make. Those who have undergone this trial and survive are afterwards easily managed.

WHAT IS CRUELTY ?

It must be admitted that the whole animal life is one of cruelty, and the subject may be classed under different heads, that is to say, cruelty may be regarded as being of different degrees, according to the various circumstances under which the cruelty exists.

The several headings under which the various forms of cruelty might be placed are—1st, what may be called, accidental cruelty ; 2nd, wilful cruelty without any provocation, or object to be gained ; 3rd, experimental cruelty with some idea, or intention, of gaining knowledge, and of becoming expert in performing operations upon living bodies ; 4th, advantageous cruelty ; 5th, necessary cruelty ; 6th, unavoidable cruelty.

At the present time there is a considerable controversy among, and disagreement in the minds of, many people who take an interest in animal life as regards cruelty. Nothing can be more laudable than the increased desire in the public mind for the prevention of cruelty to animals; at the same time the over-anxiety of many of these kind-hearted people would, if their views were carried out, involve our magistrates and other officials in the most vexatious and troublesome legal arguments. In the first place there already exists a most important and useful society established for the prevention of cruelty to domestic animals. One of the chief difficulties which magistrates, from time to time, have to encounter is, when a charge of cruelty to animals is brought before them, the vague and uncertain definition of domestic and other animals. A great difficulty would be removed if a decision in regard to this matter by the highest zoological authorities were arrived at, and this appears to me to be a very simple and easily accomplished task.

One remarkable fact is that our domestic animals, including horses, cattle, sheep, goats, pigs, dogs, cats, rabbits, guinea-pigs, llamas and camels, are all stamped by the variation of colour. All of the above-named animals exhibit the three colours, black, white, and red, varying in individuals; sometimes the colour appears to be wholly black, at others perfectly white, or red; some animals exhibit two, some three colours. This peculiar circumstance forms an extraordinary contrast with the uniform and regular colours of most wild animals.

In our domestic birds a most remarkable and similar variation in colour occurs, differing from their original colour when wild.

The great difficulty in framing a law for the protection of wild animals is to so frame it that its provisions, when enforced, would not involve the whole country in law-suits and disturbances. If this were not done no sportsman would be safe from being interfered with, because shooting, hunting and fishing are productive of and cause a vast amount of unavoidable cruelty, since the wounded beasts, birds, and fishes escape to die a lingering and painful death in spite of any amount of trouble taken by those who have inflicted the injury to rescue them.

Sportsmen, therefore, would in such cases be charged with having committed an act of cruelty, although it would be quite contrary to their intention. How could such cases be fairly dealt with?

The difficulty and trouble would be insurmountable.

As regards acts of cruelty committed by senseless and thoughtless people, there are at the present time many teachers in schools, colleges, and other institutions, who could, by constant endeavour, impress upon the minds of all young folks the necessity of practising humane and kind treatment towards all dumb animals, and instil into their nature the firm resolution to avoid acting cruelly to any animal, as far as it is possible, and a determination to interfere, upon every occasion, to prevent such act. These lessons if they were allowed to form part of the daily instruction of children, would doubtless be of much greater advantage than the attempt to make new laws that would be likely to create an amount of dissatisfaction and ill-will in every part of the kingdom.

The world is surrounded by clouds, smoke, steam, vapour, mist and fogs. Some of these elements are produced by causes over which we have absolutely no control, others we may prevent, and some are avoidable. So it is with the cruelty practised in the animal world.

Take for instance the fierce brutality of. the large carnivora, and, among birds, the savage fury of the rapacious species when seizing the helpless victims upon which they feed; but the destruction of life by these creatures is merciful, although it is frequently attended with much suffering and a lingering death, when compared with the horrible infliction of torment by which many thousands of the most harmless creatures are year after year destroyed, slowly but surely, during the summer months when the flies attack such animals as sheep, depositing beneath the wool their eggs which produce maggots in countless thousands, whose united efforts appear to be to eat away the flesh of the unfortunate living animal, until the vital parts are exposed and death ends their miserable life ; endless forms and varieties of painful existence can be found of animals tortured by parasitic destroyers, whose only mode of reproduction and existence appears so conditioned.

What purpose these cruelties in nature are intended to answer let us not stop to inquire. But let us ask ourselves the question, Are we justified in doing, under certain conditions, that which we know to be cruel? The answer must be that we are, for our only chance of maintaining our existence upon the earth depends upon our exercising our skill and power to overcome all other living creatures, to reduce their numbers and to keep under those who, unless destroyed, would in the natural course of things destroy our food, clothing, houses, and take from us the means of existence.

But with the power to kill our knowledge should produce in our minds a feeling of mercy, unfortunately not to be found in a state of nature, to be taught to, and by all fair means enforced upon, those who have it not.

Let us not, however, assume a canting, whining, sniveling, hypocritical pretence of human kindness, or " strain at the gnat and swallow the camel," but endeavour to seek out the cruel coward who wantonly, and often entirely without cause, inflicts pain, to teach the ignorant and punish the guilty.

At the same time we must not be unmindful of the innumerable methods by which pain is caused and which are constantly surrounding us. No doubt many causes are preventible, but, frightful as the statement may appear, we are obliged, however unwilling we may be, to be the instrument of torture, even to our domestic animals whose bodies contribute so greatly to our support and enjoyment.

Ask the farmer what he would do if his stock consisted of bulls, rams, boars, and stallions ; where or how could he keep them ? What would be the result if from kindly motives these creatures were not allowed to be cruelly mutilated? yet few more painful operations can be imagined than those hinted at; if we are to continue our civilization we must be cruel, or rather sanction it in our midst, as we may glean from the following letters :—

"TREATMENT OF ANIMALS IN THE CANARY ISLANDS.

" To the Editor of *The Standard.*

" Not long since I had the pleasure of residing for some months in Las Palmas.

" I regret to say I was frequently horrified to witness the cruel treatment of many of our domestic animals, horses, mules, donkeys, and others. I was astonished at the total indifference of the priests, of which there are a large number. I feel sure if they would exert themselves the unfortunate animals would be more kindly treated."

After I had written the above lines, the following letter appeared in *The Standard :*—

"A. D. Bartlett in writing the other day on the vile treatment of animals in the Canaries, said—'I was astonished at the total indifference of the priests, of which there are a large number.' But is not this attitude of indifference their usual one on the animal question? What in the name of Christ, whom they would serve, is the use of a religion that allows them to tolerate and encourage the most nauseous system of cruelty conceivable? How can you raise up a sound superstructure upon such a rotten basis? The principles that can tolerate the present practice of the laboratory are as degrading to man as they are dishonouring to God. And this is the system that Christians support in this land.

"SPERO MELIORA."

But when we come to the more serious and wanton destruction of valuable animals (in a commercial point of view) without even the slightest thought of the preservation of one fragment of the vast number destroyed, we may call it "Cruelty in Sport," which the quotation here attached (the name of the paper is lost) will illustrate:—"A hunting expedition in the neighbourhood of Kili-Manjoro have been enjoying some fine sport. They have killed fifty-two rhinoceroses, besides buffaloes, elands, ostriches, giraffes, zebras, and various kinds of antelopes. Out of thirty-two species of game which are found in that country they have killed specimens of twenty-two. Their bag in February last amounted in all to one hundred and forty-eight head."

Who could say another word against *cruelty* after reading the above destruction perpetrated by Englishmen?

MY REPORT ON THE DAMAGE CAUSED BY THE EXPLOSION ON THE CANAL, REGENT'S PARK, OCTOBER 2, 1874.

With reference to the damage done to the buildings by the explosion, I may mention that no building has entirely escaped injury; not only has the glass and, in many instances, the frame or sash been entirely destroyed, but a considerable amount of damage has been done by the cracking of the brickwork and *loosening* of the *fastenings* of *doors* and *windows*. The buildings farthest removed from the locality where the explosion occurred have suffered quite as much (or nearly so) as the buildings at the end of the Gardens nearest the fatal spot, for instance, the *reptile-house*, and *workshops immediately behind* that house, had the glass and frames *completely destroyed*. It will be observed that the reptile-house is *close to the canal*, in *reality on its bank*. That the damage was not confined to any particular spot will be gathered from the fact that the glass was destroyed at the *south entrance* on the broadwalk (which runs across the Park). I am inclined to think that the shock was *most severe along the bank of the canal;* the windows and doors at my house were smashed and blown open; the locks, bolts, chain, and other fastenings being torn out at the front and back of the premises; but, strange to say, the roof and glass lantern on the top of the roof escaped injury, probably owing to the lantern being open on all sides. The roof of the monkey-house having a similar lantern also escaped with trifling damage, while the front and ends of the same building were frightfully damaged. The parrot-house had a tremendous shaking, and a portion of the stone carving on the top of the red brick lobby was thrown down; I am inclined to think it must have been struck by some of the flying *débris*, as portions of the ill-fated Tilbury were picked up by myself, soon after the disaster, between my *office* and the *elephant-house*. Other fragments, such as sheet-iron twisted and torn about, fell in the Gardens, a fragment of stone of considerable size was found on the roof of the hippopotamus-house, and other portions of the wreck were also found in various places.

Although the work of restoration was commenced by the whole of our staff of workmen immediately after, and on the morning of, the explosion, and continued, unceasingly, up to the present time (November 3), still we find much to be done; in fact from day to day we discover damage that had escaped notice in the first instance.

The injury done to the animals, themselves, I am glad to say, has been trifling, and this I attribute principally to the utter darkness of the morning, and the impossibility, in the awful confusion, to obtain lights; two or three assistants, who are the only persons who sleep in the Gardens, and I went into the different houses, and by calling and speaking to the affrighted animals caused them to stop jumping and rushing about. As daylight gradually appeared and their several keepers arrived, they became, some but slowly, reconciled to the disturbance, and their nervous condition, in a day or two, appeared to subside. A considerable number of birds escaped through the openings in the roof of the Western Aviary. Many of them, however, returned and allowed themselves to be caught and restored to their former abode, others flew long distances and have been lost, but these do not happen to be birds of much value, and can, therefore, be easily replaced.

For many days after the explosion I received letters from people in the country (surrounding the Metropolis) informing me of strange and beautiful birds that had appeared in their gardens, etc., and, by their kindness, several were recovered.

It is impossible, at this moment, to estimate with any degree of accuracy the amount of damage sustained by the Society, but after carefully noting the repairs that have been necessary and what of them remain to be carried out, I believe the cost will be about £300.— November 3, 1874.

NARROW ESCAPE.

Having received a letter from the Society's agent at Southampton late one evening stating that a ship had arrived from South Africa with a lot of rare animals and birds alive for the Zoo, I packed up immediately and took the night mail to Southampton. Early the next morning, being anxious to see the live things on board, and wishing to have them removed without loss of time, I found my way to the docks. Finding the vessel without a gangway, I reached across with my umbrella to catch at a rope which hung from the rigging close to the gangway; having secured the rope, but forgetting that I had on a pair of leather gloves, and not noticing that the rope was covered with hoar-frost, it being mid-winter and very frosty, I threw my umbrella on the deck and swung myself off the side of the quay, thinking that I should land on the vessel, but by reason of my weight, together with the leather gloves and the frosty rope, which I could not hold tight enough, I began to slide down the rope, and all I could do, down, down I went, calling for help. Luckily a wharfinger at a distance happened to see me disappear, and ran to my assistance with a very long boat-hook, which he slipped into my overcoat just in time to prevent my feet going into the water. Then a struggle ensued because I could not hold the rope, and the water being low my weight at that depth was too much for the man; however, further assistance soon arrived, and I was rescued from my perilous position.

At that early hour in the morning very few people were about, and had it not been for that solitary man I must have lost my life.

Moral—Don't swing on frosty ropes with thin leather gloves on.

APPENDIX II.

LETTERS AND CORRESPONDENCE, ETC.

FROM among the correspondence I have selected some of the most interesting letters, which will form a series by themselves, they having no reference, one with another, to any particular subject.

Respecting the letters from Charles Darwin I took the liberty of writing to his son, Mr. Francis Darwin, upon the subject, and in answer he says—

" DEAR SIR,—I regret very much that up to the present I can only find the few letters I now send. Either I or my assistant have been systematically through my father's innumerable portfolios, and I have little hope of discovering any more. There were of course many more, and I cannot imagine where my father put them.

" Yours faithfully,

" FRANCIS DARWIN."

" *August* 24, 1860.

" DEAR SIR,—I have directed a copy of my *Origin of Species* to be sent to your address to the Zoo rooms in Hanover Square, and I hope that you will do me the favour to accept it. If you will read article on Hybridism, at page 264, you will see why I am anxious about the embryos in eggs from first crosses. I was very glad to see a donkey with a wild ass in the Gardens, for I infer from this that you intend rearing a hybrid ; if so I hope that you will look carefully for stripes on the *shoulder and legs in the foal:* you will see why I am so anxious on this head, if you will read the little discussion in the *Origin* from p. 163—167.

330

"I will let you hear about the Moscow rabbits[1] after I have heard from the young lady who brought them, whether she consents to their being sent to the Gardens. If you should hear from Hunt anything about the record of the gestation of the *Canidæ*, or about the parents of hybrid jackals, perhaps you will be so kind as to inform me.

"I was much interested by the facts you kindly communicated to me, and remain, dear sir,

"Yours very faithfully,
"CHARLES DARWIN."

"*May* 21, 1861.

"DEAR SIR,—The bearer will deliver three rabbits (if none dead on voyage) from Madeira. Will you take charge of them for me, and show this note to Mr. Sclater? They are zoologically very interesting, for they have run wild on a little island of Porto Santo, since the year 1420 : and judging from two dead ones seen by me, they have become greatly reduced in size and modified in colour and in their skeletons. I want much to see them alive, and to try whether they will cross freely with common rabbits. I am going immediately to leave home for two months. Would there be any objection to your keeping them for some time and matching them with some other breed ; or if you think fit, first try and get some purely bred?

"I may perhaps be mistaken, but I was very much surprised at many of the characters of the two dead specimens which I saw.

"If any one should die, I should like its skeleton. Pray forgive me troubling you, but I know not what to do with them at present.

"If worth consideration, I would of course pay for their keep.

"In haste,
"Dear sir,
"Yours very faithfully,
"CHARLES DARWIN."

With reference to the above rabbits, Mr. C. Darwin writes [2]—"The two little Porto Santo rabbits, whilst alive in the Zoological Gardens, had a remarkably different

---

[1] These Moscow rabbits were deposited in the Society's Gardens on September 30, 1860.

[2] *Animals and Plants under Domestication*, vol. i. p. 114.

appearance from the common kind. They were extraordinarily wild and active, so that many persons exclaimed on seeing them that they were more like large rats than rabbits. They were nocturnal to an unusual degree in their habits, and their wildness was never in the least subdued; so that the Superintendent, Mr. Bartlett, assured me that he never had a wilder animal under his charge. This is a singular fact, considering that they are descended from a domesticated breed. Lastly, and this is a highly remarkable fact, Mr. Bartlett could never succeed in getting these two rabbits, which were both males, to associate or breed with the females of several breeds which were repeatedly placed with them."

The two rabbits above-mentioned were deposited in the Society's Gardens, May 21, 1861, and entered as two females, but Mr. Darwin says they were males.

"*January* 30, 1865.

" MY DEAR SIR,—You have two rabbits of mine from Porto Santo. Will you be so good as to have one of them killed, taking great care that the skull and vertebræ are not broken, and sent as soon as you can, addressed—

'C. DARWIN, ESQ.,
'*Care of* Down Postman,
'Bromley, Kent.'

Per rail.

" I shall be very much obliged if you will inform me whether you have got young from these rabbits with the females of other breeds ?

" I want to beg one other favour ; I want to examine under the microscope the tipped feathers of *Gallus sonneratii*. Could you send me one or two ?

" Believe me, my dear sir,
" Yours very faithfully,
" CHARLES DARWIN."

"Dear Sir,—I wrote to you above a week ago to ask you to send me immediately the body of one of my Port Santo rabbits, together with some information. I have not received the rabbit, nor any acknowledgment of my letter from you. I now request you will be so good as to write to me by return of post.

"Dear sir,
"Yours faithfully,
"Ch. Darwin."

"*February* 14, 1865.

"My Dear Sir,—I am very much obliged for your note, answering so fully all my questions, and for the feathers of the *Gallus*. The rabbit has arrived safely, but most unfortunately for me the entrails have been taken out. If you catch the other, will you be so good as to send it unmutilated to me 'Care of the Down Postman, Bromley, Kent.'

"With my thanks, believe me,
"Yours faithfully,
"Ch. Darwin."

"*December* 9, 1866.

"My Dear Sir,—Would you have the kindness to send me on a slip of paper the name of the three or four Tringa-like birds in the Aquarium, which never, except once, assumed the proper summer plumage. Please just add whether you have known this with more than the three or four individuals, which you showed me.

"I much wish I could persuade you to try with different-coloured worsted or rags, whether the Bower-bird prefers gay colours.

"I thank you most sincerely for all the interesting information which you so often give me.

"My dear sir,
"Yours very faithfully,
"Ch. Darwin."

"*December* 19, 1866.

"My Dear Sir,—I was with Mr. Wood this morning, and he expressed himself strongly about you and your daughter's kindness in aiding him. He much wants assistance on another point, and if you could aid him, you would greatly oblige me. You know well the appearance of a dog when approaching another dog with hostile intentions before they come close together. The dog walks very stiff, with tail rigid and upright, *hair on back erected*, ears pointed and eyes directed forwards. When the dog attacks the other, down go the ears and the canines are uncovered. How could you anyhow arrange so that one of your dogs could see a strange dog from a little distance, so that Mr. Wood could sketch the former attitude, viz. of the stiff gesture with erected hair and erected ears. And then he could afterwards sketch the same dogs, when fondled by his master and wagging his tail with drooping ears. These two sketches I want much, and it would be a great favour to Mr. Wood and myself if you could aid him.

"My dear sir,

"Yours very faithfully,

"CH. DARWIN.

"P.S.—When a horse is turned out into a field he trots with high elastic steps, and carries his tail aloft. Even when a cow frisks about she throws up her tail. I have seen a drawing of an elephant, apparently trotting with high steps, and with the tail erect. When the elephants in the Gardens are turned out and are excited so as to move quickly, do they carry their tails aloft? How is this with the rhinoceros? Do not trouble yourself to answer this, but I shall be in London in a couple of months, and then perhaps you will be able to answer this trifling question. Or if you write about wolves and jackals turning round, you could tell me about the tails of elephants, or of any other animals.—C.D."

"*January* 5, 1867.

"MY DEAR SIR,—Many thanks about *Limulus*. I am going to ask another favour, but I do *not want to trouble you to answer it by letter*. When the *Callithrix sciurea* screams violently, does it wrinkle up the skin round the eyes like a baby always does? When thus screaming, do the eyes become suffused with moisture? Will you ask Sutton to observe carefully? Could you make it scream without hurting it much? I should be truly obliged some time for this information, when in spring I come to Gardens, or Sutton could write to me.

"Yours very faithfully,

"CH. DARWIN."

"*February* 16, 1867.

"MY DEAR SIR,—I want to beg two favours of you. I wish to ascertain whether the Bower-bird discriminates colours. Will you have all the coloured worsted removed from cage and the bower, and then put in all in a row, at same distance from bower, the enclosed coloured worsted, and mark whether the bird *at first* makes any selection. Each packet contains equal quantity. The packets had better be separated and each then put separate, but close together; perhaps it would be fairest if the several colours were put alternately, one thread of bright scarlet, one thread of brown, etc. etc. There are six colours. Will you have the kindness to tell me whether the bird prefers one colour to another? Secondly, I very much want several heads of the fancy and long-domesticated rabbits to measure the capacity of skull. I want only *small* kinds, such as Himalayas, small Angora, silver-grey, or any small-sized rabbit which has long been domesticated. The silver-grey from warrens would be of little use. The animals must be adult, and the smaller the breed the better.

"Now when any one dies would you send me the carcase, named? If the skin is of any value it might be skinned, but it would be rather better with skin, and I could make presents to any keeper to whom the skin is a perquisite.

"This would be great assistance to me, if you would have kindness thus to aid me.

"My dear sir,

"Yours sincerely,

"CH. DARWIN."

"*September* 15, 1871.

"My DEAR SIR,—As on many former occasions, I am going to beg earnestly for a little information. Judging from the structure of the beak and published accounts, I imagine that the common goose does not sift the water out of the sides of its beak like a duck. Is this so? Does any species of goose sift the water in a partial manner, as well as use its beak in tearing or biting herbage? I am trying to trace gradation in structure and habits, and this would be a very useful piece of information.

"The common goose has lamellæ on the borders of the beak, partly confluent, and which seem to serve as teeth. Now has any goose quite a smooth beak? or has any goose (and this would be more useful to me) less developed lamellæ, knobs or teeth, than the common goose? If your son Edward has a specimen not very expensive of any such goose, *i. e.* with beak nearly smooth (if such exists), I should be much obliged if he would send it to me in a paper parcel.

335

"As you are so busy, perhaps your son Edward would be so kind as to answer for you any of the above questions on which you can give me information. The beak of the Shoveller Duck which I procured from your son is one of the most beautiful structures which I ever saw.

" My dear sir,

" Yours sincerely,

" CH. DARWIN."

" *Sept.* 16, 1871.

" DEAR SIR,—I am very much obliged for your note and the specimens. I have kept two of the geese, and will the first day I send to the station return two.

" You say in your note that the Egyptian Goose throws the water, like a duck, out of the sides of the beak. Now it would be *especially* useful to me to know *positively* whether this goose can graze or tear off the herbage like the domestic goose. Will you ask your father, if he does not know, whether he could turn one of these geese out on a plot where there is fresh grass, and see whether it can use its beak well in biting off or plucking herbage.

" I shall be glad also to hear whether the Spur-winged Goose of Africa can sift the water, which does not seem possible from what you say about its beak.

" Dear Sir,

" Yours faithfully,

" CH. DARWIN.

' Mr. E Bartlett."

" *Herne Bay, Sept.* 19, 1871.

" MY DEAR SIR,—In reply to your letter which I received here yesterday I do not believe the common goose sifts the water out of the sides of the bill like a duck. But some species of geese that feed more in the water may use the bill partially in this manner, but most species of geese feed on the land ; but I think the Black-and-white Goose of Australia is the bird most likely to have the lamellæ less developed than any other goose. We have the bird alive in the Gardens. I have written to my son Edward, and asked him to look at the bird and report to you. On the other hand I think the Snow Goose of North America has the lamellæ stronger than any other goose ; they are, in fact, like powerful well-developed teeth. I have forwarded your letter to my son Edward, and you may depend you will hear from

336

him. I shall be home in a few days, and again think over the matter.

"Yours faithfully,
"A. D. BARTLETT.

"Chas. Darwin, Esq.

"P.S.—The Black-and-white Goose of Australia has the webs of the feet less developed than any other goose."

"*Sept.* 20, 1871.

"MY DEAR SIR,—I thank you truly for your letter and trouble which you have taken for me. When you return to the Zoo Gardens, if you can ascertain, or observe, whether any goose *sifts* the water, as well as uses its beak for tearing, I should be greatly obliged by being allowed to quote you. I hope that I may hear from your son Edward.

"Yours very faithfully,
"C. DARWIN."

"*Zoo, Sept.* 20, 1871.

"DEAR SIR,—I have examined a number of the geese in the Gardens and find they vary in structure of lamellæ.

"The Egyptian Goose, *Chenolopex ægypticus*, has the lamellæ well-developed on both mandibles, and uses the bill in the water like a duck by throwing the water out at the corners. (Does it graze like our goose?) The Black-and-white Goose, *Anseranus melanoleuca*, of Australia, and the Spur-winged Goose, *Plectrophanes gambensis*, West Africa, have merely the smooth ridges inside the mouth of the upper mandible and very slight points on the lower ridge. I cannot say if these birds use the bill like the duck, but will ascertain; the latter bird has less lamellæ than the former of the two.

"The *Chloephaga melanoptera*, or Andian Goose, has very slight lamellæ like the Bernicle, Ruddy-headed and Canadian and this genus.

"I will forward to you some skins for examination, and the price I will put as low as possible, so that you will be able to select any of the specimens you may think proper.

"I am, etc.,
"E. B."

"*Oct.* 15, 1871.

"DEAR SIR,—I hope that you will excuse me troubling you, but I should be *greatly* obliged if you could send me pretty soon (as my

MS. must go to the printer) any information on the Egyptian Goose, *both sifting the water and biting or tearing like a common goose the herbage.*

" Dear sir,
" Yours faithfully,
" CH. DARWIN.

" Mr. E. Bartlett."

" 70, *Delancey St.,*
" *R. P., N. W.,*
" *Oct.* 16, 1871.

" DEAR SIR,—The Egyptian geese feed in the water, they do not move their heads from side to side (laterally) like the ducks that sift the food ; their mode of tearing and biting the herbage is much the same as the common goose.

" I am sorry not to be able to send more particulars as I have had but little opportunity of watching the birds.

" I am, etc.,
" E. B."

" *Zoo, May* 16, 1872.

" DEAR SIR,—I turned a snake loose into the yard with two of Grote's Porcupines ; one of them shook his *tail at the sight* of the snake, the other did not, but gnashed his teeth and appeared much inclined to bite the snake. I then tried the Crested Porcupine ; he did not shake his tail, but set his spines up, and I thought he would attack the snake with his teeth ; he walked round the snake and appeared angry, but did not touch it. I then put the snake into the yard with the little Java Porcupine, but he was evidently frightened of the snake, and kept as far from it as possible, but did not rattle his tail. I believe from what I saw that the Porcupine if hungry and in a wild state met with a snake he would kill and eat it.

" Yours faithfully,
" A. D. BARTLETT.

" C. Darwin, Esq."

ASSOCIATED HABITS.

I take these notes from Darwin's *Expression of the Emotions*, p. 47.

"I will give only one other instance of an habitual and purposeless movement. The Sheldrake (*Tadorna*) feeds on the sands left uncovered by the tide, and when a worm-cast is discovered, 'it begins patting the ground with its feet, dancing as it were over the hole;' and this makes the worm come to the surface.

"Now Mr. St. John says that 'when his tame Sheldrakes came to ask for food, they patted the ground in an impatient and rapid manner.' This, therefore, may almost be considered as their expression of hunger. Mr. Bartlett informs me that the Flamingo and the Kagu (*Rhinochetus jubatus*) when anxious to be fed, beat the ground with their feet in the same odd manner."

MEANS OF EXPRESSION.

Again at page 113, Mr. Darwin states—

"Although sheep and goats appear such placid animals, the males often join in furious contests. As deer form a closely related family, and as I did not know that they ever fought with their teeth, I was much surprised at the account given by Major Ross-King of the Moose-deer in Canada. He says, when 'two males chance to meet, laying back their ears and gnashing their teeth together, they rush at each other with appalling fury.' But Mr. Bartlett informs me that some species of deer fight savagely with their teeth, so that the drawing back of the ears by the moose accords with our rule.

"Mr. Bartlett watched a wild boar quarrelling rather savagely with his sow; and both had their mouths open and their ears drawn backwards. Boars fight together by striking upwards with their tusks; and Mr. Bartlett doubts whether they then draw back their ears."

SPECIAL EXPRESSION.

Page 123, Mr. Darwin says—

"A similarly connected movement between the hind-quarters and the tail may be observed in the Hyæna.

"Mr. Bartlett informs me that when two of these animals fight together, they are mutually conscious of the wonderful power of each other's jaws, and are extremely cautious. They well know that if one of their legs were seized, the bone would be instantly crushed into atoms; hence they approach each other kneeling, with their legs turned as much as possible inwards, and with their whole bodies bowed, so as not to present any salient point; the tail at the same time closely tucked in between the legs."

Mr. Darwin tells us at page 138, that "Baboons often show their passion and threaten their enemies in a very odd manner, namely, by opening their mouths widely as in the act of yawning. Mr. Bartlett has often seen two baboons, when first placed in the same compartment, sitting opposite to each other and thus alternately opening their mouths, and this action seems frequently to end in a real yawn. Mr. Bartlett believes that both animals wish to show to each other that they are provided with a formidable set of teeth, as is undoubtedly the case. As I could hardly credit the reality of this yawning gesture, Mr. Bartlett insulted an old baboon and put him into a violent passion, and he almost immediately thus acted."

It was well known to all the earlier ornithologists that Charles John Andersson, of South African repute as a field naturalist, was a pupil of my father's, and that Andersson worked in Norway and Sweden by collecting all the rarer birds and their eggs which passed through my father's hands. Many of his early South African collections came

also to my father.   Some of his business letters now in my
possession date from Gottenbourgh, Sweden, June 23,
1847.   I attach one of the most interesting communications,
which was written in 1862, from Damara-Land—

"*Damara-Land,*
"*April* 23, 1862.

"Mr. A. D. Bartlett,
  "Zool. Gardens,
    "Regent's Park, London.

"My Dear Bartlett,
      "I received your letter dated London, Dec. 5, 1861, about
a month ago, and have been waiting to reply to it, in the hopes of
first hearing or seeing something of Mr. Benstead, but as there are as
yet no signs of him, either personally or in writing, I must just
scribble you a few lines in order that I may not be set down as a
negligent correspondent.

"I am sorry to say I am not homeward bound, much as I would
like it, since writing to you. Is it not so ?   I have entered into
business in Damara-land, and for the present am unable to take any
long flight abroad.   I could heartily wish that I never had had anything to do with this country beyond travelling and so forth, for of
late it has become very unsettled ; in short, I am seriously in for it.

"At present I have many thousand pounds at stake, and what is
more, I am largely indebted.   True the elements, to a considerable
extent, of making a fortune do exist, but the want of order and law
are against all serious and extensive speculations.   Still I live in
hopes of better times.   I would, however, had I the choice, unfortunately prefer to return to my wandering life.   Bad as the country is
it has many charms to a mind like mine.   In my leisure moments I
have recourse to my favourite pursuits, Natural History, but time si
scarce and the want of books of reference, moreover, is seriously felt.
However, the latter I hope soon to obviate, as I have written to
England for a large supply of books on Natural History.   I have
now by me a considerable number of bird skins, and am daily adding
something, though not quite new.   Indeed, I have scarcely obtained
anything new since I sent my first collection to you.   What I
collected on my last excursion to the interior I, in a great measure,
sent to Mr. Gurney.   By the bye, do you know if the list of Damara
birds is yet completed.   If I had it I would set to work and make
notes upon them.   Just fancy, with all my care and keen observation

341

one little antelope entirely escaped my observation! True it was discovered in a locality only once (and then hurriedly) visited by me. Messrs. Fred. and Chas. Green were the fortunate finders of it. It is of a very diminutive size, scarcely so large as a hare, and presents some curious peculiarities. It may possibly be identical with an Abyssinian species slightly known to me. I have forwarded a specimen to the Cape Museum, accompanied by Messrs. Green's remarks and observations.

"If Mr. Benstead should think proper of turning his steps this way, I need hardly assure you that he would meet with a hearty welcome, and that I would do all in my power to advance the Society's wishes and interest. But I would warn you not to be too sanguine. In the first instance the variety of animals in these parts is not very great nor their numbers. Again, the country is just now in a very unsatisfactory state, unsettled in short. Moreover, to effect anything really good a man ought to reside in the country for at least two seasons, i. e. two years. The natives are not up to the capture of wild animals, and it would take some time to initiate them. The breeding season would of course be the time for going to work. For your information I beg to state that the following quadrupeds are chiefly indigenous to Damara-Land and parts adjacent, viz.— Elephant, Rhinoceros (black and white), Eland, Zebra, Quagga, Black Gnu or Wildebeest, Jemsbuck, Bastard Jemsbuck, Harte-beest, Bastard Hartebeest (only found in the Lake region), Buffalo, Koodoo, Springbuck, Pallah or Redbuck, Denker, Steinbuck, Kliff-springer, Rock Rabbit (*Hyrax capensis*), two or three species Hares and Rabbits, two or three kinds of Hyænas, Jackals, Weasels, Wild Dog, Wild Hog, Aardvark, Porcupine, Lion, Panther, Leopard; besides these there must be one or two smaller species — Lynx, Wild Cat.

"If you could find time to tell me something about the Society's doings I would feel obliged; their doings interest me, as does everything relating to Natural History.

"What is your wonder of the day?

"I am very glad you got the situation you now hold. I fancy it would suit you very well, as it must occasionally leave you a little spare time. I am also very glad to hear that the children are enjoying health.

"Remember me very kindly to them. By the bye, do you know that I am married? If you do not I may kill two birds with one stone, for I have by this time a fine boy in addition, now some seven months old.

" Sincerely hoping this will find you in health and the enjoyment of cheerful spirits,

" Believe me,

" Very faithfully yours,

" CHAS. J. ANDERSSON.

" P.S.—Pray remember me kindly to Wolf. I hope he is alive and flourishing. I wrote more than once but never received an answer. Remember me also to Dr. Sclater."

" *Zoo, January* 1888.

" DEAR MR. BARNUM,—Your kindness in thinking of me by sending me frequently newspapers containing most interesting accounts of your good *will* and good health, and the great amount of labour you bestow in advancing mankind, causes me to think how neglectful I am, and have been, in not more frequently writing to you; it occurs to me that at the end of this year I ought to do something to make up for this apparent apathy. In attempting to do this, I am reminded that my time is limited, and that I am engaged in writing my experiences and recollections from my early life; and considering that I was born in the year 1812, you well know that much must have happened to me since that time. My book, I hope, will be published before long, and I intend it to contain many anecdotes with reference to animals, etc. etc., together with their treatment, food, and other particulars as to the management of wild animals in captivity, with illustrations. Having told you this, I am sure you will know that I have not been idle, considering that I have my unceasing duty to perform daily, but I am happy to say the work is nearly finished.

" Trusting you are well, and wishing you a happy new year,

" Believe me,

" Yours faithfully,

" A. D. BARTLETT."

" *Bridgeport, Conn., U.S.A.,*

" *February* 22, 1888.

" DEAR MR. BARTLETT,—I write in haste to say I shall be glad to get and pay for your book, when it is published, and will try to hit some American friend who will bring it over, unless you know some party who will bring it. I am certain it must be very interesting.

343

" We are very busy getting the big show ready to open in New York, March 25th. It grows larger and more marvellous annually.

" Hoping you are all well and happy as we all are,

" I am, as ever,

" Very truly your friend,

" PHINEAS T. BARNUM."

" *Walton Hall, near Wakefield,*
March 31, 1862.

" DEAR SIR,—Will you kindly excuse my troubling you with these few lines ?

" In poor Mitchell's day, I would now and then get from the keepers the cast-off sloughs of snakes. No doubt they have plenty of sloughs just now. I want the slough, or half a slough, or a little piece of the rattle-snake, or of any dark-skinned snake. I enclose a sample. The Egyptian viper would do, should the keeper have one, or a fragment of one ; please enclose it in a letter to me by post. I don't care how much it is rumpled by putting it in a letter.

" I hope this will find you in good health.

" Believe me, dear sir,

" Very truly yours,

" CHARLES WATERTON."

When I visited Charles Waterton at Walton Hall with Captain Blakeston and Andrew Downs of Halifax, poor Waterton seemed starved ; he looked as miserable as an old spider after a long winter, and although his dinner-table was supplied with everything that could be wished, and the most ample attendance we could desire, still he appeared to take so little food that I felt certain that one blackbird and two white mice could have eaten as much as he had for his dinner. At tea-time he had a little warm water with a tinge of milk and tea added : to my thinking, a sham of tea-drinking.

" *Craven Head, Drury Lane,*
" *May 2, 1851.*

" SIR,—In compliance with your desire of knowing a few of the facts connected with me, I hasten to lay the following account before you. I was born May 2, 1820, at a small village called West Somerton, near Great Yarmouth, Norfolk. My father, who was a respectable farmer, was 6 ft. 6in. in height, and married Elizabeth Dimond of the same neighbourhood ; she was 6 ft. in height and weighed fourteen stone.

"The family consisted of five daughters and four sons, all of whom attained an extraordinary height, the males averaging 6 ft. 5 in. in height, and the females 6 ft. 3½ in.

" It is sometimes a difficult and at all times an unpleasant proceeding for a man to give a description of his person owing to the simple reason so briefly and pointedly expressed by Burns, ' we never see oursels as ithers see us,' but, however, if I confine myself to facts and measurements, neither egotism nor modesty can lead me far astray.

Height, 7 ft. 6 in.
Weight, 33 stone (14 lbs. to the stone)
62 in. round the chest
64   ,,   ,,   the abdomen
36   ,,   across the shoulders
36   ,,   round the thigh
21   ,,   ,, the calf of the leg.

" Perhaps it will be necessary to inform you that in 1848, having a great desire to see the Western world, I took passage on H. M. royal mail-steamer *Canada*, and after one of the most boisterous and dangerous voyages made across the Atlantic, I arrived at the city of New York on Thursday, December 14, 1848. I remained in America two years, and during the greater part of that period I travelled in company with the celebrated General Tom Thumb.

" And now, sir, after trespassing so far on your valuable time, allow me to subscribe myself,

" Your obedient servant,
" ROBERT HALES,
" Craven Head,
" Drury Lane."

Robert Hales, the Norfolk giant, was introduced to Her Majesty, Prince Albert, and the Royal Family, at Buckingham Palace, on April 11, 1851.

EARLY CORRESPONDENCE WHICH TOOK PLACE RESPECTING
LIVE BIRDS OF PARADISE, WITH MR. A. R. WALLACE
AND THE CRYSTAL PALACE COMPANY.

" Memorandum from Secretary to Mr. Bartlett.
" Crystal Palace Company,
" May 18, 1858.

"The Board authorize you to write to Mr. Wallace and say that
they will give him £25 per bird for every Bird of Paradise which he
delivers here up to twelve birds, and £5 a bird for ten more, making
twenty-two in all ; on the understanding that no Birds of Paradise
are to be procured by Mr. Wallace for any other party than this
Company. The Board think that the males and females should
be in equal numbers.

"J. STATHAM,
"For the Secretary."

" Natural History Agency Office,
"24 Bloomsbury Street, London, W.C.,
" April 2, 1859.

"DEAR SIR,—I have lately received a letter from Mr. Wallace in
answer to mine on the subject of the Birds of Paradise for the
Crystal Palace, and the following is a copy of the reply, dated
'Ternate, Moluccas, Oct. 6th, 1858 :—

"'Mr. Bartlett and the Crystal Palace Directors have curious ideas
about getting *live Birds of Paradise,* and talk of sending them by
dozens as if they were Cockatoos or Lories. Just state the following
facts to Mr. Bartlett. 1st. The natives of Aru and New Guinea do
not know the nest-breeding-place of the Birds of Paradise. 2nd. The
few that have been obtained *alive* have been accidental, wounded
birds in almost every case. 3rd. Perhaps one Bird of Paradise in ten
years is obtained alive. 4th. At least £25 would be asked for them
here in the Moluccas—perhaps more—and would be eagerly paid by
any of the Dutch officials for presents to send to Java. 5th. In about
three hundred years that Europeans have been in the Archipelago
and trade carried on with New Guinea and Aru, why have they never
reached England or Europe but in *one* instance ? 6th. Let the
Directors offer £250 for one male bird, and have it well advertised in ·
Macassar and all the parts of the Moluccas, with a free passage to the

person bringing it home, and perhaps in the course of the next twenty years they may get one.'

"By the foregoing there does not appear much chance of Mr. Wallace getting them over *alive*, still I am quite sure if he could meet with them he would make the attempt, and trust to the liberality of the Directors.

"I am, dear Sir,
"Yours faithfully,
"Samuel Stevens."

"*Natural History Agency Office,*
"24 *Bloomsbury Street, London,*
"*Aug.* 9, 1859.

"My Dear Sir,—I received on Saturday a long letter from Mr. Wallace from Ternate, April 28th, 1859, in which he speaks of Birds of Paradise, and the following is an extract :—

"'In my next voyage to New Guinea, I think *it probable* I may get some live Paradiseas (*P. papuana*), but I must have a *definite* arrangement, or will not trouble myself with them. I hear from captain of steamer there is one now in Batavia, for which 1000 rupees (£85) is asked ; this is too much, but it shows their value here. Now I myself will not come home *on any chance*, and if sent, a person *must* come to take charge of them. If, therefore, the Crystal Palace Company want them, you must get and send me out an order for a free passage from Singapore to England *first-class*, to any person in charge of *Birds of Paradise* for me ; next they must either be put up to auction on arrival and the *Palace* get them at their market price, or they must *agree to pay as follows:* if only *one* comes alive £100, the second £50, third and others up to ten £25 each. If they will not give this price I will not trouble myself, as it would be a most difficult and troublesome undertaking. I must have their *answer immediately*, and it must be understood that they take their chance of how many are females, as in the young birds I cannot tell the difference. This is my ultimatum.'

"I shall be writing to Mr. Wallace on the 20th or 24th of this month ; perhaps you will be able to get a reply from the Company before that time.

"Yours faithfully,
"Samuel Stevens.

"Mr. Bartlett."

347

MUSIC FOR ANIMALS.

Among the various copies of letters which are in my possession, this one, written in 1895, is well worth reproducing, and the joke, which was not seen at the time, is that it was written to a gentleman of the Jewish persuasion.

"DEAR SIR,—I am frequently amused by the funny notices and sometimes silly ideas of persons who talk and write about animals. The strange fads and mistakes they circulate are very curious ; one of the fads is *Music*, another perfumes. Now most animals have ears and nostrils, and use them, and doubtless are pleased or displeased with certain sounds or perfumes ; for instance, all the cat family appear pleased with perfumes, such as *valerian, musk,* lavender and many others. It does not appear to me that there is anything very extraordinary in this. With reference to music, I live in fear lest some one should state that our animals were charmed by the sound of the *Jew's-harp,* or worse still the bagpipes, and that some kind friend might provide the keepers with a stock of these musical instruments to play in their leisure.

"Yours faithfully,
"A. D. BARTLETT."

Here we have an example of the sort of letters which were sent to my father, which he called "a real corker." It seems almost impossible for any one to think otherwise.

"*Feb.* 17, 1895.

"SIR,—I would be greatly obliged to you if you can tell me the cause, and still more, a cure for my cockatoo eating his feathers. I have had the bird ten years ; the first two years he ailed nothing. I fed him as directed by the ship's butcher, who brought him, with Indian corn, a few chili-pods, a teaspoonful of hempseed thrice a week, bread, potatoes, greens, fruit, a little milk pudding without egg, sometimes a bone to pick.

"After this my husband treated him to bacon-rind in a morning, and sometimes I gave him a taste of egg. Presently an irritation arose in his feet, he bit his toes till they bled profusely, then one claw fell off and has never grown again.

" We stopped the bacon and egg, but he has been careful to maintain an open sore on his leg ever since, will not let it quite heal. I fancy he likes the taste of blood. We have tried endless remedies without success ; any greasy ones like glycerine make him bite more fiercely. This was his sole disfigurement ; until last December his plumage was always fine. For a year previous I had been giving him lean meat once or twice a week, on the advice of an Australian who did so, and who thought his leg did not heal because he was poorly fed.

" The cockatoo suddenly began to bite the leg more than ever until it was swollen to twice its usual size, then started, not to pull out, but to bite off all the feathers on his breast and his back with some from his wings, and chew them up deliberately. A bird authority near said his blood was overheated ; his diet must be wrong ; meat was given up, even sago-pudding stopped, he has now only plain biscuits, bread, potatoes, and his seeds. The leg has returned to its former dimensions and still not quite healed, but he continues to bite off the feathers on breast, back, and wings as they grow, leaving the stumps in the flesh, and he chews these when not observed, therefore he is a melancholy-looking object, though his spirits and appetite are excellent. I have been advised to ask your advice because you study the birds under your care, and you must have had vast experience. I enclose a stamped envelope, and will be most grateful if you can tell me of a remedy, and also what you find the most suitable diet for these birds ; mine will not eat any kind of nuts. I do not know whether I have inflicted a needlessly long letter upon you, if so, my excuse must be that I thought you might understand the case better if I told you exactly how the bird had been treated.

" My cockatoo has always had a bath once a week except in frosty weather, with some of Jeyes' Purifier in it, and he is never exposed to draughts, though he is taken in the garden during the day in warm weather.

" Apologizing for the trouble I am asking you to take,

" From yours sincerely,

" FANNIE E. WOOD."

(THE ANSWER.)

" *Zoo, Feb.* 18, 1895.

" MADAM,—I fear your bird is past recovery ; no doubt the improper food has been the cause of its suffering.

" Yours sincerely,

" A. D. BARTLETT."

PORCUPINES.

(SIR CHARLES LYELL'S LETTERS.)

"*July* 6, 1863.

"DEAR MR. BARTLETT,—I have just returned from a Welsh tour and found your letter.

"I will be at the Gardens on Saturday, and try and call at your office before the band begins. I am glad you have got the Porcupine to attack a bone.

"Sincerely yours,
"CHAS. LYELL."

"*Aug.* 10, 1863.

"MY DEAR SIR,—M. Lartet I find returns to Paris to-morrow, and will call here early to-morrow morning.

"I wish particularly to show him the bones gnawed by the Porcupine. If you will be so kind as to put them up in paper I will send a servant (a man or maid) by about 5 o'clock to-day, and you will oblige me by naming the bones, whether of ox or horse, and which bone in the skeleton, if you happen to know it precisely, although no doubt Lartet would himself determine that.

"Sincerely yours,
"CHAS. LYELL"

"*Aug.* 15, 1863.

"MY DEAR SIR,—It appears to me that some of the bones of fossil animals of Saint-Prest were rolled in the bed of a river before they were streaked and marked. Are there any aquatic, fluviatile creatures which could have acted upon bones? Would an otter do anything to help us? Or perhaps you may think of some other sharp-toothed animal. I suppose an otter would not do anything under water, but it might take up a bone from the bottom of a stream, and then leave it on a bank, where a flood might sweep it away.

"I am writing a note on the subject for the French translation of my book, and shall record your experiment with the Porcupine, and Lartet's admission then anent.

"Sincerely yours,
"CHAS. LYELL.

"*Aug.* 19, 1863.

"My Dear Sir,—May I cite you for the suggestion that some burrowing animals have claws with which they may probably have scratched bones first buried by them and then torn up again out of the ground, and that a bone which I showed you from Saint-Prest suggested this idea?

" I shall be also glad to have the name of the rodents or carnivora which tore up a brick pavement, if such it was.

"Do any rodents use their claws in burrowing?

"Could you also inform me how many days the two bones, the radius and the humerus, had been in the Porcupine's cage before you took them out?

" Believe me,

" Very truly yours,

"Chas. Lyell."

"*Aug.* 28, 1863.

"My Dear Sir,—The day after I saw you last I got a letter from Paris informing me that they have given their Porcupines in the Jardin des Plantes some bones, but *they will not touch* them. So their experiment has failed.

"Now this makes it desirable for me to state exactly what were the two species of Porcupine which performed in our case, for it may be that *all* the work was done by *one* of the two species?

" Will you be so good as to write me word as soon as you can the *names* and countries of the two species; *Hystrix* I think is the genus.

"The names ought to be printed and stuck up in the cages, but I rather think they are not, but you will be able to find them out for me.

" I was also directed by M. Lartet to some bones in the British Museum of the age of *Elephas meridionalis* having marks on them. These I saw before leaving town, and if I had had a day to spare I would have asked you to drive with me to the Museum that you might better understand the very curious and perplexing phenomena which we want to interpret.

" If you could ascertain by future experiments whether both of the species of Porcupine, or which of them, do the work, it would be well.

" I am, my dear sir,

" Very truly yours,

"Chas. Lyell."

"*Oct.* 5, 1863.

"DEAR SIR,—I will call to-morrow, Tuesday, at the Gardens (at your house), at 4 o'clock, in hopes that you may be able to be there and show me the bones which have been gnawed, and about which you wrote to me when I was in Scotland. I imagine from what Mr. Thompson told me yesterday that the beavers did nothing.

"Yours very truly,
"CHAS. LYELL.

"I hope you separated the two species of Porcupine, which may help to explain the French failure."

BUFFALO OF MINDORA.

"*Zool. Soc. Gardens,*
"*Regent's Park, London, N. W.*
"*Nov.* 18, 1878.

"DEAR SIR,—About thirty years since, a collector of natural history specimens, named Nappar, wrote to me from the Philippines to say that there existed on the island of Mindanos, or Mindora, a small kind of Buffalo extremely wild and difficult to obtain. I engaged him to obtain specimens, and, after much trouble and expense, he sent me an adult bull, a cow and a calf that he had shot and skinned. They were offered by me to Dr. Gray for the British Museum, who declined them, as he was of opinion they were only small varieties of the common Manilla or Water-Buffalo; and this was my own opinion, and also that of every one who saw them. I kept them a long time, and, not finding any one who would have them, I at last sent them to Stevens's sale-room, where they were sold for a few shillings. I can assure you that these animals were not like the *Anou,* but much larger, and had all the appearance of a common Indian Buffalo of small size.

"Yours faithfully,
"A. D. BARTLETT.

"The Secretary Zool. Soc."

THE AYE-AYE.

While preparing my notes on the habits of the Aye-aye I received this letter :—

"*British Museum,*
"*Sept.* 8, 1862.

"DEAR SIR,—You would oblige me by comparing the enclosed proof with your living Aye-aye, and noting any discrepancy in my description from the specimens in spirits ; the colour of the palm and sole ; whether M. Vinson's account of the sleeping posture accords with that of our living specimen.

"And an early return of my proof would be acceptable to the Editor of the *Trans.*, and to yours very truly,

"RD. OWEN."

THE AARD-WOLF.

"*January* 14, 1896.

"DEAR SIR,—I believe that a good many years ago, somewhere in the winter, a specimen of the Aard-Wolf (*Proteles cristatus*) lived for some time in the Gardens. At this distance of time it may seem at first sight unreasonable to ask if you can recall the nature of the food you used to give it, but if you can I shall be much obliged to you, as I am making an effort to procure some living specimens from Suakin.

"Yours sincerely,
"JOHN ANDERSON."

"*Zoo, January* 15, 1896.

"DEAR SIR,—On Oct. 26th, 1868, an Aard-Wolf was brought here, and supposed to be the first of the species ever seen (alive) in Europe.

"For some days the animal refused food, and I was in fear that it would die. Various kinds of food were offered to it, but without result; at last I made a mixture of finely-minced tripe boiled with milk, this it would not touch ; almost in despair, I, with my hand, sprinkled this mixture all over the animal, the creature at once began to lick itself, and thus having tasted this food, gave me no more trouble. I have had two or three individuals of this species since, and have fed them on well-cooked meat and soft food.

"Yours faithfully,
"A. D. BARTLETT.

"Dr. J. Anderson."

APPENDIX III.

ZOOLOGICAL NOTES.

ANIMALS IN REGENT'S PARK DURING THE SEVERE WEATHER. THE TARANTULA SPIDER, ETC.

WE are just recovering from the terrible war of the elements that broke out and came so suddenly upon us. When the enemies of life, to wit, frost, snow and cold winds threatened us with destruction, we were taken by surprise, and all our available strength was called out; we had fire and water in full force on our side, and by their powerful aid we thought to keep our ground. The latter ally, however, after a few days, was unfortunately defeated. This loss caused us much apprehension, and it was only by the greatest and most determined exertions that a fresh supply was brought up. Still for many days the struggle continued. Our only hope lay in the arrival of General Thaw, and this consummation so anxiously wished for took place on Jan. 27, 1881. After the battle comes the list of casualties—the killed, wounded, and missing, and the usual endeavour to offer some kind of consolation that many hope for and expect, that the *loss on the side of the enemy was very great*. In our case this consolation (if it can be regarded as one) is denied to us—the enemy not being human forms—it is, however, satisfactory to know that our misfortunes and losses up to the present time are small considering the overwhelming force against us ; our only consolation is in the fact that the enemy has retired, after having slaughtered and damaged, unmercifully, the helpless and infirm, and inflicted upon our water and other works and contrivances an incalculable amount of damage, leaving us to replace, restore, and repair as best we can. I shall say no more at present upon this unpleasant subject, but at once tell you that I have been very much interested in witnessing the change of skin in the Tarantula spider. On Tuesday last, about two o'clock, the creature turned upon his right side, and by repeated jerks and convulsive efforts broke open the carapace, or covering over the head and upper parts of its body. Soon afterwards the two front legs were withdrawn from their former covering, and the fore-part of the animal thrust forward and backward, away from the old skin. These jerking movements continued, the animal resting from time to time until four o'clock; by this time it was perfectly free and able to drag its body forward, but was too soft and weak to walk about. I removed the cast skin, which is quite perfect, the eyes and every part most clearly to be seen, and this beautiful specimen is now safely preserved for inspection. Mr. or Mrs. Spider has this morning commenced hunting cockroaches. They will have a lively time of it for some weeks. I am perfectly aware that there is nothing new in saying that spiders shed their skins after the fashion of lobsters, crabs, and other crustacea, that to most observers the two former are the more wonderful considering that the flesh of the large claws must be drawn through the narrow neck of joints in order to escape from the hard and almost stony covering, and that the animal, almost in a fluid state, on emerging from its old shell is weak and helpless, and hides itself until its outer covering becomes hardened, for if met by a hungry fellow of its own species he becomes, as is frequently the case, a prey to his hard-shelled opponent.

It is extremely interesting during the season when the various species of crabs are shedding their outer shell to find them under stones near the water's edge; above or beside the cast shell rests the creature, whose enlarged size is most remarkable, for as soon as the animal is free from his old shell his soft skin-like covering becomes inflated or expanded in a most extraordinary degree, and in a few days hardens, and the animal comes forth to feed.

A very curious sight, and one almost ridiculous, is to see, in a state of terror, a fine large lobster, in the soft condition in which he has probably a day before left his old hard covering, meeting a hungry hard-shelled fellow of his own species, but not half his size, who is about to attack him; the big fellow knows his weak and helpless condition and tries his uttermost to frighten off his dreaded foe, making great efforts to lift and open and shut his large claws, but this menacing does not always succeed, for if once the attacking one has the chance of feeling the soft condition of his opponent he quickly nips off one of the claws of the unfortunate owner, and quietly makes a meal off it without further trouble—such is lobster life.

APPENDIX IV.

FEEDING ANIMALS AND BIRDS.

FOOD AND FEEDING ANIMALS.

In the matter of food I may possibly be told that in a vast number of the different kinds of food proposed to be used, there are the same, or they contain the principles of the same, ingredients, such as starch, sugar, etc.

This may appear perfectly true, as, for instance, when I propose rice, wheat, barley, oats, pea-flour, Indian corn, canary seed, millet, etc. It must, however, be borne in mind that the various kinds of food differ much in the proportion of each chemical ingredient, and as in many instances an animal that thrives upon rice would die if fed upon pea-flour, although both rice and pea-flour may contain starch, etc.,—still the proportions of the chemical elements are so different in each, that it can only, by long experience, be ascertained upon which kind of food certain animals herein mentioned thrive best.

The most pig-headed feeder of swine will soon find out whether his animals do best on oat-meal, barley-meal, rice, or peas—and in the end he may discover that he has done best by a change, occasionally, from one kind of food to another. This fact has taught me how important it is to have at hand any number of different kinds of food to offer, at any moment, when I have seen it necessary for the well-being of the animal under my charge.

How often have I put the question to the keepers when an animal was not doing well, "What have you tried as change of food ?" The answer has been frequently, "We have tried everything." That word *everything* always enraged me, for the very first article of food I mentioned, I was sure to find had not been tried, in fact, I nearly always found the word "everything" meant next to "nothing," and, in endless instances, as soon as the change I proposed was tried the animal began to improve.

This want of thought and of knowledge on the part of those who undertake the charge of animals is doubtless the cause of most serious losses and disheartening failures on the part of the owners. This has been my experience and has caused me much trouble and anxiety ; others from the same causes have ceased to collect, or to keep collections, added to which is the want of proper information and the difficulty and impossibility of obtaining persons who had sufficient knowledge of the subject.

ANIMAL SUBSTANCES USED AS FOOD.

Beef or horse-flesh, sheep, goats, rabbits, guinea-pigs, rats, cats, mice, frogs, snakes, fish, living and dead, shrimps, meal-worms, earth-worms, Thames-worms, gentles, grass-hoppers, snails, eggs, ant eggs, Liebig's condensed beef, milk, pigeons, ducks, fowls, sparrows, and cod-liver oil.

VEGETABLE SUBSTANCES USED AS FOOD.

Hay, straw, clover, grass, cabbages, lettuce, tares, marrows, pumpkins, carrots, potatoes, mangold, onions, apples, pears, oranges, grapes, bananas, figs, dates, raisins ; in summer—cherries, gooseberries, strawberries, and other fruit, nuts of different kinds, wheat, barley, buck-wheat, oats, canary, millet, rape, hemp, flax and maw seed, Spratt's poultry food, beans, Indian corn, oat-meal, barley-meal, rice, arrowroot, bread, biscuits, rye-bread, German paste, pea-meal, cayenne, ginger, sugar, treacle, honey, oil-cake.

The food required for the following animals :—

GAZELLES, PRONG-HORN ANTELOPE, JAPANESE AND OTHER DEER, KANGAROOS.

Oats, bran, dry clover, meadow hay, a little green food, carrots, potatoes, mangold, grass, a little fresh tares or green clover. For antelopes and deer a block of rock-salt should be placed in the trough, or feeding-box.

The food required for the following birds :—

NICOBAR PIGEON, BLUE-BACKED JAYS, BLUE ROBIN AND LIOTHRIX.

Mixture of hard-boiled eggs, boiled rice, potatoes, carrots, maw seed, bruised hemp seed, boiled Indian corn, raisins and currants, and ground or monkey nuts.

GOLD, SILVER, AMBERST, IMPEYAN AND REEVES PHEASANTS, ETC., SNOW PARTRIDGE, AND CURASSOWS.

Indian corn, wheat, barley, hemp seed, bread, buck-wheat, biscuit, green food, such as cabbage, lettuce, and onions, boiled potatoes and carrots, raisins, a few earth-worms, etc., and ground or monkey nuts.

PARROTS, PARRAKEETS, MACAWS, AND COCKATOOS.

Boiled or crushed Indian corn, hemp seed, canary seed,

scalded bread or biscuit, nuts, fruit, and a little green food, such as lettuce, chickweed, etc.

SCREAMERS.

Green food, cabbage, lettuce, grass, boiled Indian corn, barley, bread, biscuits, boiled rice, etc.

FLAMINGOES.

Wheat, soaked or boiled, shrimps, bread, a little fish cut up small.

VARIEGATED SHELDRAKE AND OTHER DUCKS.

Barley, buck-wheat, crushed maize, bread, and a little chopped green food.

SWANS.

Food for newly-hatched swans :—a mixture composed of Spratt's poultry food, hard-boiled eggs, grass or lettuce chopped fine; duck-weed collected from ponds or stagnant ditches.

THE MODE OF PREPARING THE FOOD FOR AND KEEPING THRUSHES AND SOFT-BILLED BIRDS INTENDED EITHER FOR SHIPMENT OR THE AVIARY.

In attempting to carry out this object, the greatest attention to the comfort and wants of these birds is essentially necessary to secure success.

They must be provided with sufficient good and suitable food, and changes of food, and also with the most complete cages in order to enable the person who takes charge of them to keep them clean, and feed them with the least possible difficulty. By these means they may be preserved in good health during their captivity.

THRUSHES AND OTHER ALLIED FORMS OF SOFT-BILLED BIRDS.

Before obtaining the birds it is necessary to have a small room or aviary prepared for their reception, as follows :— Place in and about the room perches or bushes, especially in the corners, for the concealment of the wild birds ; have a fine net strained over the window-frame, at sufficient distance from it to prevent them striking against the glass. Let the floor be sprinkled with grit or coarse gravel. Throw about the floor apples or pears, if a little decayed the better, chopped meat, bread-crumbs, worms, snails, etc. One or two shallow pans of water must be placed in the lighter parts of the room or aviary. One or two tame birds of any kind, accustomed to the food, will be found of great advantage in the room. Everything thus ready, the birds cannot be too freshly caught, and they should be turned into the room with as little delay as possible after their capture. Before turning them loose into the room cut, with a pair of scissors, the first six feathers of the wing, and also the whole of the tail. Do not, however, cut them too short, so as to injure the hollow quills. The object in cutting the wings and tail is, firstly, that you prevent the birds dashing about and injuring themselves, and, secondly, they get tame sooner, and are ready to go into a small cage without and feed, and thus get accustomed to the cages before the door is finally closed upon them. By this treatment the birds are never much reduced in condition or in any way weakened, which is sure to be the case should they be put into small cages when fresh caught.

It is always a little difficult to get birds to feed immediately after capture, but the above method has been found to answer admirably. It is of the greatest importance that the birds should not pine or get weak, as they seldom or, perhaps, never quite recover from the effects, but frequently linger for months, and such birds would be quite useless for the purpose intended.

Experience gained during a long course of experiments, in order to ascertain upon what food these birds might be kept in perfect health and good condition, has led to the use of a much larger number of ingredients than may be required or necessary. But, taking into consideration the chances of any accident or delay that might happen on board ship, it is well to know, by a fair trial, what can be used without risk, and, at the same time, it is certain that the more the food is changed and varied the greater the chances of success in keeping the birds in good health, taking into consideration the nature of their food in a wild state, varying as it must do at different periods of the year.

In the foregoing remarks allusion is made to the cages intended to convey these birds abroad, and this part of the subject requires especial notice and description. In speaking also of cutting the wing and tail feathers, which operation of course renders the birds unable to fly for a time, but only until they moult, which all birds do at least once every year, the advantages of this painless operation will be readily seen, because not only does it prevent injury to the bird, as before stated, but, in the event of it escaping from its cage, it is unable to fly, and, therefore, is easily caught and returned to confinement.

The following is a list of articles used for food, and the instructions for preparing the same are, it is hoped, so simple and clear as to be easily understood. The use of them can be safely recommended from long personal experience.

ANIMAL SUBSTANCES.

Meat, fresh or cooked, of any kind except salted.
Liver, prepared according to instructions.
Eggs, boiled. Insects.

VEGETABLE SUBSTANCES.

Peas and pea-meal. Barley, wheat, oats, Indian corn, or the meal of any of these. Rice, whole or ground. Fruit of all kinds, fresh or dried, raw or cooked. Potatoes, cooked. Carrots, raw or cooked. Bread, biscuit, bran, or pollard. Hemp seed.

METHOD OF PREPARING THE FOOD AND USING THE SAME.

In order to prepare a quantity of food required for a large number of these birds two machines have been employed, one the mincing or sausage machine, the other

363

a coffee-mill. The necessity of these will appear by looking over the list of food, and the manner of mixing, etc. Not only is the amount of labour much reduced by the use of these machines, but the food is more equally prepared, and better adapted for the birds than it can be if made by hand.

Of each kind of food, the instruction having been given as to its use, etc., it may be only necessary here to state, that any of the different kinds of meal mentioned may form the basis of the food, and the other ingredients may be added, such as meat, fruit, etc., according to circumstances and the judgment of the person who has charge of the birds, as a change of climate and circumstance may lead to variation in their condition, which must be carefully attended to.

I find the quantity of food required for each bird to be about one ounce and a half per day, with the same quantity of water. At the same time, in very hot weather, a larger quantity of water might be required.

Gravel, sand, grit, ashes, or dry earth is always required in the bottom of the cages.

ANIMAL FOOD.

MEAT.

Flesh of almost any kind, raw or cooked, will answer (always avoiding that which has been salted). A small quantity of fat is not objectionable. It must be well mixed with meal, as too much fat would be injurious. As fresh animal food is not always at hand, liver can be prepared in the following way, which is found to agree well with the birds, and it can be kept any length of time :—Cut a bullock's liver into slices, boil it half-an-hour, then cut it up in a mincing machine, place it in shallow dishes or tins, and put it into a slow oven until quite dry. In this state it will keep in tins or, better still, in jars.

EGGS.

Eggs boiled hard and chopped fine or ground, are excellent for most birds, and can be mixed with almost any kind of food.

INSECTS.

These are eaten by most birds. A few are good for them, such as earth-worms, caterpillars, meal-worms, flies, maggots, grasshoppers, etc. Do not, however, adopt the too frequent use of living food, as birds are apt to crave after this kind of food and refuse to eat that prepared for them. Snails can be kept a long time, and as they form a large portion of the food of thrushes in a wild state, their use is good; as they can be chopped up and mixed in the other kinds of food.

CHEESE.

Cheese can be occasionally given with the other food, but sparingly. In the event of liver or other animal substances failing, cheese (ground or minced fine) will answer.

VEGETABLE FOOD.

PEAS, OR PEA-MEAL.

Perhaps the best method of using the above is in the form of German paste, viz. fried with fat or oil, to which

365

may be added sugar or treacle. In this way it may be kept a long time in tins or earthen jars. It can also be used in many other ways; for instance, mixed with moist food, such as soaked bread, meat, fruit, potatoes or carrots. The peas can be soaked or boiled, and then ground and mixed with other food. In fact, peas ground afford a good and wholesome diet, and can be strongly recommended for all birds that will eat them; and, as they can be prepared in several ways, they are almost indispensable.

At least one-half of the pea-meal I would prepare as German paste, and have it packed in stone jars; and the liver must also be prepared according to the instructions.

GROUND BARLEY, OATS, WHEAT, AND INDIAN CORN SOAKED OR BOILED (BEFORE GRINDING).

Any of these can be used, and, mixed with fruit or meat, etc., form a good and wholesome food. Care is necessary not to give too large a quantity of them, especially when ground into fine flour, as it is liable to get too cloggy. The introduction of bran or, better, pollard (fine bran), will prevent this; but always use meat, fat, or fruit when flour is used.

RICE.

Rice is best used with pea-meal, or some other food. By no means attempt to use it alone. Boil it until soft, and then mix with meat, fruit, meal, etc., or it may be fried in fat or oil, after having been boiled to make it soft. Ground rice can be mixed after having been scalded, but it is better to boil it until it is well done.

BREAD, BISCUITS, ETC.

In feeding with these, if the bread or biscuit be stale, or hard and dry, scald or soak in water until quite soft, then rub up with pea or barley-meal, etc., until the required condition is obtained; then add meat or fruit, etc., if thought desirable, according to the condition of the birds.

HEMP SEED.

For many birds this seed is invaluable. It must not, however, be used too freely, for its stimulating power is apt to produce disease. In order to regulate its use it is well to bruise or grind it, and then mix with scalded or soaked bread, or other soft food. The reason why this is recommended is because some birds will not eat it whole; and, on the other hand, some birds will pick it out from the other food and eat nothing but this seed, and a fit of apoplexy generally follows. Still it is strongly recommended in moderate use, and a drooping bird will frequently be recovered by it. Care must be taken to see that the seed is good. This may always be known by bruising it; when crushed it ought to be quite white inside and oily; if yellow or brown it is rank and poisonous. Many valuable birds are lost by using bad hemp seed.

BRAN AND POLLARD.

Experience has shown that these may be used almost constantly. The birds are prevented getting too fat during their captivity by mixing bran or pollard with their food, and it is especially good with meat or boiled rice, fruit, or fat.

FRUIT (RAW, COOKED, OR PRESERVED).

Fruit of almost any kind appears to answer, and when prepared and mixed with any or all the different ingredients mentioned in this paper, forms a food at once acceptable to these birds; and, judging of their condition after some months' experience, there can be no doubt of the beneficial effects of the fruits employed, viz. apples, pears, oranges, raisins, figs, currants, etc.

The manner of mixing has been with meal, bran, or flour, and passing these together through a mincing machine, by which they are chopped or ground fine enough to mix with the other food, the admixture of the meal preventing the loss of the juices of the fruit.

POTATOES AND CARROTS.

Potatoes require to be boiled or baked, and then ground or mixed with meat, fruit, meal, etc.

Carrots may be boiled and then mixed; or if first ground and put into a pan to stew or bake, then mixed, they answer instead of fruit very well.

INDEX

B B

THE END

RICHARD CLAY & SONS, l
LONDON & BUNGA

WILD ANIMALS IN CAPTIVITY

Being an Account of the Habits, Food, Management and Treatment of the Beasts and Birds at the " Zoo."

With Reminiscences and Anecdotes by

A. D. BARTLETT,

LATE SUPERINTENDENT OF THE ZOOLOGICAL GARDENS.

COMPILED AND EDITED BY EDWARD BARTLETT, F.Z.S.

With Illustrations by A. T. ELWES, and Portraits.

Large Crown 8vo, 7s. 6d.

The Times says : "All . . . will find 'Wild Animals in Captivity' a delightful volume, and Mr. A. D. Bartlett a bookshelf companion of whose stories and recollections they will never tire."

The Athenæum says : "An eminently readable volume. . . . One of the most interesting works of its class that we have read for a long time ; it is also one of the most instructive, for its author was a man who thought out every question for himself, and took no statements on trust—a perfect Mr. Gradgrind for facts."

The Academy says : " Mr. Bartlett lived a life unique and striking to the last degree. He was doctor and surgeon to his flock. He was also their dentist at a pinch. . . . Lancing Jumbo's cheeks was no child's play ; that is a story of real bravery on the one side and touching docility on the other. Many of Mr. Bartlett's remarks in the character of a naturalist are most interesting. . . . Mr. Bartlett was master of his calling, a true naturalist and friend of naturalists."

The Illustrated Sporting and Dramatic News says : " Mr. Bartlett has left us an entertaining book upon some of the animals he had under his care during the past forty years. His book is very readable."

The Manchester Courier says : "There is plenty to amuse the reader as well as instruct. No one must imagine that the office Mr. Bartlett held was in any sense a sinecure. He had a multiplicity of duties to perform, and many of them were of a highly dangerous character. Who, for instance, would lightly undertake the task of lancing an elephant's upper jaw ? or abstracting a baby hippopotamus from its doting mother ? The Superintendent performed these and many other risky feats, such as taking a bone from the mouth of a lion, where it had become wedged, helping to get a rhinoceros out of its frozen pond, and catching escaped wolves and bears. Boys will delight in this interesting volume. The story of Jumbo and his bereaved Alice is related, and some amusing accounts of the zoological home experiences of the late Frank Buckland are given."

The Manchester City News says : " Mr. Edward Bartlett has done really valuable service, both to scientists and to those whose business it is to have the care of wild creatures in confinement, by gathering into this volume some of the numerous papers and monographs on natural history topics, which his father wrote during a long and busy life. Much of the fruit of his ripe experience in the treatment of fauna under unnatural circumstances is here gathered together. It will be also none the less acceptable for the gentle humour which now and again ripples across the page ; for its wealth of amusing anecdote, and of narration of strange, and often dangerous, adventure which befell the author in his dealings with the beasts of the field."

The Daily Telegraph says : " Our only fault with the book is that there is not more of it."

The Daily Mail says : " Exceedingly interesting volume."

CHAPMAN & HALL, LIMITED, LONDON.

CHRISTMAS STORIES

FROM

"HOUSEHOLD WORDS" AND "ALL THE YEAR ROUND."

Edited by CHARLES DICKENS.

A pocket reprint of the Christmas Stories which comprise the Extra Christmas Numbers of "Household Words" and "All the Year Round" during the years 1850–1871 under the Editorship of CHARLES DICKENS. These Christmas Stories are entirely distinct from his Christmas Books. The latter were written entirely by Dickens himself, whereas in the former he was assisted by other writers. These were many and excellent. Mr. Andrew Lang, in the Gadshill Edition of Dickens's works, says:—"Some, like Mr. Sala, of genial memory, imitated the master; some, like Mrs. Gaskell, worked on their own lines. . . . The framework Dickens himself devised and supplied, while his allies contributed many of the stories which it enclosed."

The portions of these stories which Dickens himself wrote have appeared in the various editions of his collected works; but the series of stories complete as they were originally written are now being issued in a convenient form for the first time.

The volumes will be printed on wove paper, with a decorative title-page and a frontispiece, drawn by A. JULES GOODMAN, and reproduced in photogravure.

The size of the volumes will be *Pott 8vo*, and they will be bound in two styles of binding:—

> *Cloth, gilt top, at 1s. 6d. per volume.*
> *Limp leather, gilt top, at 2s. net per volume.*

The First Five Volumes are :

The Seven Poor Travellers.
By CHARLES DICKENS and others: Being the Extra Christmas Number of "Household Words," 1854.

The Wreck of the Golden Mary.
Being the Captain's Account of the Loss of the Ship, and the Mate's Account of the Great Deliverance of Her People in an Open Boat at Sea.
By CHARLES DICKENS and others: Being the Extra Christmas Number of "Household Words," 1856.

Somebody's Luggage.
By CHARLES DICKENS and others: Being the Extra Christmas Number of "All the Year Round," 1862.

Mugby Junction.
By CHARLES DICKENS, ANDREW HALLIDAY, CHARLES COLLINS HESBA STRETTON, and AMELIA B. EDWARDS: Being the Extra Christmas Number of "All the Year Round," 1866.

No Thoroughfare.
By CHARLES DICKENS and WILKIE COLLINS: Being the Extra Christmas Number of "All the Year Round," 1867.

CHAPMAN & HALL, LIMITED, LONDON.

CHRISTMAS BOOKS

By CHARLES DICKENS.

A new pocket edition of CHARLES DICKENS'S famous Christmas Books, printed by Messrs. T. & A. Constable, of Edinburgh, uniform in size and style with the reprint of Christmas Stories on preceding page.

Each volume will contain a coloured frontispiece and decorative title-page, drawn and designed by F. D. Bedford.

Pott 8vo, issued in two styles of binding.

Cloth, gilt top, 1s. net; Limp leather, gilt top, 2s. net.

A Christmas Carol in Prose, being a Ghost Story for Christmas.

The Chimes: a Goblin Story of some Bells that rang an Old Year out and a New Year in.

The Cricket on the Hearth: a Fairy Tale of Home.

The Battle of Life: a Love Story.

The Haunted Man and the Ghost's Bargain: a Fancy for Christmas Time.

CHAPMAN & HALL, LIMITED, LONDON.

Lightning Source UK Ltd.
Milton Keynes UK
UKOW04f1411231217
314931UK00010BA/567/P